AF600234

TRANSNATIONAL IDENTITY AND MEMORY MAKING IN THE LIVES OF IRAQI WOMEN IN DIASPORA

STUDIES IN GENDER AND HISTORY

General Editors: Franca Iacovetta and Karen Dubinsky

Transnational Identity and Memory Making in the Lives of Iraqi Women in Diaspora

NADIA JONES-GAILANI

UNIVERSITY OF TORONTO PRESS
Toronto Buffalo London

Toronto Buffalo London
utorontopress.com

ISBN 978-1-4875-0316-1 (cloth)
ISBN 978-1-4875-1732-8 (EPUB)
ISBN 978-1-4875-1731-1 (PDF)

Studies in Gender and History

Library and Archives Canada Cataloguing in Publication

Title: Transnational identity and memory making in the lives of Iraqi women in diaspora / Nadia Jones-Gailani.
Names: Jones-Gailani, Nadia, 1982– author.
Series: Studies in gender and history ; 52.
Description: Series statement: Studies in gender and history series ; 52 | Includes bibliographical references and index.
Identifiers: Canadiana (print) 20200208047 | Canadiana (ebook) 20200209140 | ISBN 9781487503161 (hardcover) | ISBN 9781487517328 (EPUB) | ISBN 9781487517311 (PDF)
Subjects: LCSH: Iraqis – Migrations. | LCSH: Women – Iraq – Biography. | LCSH: Iraqis – Jordan – Amman – Ethnic identity. | LCSH: Iraqis – Jordan – Amman – Social life and customs. | LCSH: Iraqis – Michigan – Detroit – Ethnic identity. | LCSH: Iraqis – Michigan – Detroit – Social life and customs. | LCSH: Iraqis – Ontario – Toronto – Ethnic identity. | LCSH: Iraqis – Ontario – Toronto – Social life and customs. | LCSH: Belonging (Social psychology) | LCSH: Group identity.
Classification: LCC DS79.66.A2 J66 2020 | DDC 956.7044092/52 – dc23

This book has been published with the help of a grant from the Federation for the Humanities and Social Sciences, through the Awards to Scholarly Publications Program, using funds provided by the Social Sciences and Humanities Research Council of Canada.

University of Toronto Press acknowledges the financial assistance to its publishing program of the Canada Council for the Arts and the Ontario Arts Council, an Ontario government agency.

Canada Council for the Arts
Conseil des Arts du Canada

Funded by the Government of Canada
Financé par le gouvernement du Canada

Contents

Acknowledgments vii

Introduction: Narrative, Memory, and Identity 3

1 Gendered Narratives of State: The Project for the Rewriting of History 21

2 Resisting the State: Shi'a, Chaldean, and Kurdish Women's Counter-narratives 40

3 Towards an Affective Methodology: Interviewer, Translator, Participant 61

4 *Qahwa* and *Kleiche*: Cookbooks, Coffee, and Conversation 83

5 Policing Women's Bodies in Diaspora: Toronto and Detroit in Comparative Context 104

Conclusion 127

Notes 135

Index 177

Acknowledgments

First and foremost, I offer heartfelt thanks to all of the Iraqi women who have contributed to my research. I am enormously indebted to their generosity and friendship throughout the process of collecting and collaborating in the many spaces I was fortunate to inhabit as a researcher. Navigating the blurry grey areas between personal and professional realities allowed me to transcend the usual bounds of an oral historian, though this did not come without significant sacrifices that were made on my behalf. I thank in particular Shehada Al-Ali and Yasemin Al-Gailani, who have supported my work every step of the way.

There is a debt I can never repay to my feminist mentors and interlocutors, who have provided the biggest challenges and the strongest support for this research. Foremost among these are Franca Iacovetta, whose work and influence can be recognized in all parts of the book. I can never adequately repay all of the hours of advice, editing, suggestions, and critiques Franca has offered over the years, but I take seriously my indebtedness in extending to my students the same kind of supervision. Other mentors and colleagues who offered critical guidance at various points in the advancement of the manuscript are Giovanna Benadusi, Mark McGowan, Russell Kazal, and Nadje Al-Ali.

The initial research upon which the book is based was conducted with support from the Ontario Graduate Scholarship Fund, the University of Toronto Scace Graduate Fellowship, and the Vivienne Poy Chancellor's Fellowship for the Humanities and Social Sciences (University of Toronto). Support for the initial stages of the inception of the manuscript was provided by the Provost Postdoctoral Fellowship for the Social Sciences and Humanities at the University of South Florida. This book has, however, been written without institutional support or the benefit of academic leave. I would instead like to acknowledge how my relationship with Central European University (CEU) has shaped the genesis of the book manuscript. When I arrived as a visiting professor, the institution – funded by philanthropist George Soros – was on the cusp of entering an ideological war with the increasingly authoritarian state-government. Founded upon the principles of "open society," CEU has played an important part in providing scholarships for students, as well as a framework for civil society organizations in Eastern and Central Europe. The manuscript was compiled during a period of frenzy and chaos, since the Hungarian government passed a law (lex CEU) that effectively means foreign universities can no longer operate autonomously without the cooperation of the government. The last copy-edits were submitted in the final semester of my tenure here as a (now) professor at the Budapest campus.

There is both a terrifying poignancy and an urgent immediacy to the task of uncovering the lives and experiences of women who fled the authoritarian Ba'ath regime, as I am in the process of leaving Hungary for what I hope will be a safer home in Austria. As a historian who remains fascinated by the ways in which memories are manipulated and contested at local, national, and transnational levels, I find it frightening to witness the rapidly evolving use – and misuse – of historical memory during heightened periods of political change.

I would like to acknowledge the patience and guidance offered by the University of Toronto Press team during what has been a difficult few years and a number of unforeseen delays in advancing the book to publication. In particular, thank you to Terry Teskey's patient and impeccable copy-edits, which have immeasurably improved the readability and accuracy of the text and notes. And sincere gratitude for the patient indexing work – and uncompromising support – of Mert Koçak.

If it is always darker before the dawn, as goes the adage, then I must pay tribute to those individuals who have filled my life with light and love during the blackest hours. To my students and friends at CEU, without whom I would lose all hope and the will to fight each and every day for the freedom of expression to produce critical knowledge. In solidarity, we have stood side by side and fought for the right to exist as an independent and open institution. To my patient and ever-loving partner, Quentin Williamson, who was present for each stage of the manuscript as we migrated together across borders. And finally, to my mother, Katharine Jones, and grandmother, Cynthia Jones, who are the maternal pillars upon which the foundation of my existence stands; I could not have survived through this period of my life without you.

TRANSNATIONAL IDENTITY AND MEMORY MAKING IN THE LIVES OF IRAQI WOMEN IN DIASPORA

Introduction: Narrative, Memory, and Identity

Home is not where you were born
It is where all your attempts to escape cease ...

– Egyptian poet Naguib Mahfouz

On a cold afternoon in January of 2010, I took two subways and a bus to reach what was then the Center of the Assyrian-Canadian Federation located in Toronto, a modest operation run out of a family restaurant. I was there to meet Sahena, a recent Sunni refugee woman from Mosul who worked with the municipal school board to help with the integration of immigrant children. In keeping with the custom of lavishing upon guests an impressive array of dishes,[1] the executive members of the federation had prepared for us their most beloved Iraqi dishes. Food – its preparation, planning, and consumption – plays a central role in the negotiation of identity in the Iraqi diaspora. As we came together to eat and share stories, the men from the executive discussed how shared foods provide a sense of sameness and belonging for the disparate threads of Iraqi migrants who have in one way or another been forced to leave Iraq. Food also emerged as a means of negotiating counter-narratives and memories of home in the life narratives that I collected with Iraqi women in Toronto, Detroit, and Amman. Women consistently invoked sensory metaphors as a way of expressing, in affective terms, their lived realities and memories, their stories serving as well to decentre the male authorial voice. Through these metaphors, women also sought to reconcile past and present understandings of difference based on ethnic and religious histories and lineages in Iraq. When I asked Sahena why she thought ethnic and religious group identity held such salience for Iraqis in diaspora, she paused and then, pointing to the bowl of *bamieh*[2] on the table, said:

> Iraq is like this dish. If you put many things together it is not plain and it keeps getting more delicious. In Iraq you have different labels, yes, but these all belong to the same dish. Without one of these ingredients, the dish will not taste good anymore. All of the parts of the dish are different but they are all important. After the war, the people were not together as an Iraqi community, some people – their mind is changed. When they leave Iraq now they are trying to get their own rights for Kurds and Chaldeans ... If Iraqi people start to think of themselves as Iraqi again it will be better. Iraqis have to stop thinking of themselves selfishly by ethnic group, because really we are all part of the same dish, and we are all Iraqi.[3]

This metaphor illustrates the central role of food in Iraqi culture. It also underscores what many of the women I interviewed assumed in their narratives that the history of interconnectedness between Iraq's ethno-religious communities far predates the more recent sectarian divides that have largely been the result of state-defined and -imposed nationalism and imperialist interference in the region. Just as Sahena's metaphor offers a pointed discourse on the complex articulation of Iraqi identity, she uses a language of emotions, expressed through food, in order to map the sociopolitical locations of ethnic and religious Iraqis both in the homeland and in the wider diaspora. Drawing upon an imposed state narrative of collective memory, Sunni women like Sahena advance narratives that serve to support the concept of a cohesive national identity promoted by the ruling Arab Socialist Ba'ath Party between 1968 and 2013. As I will expand upon in subsequent chapters, this state-led nationalism effectively relegated all other ethnic and religious groups to the sidelines. By contrast, Kurdish, Chaldean, Assyrian, and Shi'a Iraqi women provide counter-narratives that effectively challenge the hegemonic, state-imposed Sunni narrative of a collective Iraqi identity that was such a defining feature of the nationalist politics of the Ba'ath regime. Giving voice to their subjective recollections of "home" through affective memories, these narratives are replete with themes of longing and silence. Using rumour, gossip, and metaphor, the women address the pain and pleasure of lives lived through periods of intermittent war.

From 1968 to 2003, the Iraqi Socialist Ba'ath party, led by Saddam Hussein from 1979 onwards, sought to create a stable and collective nationalism that promoted an ahistorical narrative of Sunni ascendancy. In an effort to safeguard their ambitious and nation-building aims, the state used political, social, and cultural institutions – including women's organizations – in an effort to remake Iraq's history in the national imagination. Since 2003, Iraqi migrants and refugees have watched from afar as the actions of outside actors exacerbate the internal cleavages between Iraq's diverse and historical populations. The focus of this book is on oral histories collected with migrant and refugee Iraqi women from Sunni, Shi'a, Kurdish, Assyrian, and Chaldean backgrounds. Cleavages that were nurtured during the Ba'ath administration are now appropriated in the ongoing civil conflict and, as I demonstrate here, are in many ways replicated in diaspora. During my five years of fieldwork, I travelled back and forth between Aman, Detroit, and Toronto (2007–2012) and collected a total of 112 interviews, of which over two-thirds are individual interviews, and others are in groups or part of group interviews with natal families. Additionally, I conducted interviews in all three locations with twenty-two individuals (men and women) from key organizations that were assisting Iraqi migrants and refugees. By exploring the intersections of memory, migration, and subjectivity through the narratives of Iraqi women, the book draws upon a reflexive feminist methodology in order to understand how the women negotiate identity outside of Iraq. As I will discuss, in diaspora, women participants who had previously belonged to "dispossessed" groups find new platforms from which to advocate for the survival of their community. No longer parts of a cohesive "dish," Iraqi women form elements of a mobile and scattered web of individual ingredients that are fighting to once again coexist.

Iraqi women's life narratives constitute sites of struggle and are emotional testimonies of subjective experiences that give voice to women's multilayered identities. The participants who shared their narratives with me recounted their pasts by threading painful memories through happier recollections, and used rhetorical strategies to help them communicate feelings of loss, love, and belonging.[4] As Peter Burke and others have noted with respect to oral history, we need to be clear about who wants to remember and whose past is preserved.[5] First and foremost, this book is an exploration of the intersections of memory, nation, and identity in the narratives of Iraqi migrant women. Asking women to remember "home" elicited memories that they shared in intimate exchanges, usually over many cups of strong Arabic coffee. These memories were communicated through highly selective and malleable recollections of lived pasts, providing a rich and complex jumble of events, details, and recollections from their lives.[6] Iraqi women's histories have rarely been written, nor have their stories been collected, preserved, and cherished. The project of decentring men from the historical record is a long-term one, and the second and related aim of this book is to contribute to the disruption of the hegemonic "truth" of Iraq's recent past with a history of resistance as told through the storied lives of women.[7] Adopting a pluralistic model of memory, the methodology draws upon the insights of feminist holistic reflexivity in order to interpret women's memories and the ways they use their stories to contest and resist the imposition of state-centred nationalism.[8] The personal is political; I draw on the diasporic memories of my own family, who over two generations have been divided and dislocated within this same transnational web. The ethnographic fieldwork was conducted with women at three sites of settlement, Toronto, Detroit, and Amman, in an effort to trace multigenerational modes of memory – including inherited memories – and assess how the temporal and material realities of living transnational lives shapes the subjective.

Since at least the late 1970s, successive waves of refugees and migrants forced to flee Iraq have moved to these three sites, in each case seeking to recreate communities within established networks of family and friends. As Iraqi women negotiate a place within these existing networks, the politics of "home" continues to shape multigenerational memory and feelings of belonging. Place matters, as the site of resettlement provides the outside stimulus that helps to shape what is remembered and why, and how the internal dynamics of individual, familial, and community relationships develop. By engaging the work of transnational migration and feminist scholars, the book, thirdly, seeks to understand how the local affects the global in the process of "locating diaspora' in the memories of Iraqi migrant women.[9]

Quantifying the Iraqi Diaspora?

The persecution of ethnic and religious minority groups in Iraq that has occurred as part of a broader nation-building and consolidating project has left deep and lasting scars on all three generations of women that I interviewed. A series of brutal autocrats have led security forces to murder, maim, and erase the legacy of its numerous ancient peoples, forcing many in these groups to migrate to Western states as well as across the Middle East and North African (MENA) region. What began as international intervention (and invasion) has become a civil conflict that continues to affect all Iraqis regardless of their location. After 2003, the members of Baghdad's Sunni professional class – many of whom escaped the violence of the Ba'ath administration – initiated a new wave of Iraqi migrants to Jordan, Canada, and the US. My family – the Al-Gailanis – are part of this most recent and populous wave of refugees. The disintegration of basic security and infrastructure forced them to flee in 2004 first to Syria, then to a paid residency in Jordan. They waited for two years in Jordan before resettling in Ontario under the auspices of the United Nations High Commissioner for Refugees (UNHCR).

As I set out to trace Iraqi settlement through Jordan and on to Canada and the US, a major challenge was finding accurate statistics on Iraqi migrations after 1945. Since the Geneva Convention was passed and protections for refugees were established in the aftermath of the Second World War, there have been three significant waves of Iraqis to Canada and the US. The first wave were the Christians and Jews who came during the period 1945–79. Of the different ethno-religious groups of Christians included in this study (Assyrians, Syriacs, and Chaldeans), Chaldeans are currently the largest group of Iraqi Christians in North America and feature prominently throughout this book.[10] Migrations of Shi'a and Kurds attempting to avoid military service (for conflicts with both Iran and Kuwait), and fleeing in the aftermath of the Intifada (a series of failed political uprisings from 1990 to 1991) and genocidal Anfal campaign, have contributed to a second wave of Arab Muslims and Kurds across these three sites of settlement.[11] Worsening economic conditions resulting from the crippling effects of the decade-long US-led international sanctions against Iraq also precipitated migration from the country throughout the nineties.[12] The third and most recent discernable wave of Iraqi immigrants includes many of the former aristocratic and political elite families of educated Sunni Arab Iraqis. It was as part of this most recent wave that my family arrived in Hamilton, Ontario, where they settled among relatives, old friends and colleagues who have similarly recreated their communities and networks outside of Iraq.

Although Toronto and Detroit are the largest sites of Iraqi migration in North America, I soon discovered that it would be virtually impossible to calculate and compare the numbers of migrants arriving in each "wave." Population statistics obscure the aggregate numbers of migrants since questionnaires allow each individual to decide how they are counted – by national origin or by ethnic group affiliation.[13] In both countries, the national census presents problems because of how immigrants are officially recorded as compared to how Iraqis of various backgrounds self-identify. In each case, there is a disconnect between the census, which groups immigrants by ethno-nationality (with religious affiliation often listed as "other"), and how Iraqi immigrants identify themselves, which is by reference to ethnic, religious, or national designations or some combination thereof. These inconsistencies mean that migrants designate according to the category they fit "best" on a census that cannot account for the complexity of overlapping forms of identification.

When I started this research in 2007, official documents for Arab, Muslim, and Middle Eastern populations living in both Canada and the US had already been heavily restricted and censored. As I came to understand, the restrictions were not only a post-9/11 reaction to "sensitive" material, but the result of the decision to place certain groups, including Iraqis, under surveillance on the grounds that they posed a potential threat to national security.[14] Multiple frustrating research trips ultimately proved a useful exercise as they helped explain how some ethno-national/ethno-religious groups were more successful than others at campaigning for self-determination on the basis of mitigating circumstances in the homeland and the presence of support from settled communities in North America. Since national census material failed to identify Iraqis adequately in terms of either national or ethnic designation, I could not provide a detailed comparison of Iraqis in Michigan and Ontario.[15] The fact that Iraqis could be recorded as Iraqi, Arab, or Muslim or some combination of the three precluded any precise accounting of the people involved. Another major aim of this book is to unravel, as I work against the essentializing of collective identities, how divisions within and between Iraqi communities are transposed and renegotiated in the diaspora. In recreating the complex realities of over 112 individual migrant women who shared their stories with me, this book aims to address the national, ethnic, and religious differences that have shaped distinctive Iraqi communities in transit through Amman and on to more permanent settlement in Toronto and Detroit.

Emigrant; Immigrant; Migrant

Studies of transnational feminisms and diasporic subjectivities build upon the legacy of social and cultural histories that have transformed how we think about migrants in the past, as well as how we relate to – and police – migrants and refugees in the present. In contrast to earlier studies, which portrayed migration as a unidirectional movement from a place of origin to destination and resettlement, practitioners of the transplanted model shed new light on migrants' links back to their homeland and on the global networks of migrants that emerged in eras well before our postmodern age.[16] During the sixties, the rise of the "immigrant paradigm" in American and Canadian migration literature, which sought to understand immigrant strategies, transnational family economies, and identities rather than simply assess migration in terms of nation state priorities, "challenged scholars to rethink linkages between national history and the histories of sub-national ethnic groups and to write the histories of particular ethnic groups."[17] The focus in migration studies has shifted away from a discussion of immigrants and emigrants to one of *migrants* that included the complexities of linkages back and forth across nation state borders.[18]

Drawing upon methods emerging from the study of oral history and ethnography, New Left migration historians transformed our thinking about migrant lives, stressing the central importance of ethnic persistence and the multiple ways of "being American" or "Canadian."[19] Ethnic and working-class histories that followed further demonstrated how attention to ethnic subjects both broadened and revised conventional understandings of national histories.[20] Feminist historians of women led the charge in calling for a new kind of migration history by focusing on the transnational links that connected both men and women, in the process also opening up the field to explorations of migrant women's narratives and life histories.[21] Gendering the experiences of migration led to critical insights regarding the power dynamics of immigrant family economies, community building, and labour activism.[22] The collaborative works of Franca Iacovetta and Donna Gabaccia in particular have informed the multidimensional and intersectional framework adopted here to understand Iraqi women in diaspora.[23]

The interdisciplinary character of the transnational turn in migration has meant a greater focus on the intersections of space, geography, and human movement.[24] Ongoing efforts to redefine the parameters of the field have challenged previous assumptions regarding the centrality of nation and nationalisms and given rise to analyses that highlight the fluidity of ethnic diasporas with respect to their ongoing relationship to the homeland. Studies that have gendered these diasporas have been a critical part of this process. [25] The "exile" motif – the idea of being part of a forced dispersal or diaspora – is an important theme in Iraqi women's narratives, revealing much about how they imagine their place both in the "nation" (Iraq) and in their new homes in Toronto and Detroit.[26] My research reaffirms the insight that transnational movement is intricately connected to the discourse of globalization and global migration, shaping new diasporic identities that reimagine national identities.[27] By exploring the politics of "imagined community" in terms of how national rhetoric is used to construct diasporic imagination within imagined geographies, this book examines how allegiances to "old world centers translate into emergent new world nationalisms."[28] This is a study of how individuals as members of groups claim a space for themselves within different contexts shaped by the Ba'ath regime in

Iraq and the conditions and institutions of their host countries. As old and new Iraqi groups and communities come into contact in diaspora, they renegotiate the boundaries of belonging. "Located" or rooted in a particular temporal and spatial reality in the host country, they orient their focus towards home and the "transnational nation" or vision of that place in the communal imaginary.[29]

The dangers of falling into the trap of methodological nationalism are nevertheless still present. Following the interventions of social scientists Andreas Wimmer and Nina Glick Schiller, this book seeks to disrupt the assumptions that nation and state are natural forms of social and political order. If we are willing to concede that transnationalism is not a by-product of globalization but has always been a constant in modern life, then it is possible to participate in research that decentres the one-nation-state focus. The politics of nationalism has shaped the history of relatively "new" modern states such as Iraq; it has also manipulated the process by which some, but not other, ethnic and religious communities became part of the naturalizing of nation states. By treating the history of "nation" and "state" as two separate objects of inquiry, we can separate the study of "national culture" from an examination of how the political apparatus in Iraq worked to produce "an alterity that contributed to build unity and identity." [30] In other words, our analyses are not burdened by notions of an internal homogeneity that somehow links a transnational community of Iraqis. Another purpose of this work is to address, on an individual level, how the process of a state-sanctioned nationalist policy that sought to circumvent longer histories of cohabitation and intercultural exchange has affected the ways in which women connect to "home," including how they remember the past through the framing of nation, state, and community.

Will the "Real" Iraqis Please Stand Up?

Edward Said argued that people have always moved, and that all contemporary life is characterized by a "generalized condition of homelessness."[31] Being a nomad is perhaps the best perspective from which to explore transnational mobility and culture. As someone who has moved multiple times across national borders, I feel an affinity for migrants and displaced peoples who narrate stories of "uprootedness" and "exile" through the use of metaphor, humour, and the telling of contradictory historical accounts. By the time I embarked on this multisited research, I had already moved from Iraq to the UK and later to Canada. The research project meant periods of intensive work in three different countries, with time also spent in Syria observing the early refugee management in UNHCR camps. The challenge of finding stable academic work has further increased my state of mobility. As a result, I have completed this book amid multiple relocations from Canada to the US, and most recently to Hungary. As academic nomads or transnational migrants, we as part of the academy can also play an important role in reorienting the study of migrants from the assumption that cultures are, out of moral and spiritual necessity, "rooted in place."

The question that led many of the women interviewed in Amman, Detroit, and Toronto to reflect on how they contribute, both individually and as part of a web of dynamic interactions and relationships, to the concept of a collective Iraqi identity was: What does it mean to *be* "Iraqi"? In her answer, Bana, who is Kurdish-Iraqi, challenged the notion that new hyphenated realities can reshape one's internalized understanding of what it means to be Iraqi:

> Okay, you want to ask me who I am as in what's my identity? Then you must ask me this for each place ... who are you in Iraq, who are you in Canada, and who are you in the rest of the world, no? We come from Iraq because it is on our passport and we are taught always to believe that we are the best and most advanced Arab race – yes! It is actually true! You cannot disagree with Saddam about this – no?! ... You are laughing at me, but to me I will never say I am not Iraqi because my family is from this part of Iraq – Erbil – and we have always been there. But if you ask me who I am in Iraq, of course I will say I am Kurdish – of course! In Canada I struggle for the rights of Iraqis, but I do not introduce myself as Iraqi – no – I am Kurdish first of all. You must understand this, because it is important – the seed of your personality is planted in your birth, the food and the water and the sun make the plant grow, yes? What if I take one away? Maybe the plant will grow, but it will be made in a different way – do you see? Because now we were forced to leave, and many of the Kurds are all over the world, they are growing, yes, but it is all in different ways. The plants are all different now – maybe if I go back, I don't know how to be Kurdish anymore?[32]

Drawing upon two distinct rhetorical devices – metaphor and (dark) humour – Bana creates meaning out of the confusion and frustration of articulating a fractured and hyphenated migrant identity. When individuals are forced to migrate, and are essentially ripped from the surroundings, people, and history to which they feel they belong, the use of metaphor becomes a useful tool for conveying meaning by distancing the details and particularities from the argument they are making. Like other migrants who articulate their emotional ties to soil and the territorialized concept of nation, Bana expresses what Liisa Malkki argues is a "deeply metaphysical" link between people and place.[33] Bana demonstrates how self-identity depends upon a "situated intersubjectivity," or the interchange of thoughts and emotions between people. As Bourdieu explains, one's internal "self" is in some ways constant even as it is negotiated against internal and external forces.[34] Lamees Al-Ethari in her illuminating discussion of Iraqi women's identities in North America through popular literature and media refers to this process as one of "defragmentation" in which "even the act of migration itself renders these women's identities in a state of constant alteration."[35]

In the process of recording the memories and life histories of Iraqi women, I began to realize that this idea of "Iraqi" identity was part of the more constant and imposed "self," whereas their subjective self-categorization shifted based on new developing relationships with the spaces outside of Iraq that they now occupy. Al-Ethari documents through films such as *Baghdad Twist* how women's narratives blend personal and political ways of expressing "Iraqiness." The film focuses on how one Jewish-Iraqi woman's struggle to maintain her Iraqi identity as mother and wife was informed by the family's exile from their home. As she describes it, Valentine Balass, who is interviewed by her son Joe Balass, documents her past through an appeal to the same sense of Iraqiness that women from all of the ethno-religious groups I investigated also expressed. Even after forty years of exile, the disruption to the inner self is still acute, and the audience witnesses the son asking his mother, "Did you ever question the fact that you were Iraqi?" In response, she insists: "No, I did not. I was Iraqi and that was it. I was Iraqi, I was a Jewish Iraqi. The two always went together. I am Iraqi, I am Jewish. That is how it was."[36] In their reflections, the women I interviewed similarly insisted upon their Iraqiness as a central part of how they understood themselves. This Iraqiness had little to do with a territorialized and bordered community; rather, it reflected an unbounded understanding of Iraq as an integral component of new identities in formation.[37]

At first, I struggled to understand Iraqi identity beyond the women's frequent characterization of a highly homogenized Iraq. The modern state of Iraq is in many ways a fictive and ahistorical construction by Western imperial powers that in more recent decades has been held together by the force of an autocratic regime.[38] Continued fieldwork with migrant women and their families offered new insights into the fluidity of ethnic and religious groups as they migrate, settle, and in many cases resettle in different locales, each time renegotiating their relationship with Iraq.[39] In scrutinizing the ways in which the women's memories are shaped by changing temporalities and topographies, I seek to challenge current categories of race and ethnicity in North American migration studies.

Ethnic and Religious Diasporas

An understanding of ethnic as well as religious identities is critical to understanding the state-led persecutions that led Iraqis to flee their homeland. With a focus on ethnic diasporas, Floya Anthias and others have called for including the relevance of ethnicity – in addition to race and nation – as an analytical category in diaspora studies.[40] In the case of diasporas from the Levant region, the durability of ethnicities in certain socio-economic and political processes is heightened as a result of migration where groups can resettle and reimagine a bounded ethnic community. The perceived ethnic homogeneity is not a cause but a result of a long history of a top-down political process that sought to enhance national unity by engineering a collective national identity.[41] Belonging to a national, ethno-national, or ethno-religious group depends ultimately upon ideas of common blood and lineage.[42] Such characterizations of ethnic groups tend to categorize "new nationalisms" as the reproducers of ethnic hatred, and they promote a "civic nationalism" that is a more constructive end to reconciling rights and reconstructing community.[43] Drawing upon these insights, I consider whether and how women migrants who formerly lived under the socialist regime in Iraq have articulated a "new nationalism" rooted in notions of ethno-nationalism and ethno-religious identity.[44]

As Vijay Agnew and others have argued, cultural phenomena are reproduced in diaspora, informing the "racialized, sexualized, gendered and oppositional subjectivities" that "shape the cosmopolitan intellectual commitment of scholars."[45] Since the memory and self-identity of diasporic groups depend upon the "political unreality of one's present home," this identification can be surpassed only by the "ontological unreality of one's place of origin."[46] Because this location (imagined or real) promises "neither transcendence nor return," diasporic individuals, like ethno-religious Iraqis, live in a permanent limbo between a metaphorical and physical "home."[47] Postcolonial and critical race studies of racialized women have been influential not just in opening up spaces to discuss not just the intersections of race and gender, but also the important role of religion as an alternate lens in studies of the subaltern or marginalized.[48] A consideration of how women's political subjectivities have been informed by their religious identity and practice has until relatively recently occupied a secondary place in feminist social histories of migrants in North America, with the exception of select works on religious orders and feminine religiosity.[49]

Early studies of Arabs from the Middle East, many of them also focused on Muslims, have homogenized religious women in a different kind of way: by reinforcing the "sameness" of Muslims in North America, they reinforced the trend amongst secular academics that overlooks the diversity and difference within these communities.[50] Many theorists have criticized such studies for overlooking the construction of geographically and socially distinct localities of "Muslim" populations in Western metropoles.[51] Defining diaspora as "an agent of social and cultural change as well as a political reaction to new realities," Haideh Moghissi has proposed a framework for exploring "Muslim diaspora" that demonstrates how cultural or racial exclusion in host countries often leads to politicized identities rather than vice versa.[52] As Moghissi notes, even though Muslim diasporas are rarely driven by political or religious exile, the second and third generations in Canada, Britain, and the United States take on a politicized and religiously oriented identity.[53]

This is not to say that the diverse communities of Muslims who may share a common geographical origin or ethnicity are necessarily linked by nostalgic connections to the land of origin. Rather, it is the emergence of a group consciousness that they are part of a global *ummah* or community of Muslims that binds them together in protest over their marginal location at sites of resettlement outside of Muslim-majority societies. Muslims that migrate and settle across the Western Hemisphere have become another example of a population against which "ethnic absolutism" is applied with destructive effects, as we have seen in the growing racial hatred and violence aimed at Arabs and Muslims globally since 9/11. Studies of Arab Americans have highlighted the complexities involved: Muslim Arabs are racialized according to religion, but they self-identify ethnically (or racially) as white/Caucasian. In the case of Chaldeans, there is an interesting shift in the Detroit community towards a "white ethnic" agenda that separates them from newer communities of Muslim migrants and refugees in Michigan.[54] Since "race" can be "ethnicized" and vice versa, the interchangeability of these factors allows hostile host societies to construct homogenous and static ideas of Islam and of Muslim rituals and practices.[55] Iraqi women's experiences in diaspora are defined by the recognition of diversity within these communities, and not in spite of their differences.[56] Since diasporic experiences are typically characterized by "sociocultural marginality, racialization, and denial of access to political and economic power," the "ethnicity" of groups that are "visible" in the host country as a result of skin colour, religion, language, and accent is absolute.[57] This "ethnic absolutism" maximizes cultural, social, and historical differences and assumes an unbridgeable, imaginary gap between specific groups that no amount of counter-evidence can bridge.[58] In this sense, policy makers and social service organizations' homogenization of Muslim and Arab groups has allowed those groups to fall victim to powerful cultural practices that structurally exclude racialized minorities.[59]

In order to understand Muslim women's participation in North American society, we must look to multiculturalism's rich and complex ideological and policy implications as "the backdrop against which Muslim women's negotiations takes place." Shahnaz Khan suggests that "in moving away from assimilationist paradigms," multicultural policies "continue to be a positive step in the validation of 'difference.'"[60] But by focusing on difference, are we not simply reinforcing the marginalization of "other" cultures and the outsider status of Arabs and Muslims in the West?[61] Although multiculturalism frames a place within which diversity can prosper and communities can foster an identity, difference is often defined as the superfluous elements of cultural identity while ethnic communities are assumed to be homogenous and static, unchanging over time.[62] Muslim and Arab women are therefore stereotyped either as active promoters of religion or as the victims of patriarchal religious ideologies.[63]

One danger of grouping Muslims as a "religious diaspora" is that the drawing together of all Muslim men and women into the *ummah* perpetuates these homogenizing efforts. Some migrants are drawn towards this idea of a larger Muslim community, the result of which is an intensification of their religious identity in diaspora. The *ummah* is itself viewed as an imagined nation of sorts, one that is typically differentiated from a national or politically identified community (that Islamist groups such as Daesh are fighting to establish as a bounded and political nation state under one caliph). For some young Iraqi women in diaspora, religious identity and a commitment to the *ummah* is performed through the act of wearing the hijab. Thus, the "proper" behaviour of women is delineated by a collective set of regulations, which divides those who meet the regulations from those who don't (and thus fall outside this community).[64] Symbolic and chaste women are at "the core of an identity politics" and become the focus of extremists who attempt to assert social and sexual control over their bodies. Imposing a "Muslim" community on female migrants in Western countries forces these women into manufactured categories: Arab, Muslim,

Third World/developing women, "ethnic," and so on. Paradoxically, as we shall see, such categories, self-imposed or otherwise, do matter a great deal.

The "Third World" both as geographic location and as a site of "particular socio-historical conjectures" has since the 1990s been reframed by postcolonial discourses that seek to redefine feminism in its many forms.[65] The exploration of women in transnational contexts has reoriented "imagined communities" of women who are "woven together by the political threads of opposition to forms of domination that are not only pervasive but also systemic."[66] A reductive "universal sisterhood" ignores the many ways in which these women are divided by class, nation, ethnicity, religion, region, sexual orientation, and other differences.[67] Analyses of patriarchy need to acknowledge the fact that women are not all marginalized in the same way or to the same extent, even within the same society at a specific point in time.[68] Iraqi women are not passive recipients or non-participants in the determination of gender relations; they are active agents reframing new lives and identities.[69] As Dorothy Smith argues in the context of British-Indian relations, "systems of racial, class and gender domination do not have *identical* effects on women in third world contexts."[70] "Women" and "gender" do not represent a shared experience across space and time. Instead, the categories of gender, sexuality, class, race, ethnicity, and nationality are always constructed, reproduced, and resisted through intersections with one another and, importantly, transnationally.

As historians who record the memories and experiences of racialized migrant women, we should also be aware of how the dispossession of the body in popular media frequently serves to portray women of colour (as well as Indigenous women) as non-intellectual, emotional, and mindless nurturers. Critiquing these "unitary categories of gender, race, or class," Himani Bannerji and others call for an integrative analysis informed by feminist Marxist theory that recognizes that race, class, and gender "operate simultaneously in the oppression of racialized women."[71] It is this integrative analysis that I bring to this study of Iraqi women, whose lives are uniquely shaped by the imperial (British) context of an independent Iraq nation state as well as the middling place that Iraq occupies as a neither developed nor entirely developing nation. This much was true until the US invasion in 2003, after which the country has been in the grip of civil turmoil with a weak government unable to hold together competing political agendas.

The current situation in the MENA region has intensified popular and scholarly feminist debates about Muslim and Arab women's rights and their so-called subjugation by Muslim/brown men.[72] New developments in gendered religious conservatism affect the autonomy, rights, mobility, health, and livelihoods of women living in volatile pockets of the Middle East and North Africa. As the second part of the book demonstrates, these trends also affect women's everyday experiences and their modes of integration in North America. Even as religious militias in Iraq hide behind a façade of "honour," they carry out violent public acts against women, reinscribing patriarchal ideologies by policing women's bodies and creating a climate of fear.[73] In diaspora, Iraqi migrant women remain closely linked to family and friends in Iraq, but they are affected both by a new rhetoric of Islamism in Iraq and by the ongoing violence in the region. This is particularly so for those transmigrants who live in between several sites including Iraq.

Iraqi women and their histories remain relatively understudied, but a growing number of innovative works explore women's lives in Iraq and in the diaspora. Nadje Al-Ali and Nicola Pratt's work has broken important ground by exploring the long-lasting consequences of state building and the impact of international sanctions on women in Iraq, as well as the women's continued connection to home through the diaspora. Noga Efrati and Orit Bashkin examine the effects of the earlier period of British Mandate and monarchy on the lives of Iraqi women, filling this important gap in the historiography.[74] In diaspora, female refugees and migrants are empowered by the new freedom of speech to address the past, reinvent their position in the community, and redefine their relationship to traditional values as expressed by, for example, religious observance, female modesty, and family reputation. Analysing these trends takes time, and it involves looking comparatively at these processes and their impacts on women both during the socialist period and after 2003. Zahra Ali's recently published book *Women and Gender in Iraq: Between Nation-Building and Fragmentation*[75] provides an important contribution through its sociological focus on political activism and Iraqi women's social, economic, and political experiences since the formation of the Iraqi state.

The destabilizing of nationalisms within global migrations of capital and people forces us to look beyond national ties to understand the "spaces of dynamic encounter" mapped in the liminal state between nations, languages, and cultures.[76] The "politics of dislocation" creates a polarized climate in which women are trapped between, on the one hand, masculine ideals of nation states and, on the other, mainstream feminist ideals that Orientalize and recolonialize their identities. Diasporic religious women are in many ways caught between oppressive systems of patriarchy (Arab and Western) and imperialisms that victimize them, a predicament that threatens to silence their subjectivities and marginalize them within the historical record. The Iraqi women of this study, however, are active participants in collectivizing and recording communal memory, not only as individuals but also as members of kin networks and ethno-religious global families. Furthermore, in different and often dissonant ways, these women articulate their identities within existing frameworks of Canadian and American pluralisms. Mapping transnational feminisms has opened up a dialogue that seeks to bridge the proverbial gulf between secular and religious feminisms. Articulating transnationality within the context of nation, sexuality, and class has helped us advance our analysis of diasporic women beyond simply the lens of gender in studies of postcolonial and poststructural identities.

The first chapter of this work employs an intersectional analysis of how multiple, overlapping, and discrete forms of oppression are amalgamated into the construction of a master/meta narrative promoted by the Ba'ath socialist state in Iraq. Zeynab's life narrative provides an example of Sunni elite women's memories and interventions that promoted state nationalisms whilst also exposing the fluid imaginings of "home" against which their self-identity is negotiated.[77] Drawing upon Eric Davis's framework of "memories of state," the first chapter traces the historical trajectory of collective national memory production.[78] The first two chapters explore the historical imaginaries of Kurds, Chaldeans, and Arab (Sunni and Shi'a) Muslims as they frame their memories and identities against the spectre of the nation state. Taking as its *problema* the issue of sectarianism in historical perspective, chapter 1 traces the origins of a modern imagined "Sunni state" glorified in the pan-Arab past, where women bear the responsibility of reproducing the nation and conveying through oral traditions a "national" identity.[79] The second chapter, which addresses questions raised in the first, provides an assessment of women's counter-narratives, which are read "against the grain" of imposed state and collective commemoration. It explores how a spatialized production of knowledge can subvert the means by which self-identity is conveyed through narratives that resist the state. In their counter-narratives, non-Sunni Iraqi women rejected the position of gendered obedient subjects of the state and provided multiple and overlapping ways of mapping loyalties and ties that did not conform to state nationalism.[80] This chapter traces "testimonies of the disenfranchised," by assessing the patchworks of rich oral histories and life narratives posed by Shi'a, Chaldean, and Kurdish refugee women in opposition to the dominant Ba'ath "memories of state."[81]

The second part of the book focuses on the process by which women structure their narrative through metaphor and meaning. It examines how the women I interviewed drew upon the rhetorical devices of dark humour, inherited or multigenerational memory, and food metaphors to weave together competing and dueling narratives of memories that disrupt a collective informed by the state. Chapter 3 explores affective methodology, drawing out the many challenges of conducting research that aims to understand the emotional content of the interviews. In this chapter, I clearly situate myself as researcher and interviewer in terms of my relationship to and with certain individuals and communities in the study. The chapter focuses in part on the use of a translator as that "difficult" third person in the interview. The substantive methodological discussion addresses several themes, with a focus on two in particular: the first is my "hybrid" status as a researcher and how my positioning as both "inside" and "outside" of the communities I study affected the interview process and overall project, and the second is how postcolonial feminist perspectives can help us to think through the "gender" component of designing and conducting intensive ethnographies with women migrants.

In chapter 4 I examine how multiple and overlapping ethno-religious identities shaped the way in which women manipulated the spaces of the interview. As the chapter demonstrates, women of all backgrounds covertly used the "ceremony" of serving coffee to initiate shared intimacies and to realign the power dynamics of the interview space. In order to draw out the broader implications of food as central to Iraqi culture, the chapter assesses Iraqi immigrant cookbooks as well as the role that food metaphors play in promoting distinctive disparities between communities and individuals in the diaspora. My inquiry into the cookbooks is focused on how women thread joy, loss, and sensory memories through recipes and histories, creating somewhat of a catharsis through familiar images and understandings of recipes beloved by many different groups. By engaging with both the oral and the aural, the Iraqi women that I interviewed invariably drew me into their storytelling, and in so doing made me a complicit part of this intimate sharing. Here, I return once more to "reading against the grain" as I document how women used metaphors of food and drink to tell stories, but also how they manipulated the way in which their narratives were collected by circumventing the "formal" space of the interview. I also ask questions about the central role of food in "memory making," since foodways or food memories are a site for negotiating, subverting, and challenging existing power structures. Since systems of food and drink often present competing discourses of power, the focus of this exercise was to enable these women participants to produce new knowledge that in turn produces new power relations within the interview space. The chapter's aim is to explore how remembering through consumptive metaphors becomes a form of resistance, since women used the centrality of food and drink in social rituals to draw metaphors and make claims to national symbols such as beloved dishes (and their preparation). Negotiating memory through food reveals contrasting and often competing facets of national, regional, ethnic, and gendered identities, triggered as they are through different sensory recollections.

The final chapter examines how multigenerational groups of Iraqi migrant women negotiate their bodies within new spaces where the expectations and policing of their bodies give rise to new expressions of feminism. Since the topics of "reputation," "modesty," and "virginity" all feature prominently in the anxious reflections of Iraqi women in diaspora, and especially so for recent female refugees, I question how "the phenomenon of 'honor and shame' bears a direct relation to family ties."[82] Exploring the active role Iraqi women play in maintaining reputation and protecting female modesty, I examine how their actions reflect traditional ideals of Iraqi womanhood within the context of developing ideas about female modesty. Addressing the public and private religious lives of women, and in other cases the not-so-religious break with ethnic/ethno-religious rituals, the chapter illustrates the different ways in which diasporic women confront, and in some cases reconcile, differing cultural perceptions of the female body in North America. A key argument is that as "homeland" rituals are remade in the process of (re)inventing new traditions, these women – as migrants – challenge many of our assumptions about fixity and stasis in the internal self or subjective narrative.

Chapter One

Gendered Narratives of State: The Project for the Rewriting of History

A fundamental questioning of the privilege and politics of knowledge has made any representation problematic. There is now no escaping the questions "who is speaking here? And who is being silenced?"

– Amitava Kumar, *Passport Photos*

On a cold Saturday in January 2010, Leyla, a young Sunni Iraqi refugee woman and I, sat on hard plastic chairs in a Toronto mall exchanging personal stories over a cup of coffee. As I put away my tape recorder and gathered my things to leave, she hesitated, surveying the crowd, and then leaned towards me to ask, "Do you know my greatest fear?" I shook my head no. "When the phone rings at night," she whispered, "My heart stops, and I think they will say my father is dead." For a moment, I thought I had imagined her words, the jovial bustle of the food court where we sat contrasting so sharply with their gravity. When I asked why her father was still living in Baghdad, she replied: "You see, he must, because otherwise they will take everything – the house, the business, our things. You know, they have tried to kidnap him several times before." "The Shi'is," she practically spit out, "they are the ones – always they are the ones ... the cause of all our problems. They come from Iran and take over our country and kill our people." "They are not Iraqis," Leyla insisted, "but in the end they will have Iraq for themselves." Getting up and adjusting her hijab, she added with a sad smile, "This is the way for the Iraqi women. What can we do? We must sit and pray for the men to be safe."[1]

Leyla's narrative illustrates the persistence of a century-long process of "Sunnification" through ethnic oppression and historical manipulation by the political elite, and after 1968 as part of the state nationalism promoted by the Arab Socialist Ba'ath party of Iraq. Despite being

Iraq's majority ethno-religious population, Shi'a Iraqis have long been treated as second-class citizens, systematically prevented from participating fully in the social, religious, political, and economic life of the nation state. Over the past half-century, an ideology that has promoted pan-Arabism has legitimated exclusionary power structures in prominent Arab Sunni areas such as Baghdad. Initially supporting a cross-sectarian and cross-religious ideology of Arab unity, the Iraqi Ba'ath Socialist Party – whose original Iraqi branch was established by a Shi'a Iraqi from Nasiriyah in southern Iraq – initially had strong support from Shi'a who populated many of the radical leftist revolutionary groups in Iraq during the 1950s and early 1960s. The 1968 coup began a thirty-five-year rule whereby a tribal group of Sunni military men exercised control over the party's foremost resources. Once in control, Saddam Hussein ruthlessly hunted down his Shi'a and communist rivals in Iraq and launched a war with Iran in 1980 and another in 1991 with Kuwait in an effort to further his pan-Arab Sunni agenda. Efforts to repress Iraq's Shi'a population have been in effect across multiple generations, and the impact of a top-down statist approach as well as a campaign of grassroots and popular movements have enabled the elite status of Sunnis in Iraq to prevail.

Stories such as Leyla's give us a glimpse into the process of memory making as migrants negotiate new identities in diaspora. For recent migrants forced to flee Iraq, narratives tell a particular lived truth through which they make sense of their displacement and seek to re-establish identity. Since 2003, most migrants from Iraq who have sought refuge outside the region have been Sunni Muslims, and they make up the largest group in my research sample. As recently displaced migrants, Sunni Iraqi participants, like Leyla, seek to restore meaning and cohesion to fractured lives by telling stories that address the current conflict, and how they are positioned within the context of national belonging. These are organic and evolving narratives, since refugees are "in the midst of the story they are telling, and uncertainty and liminality, rather than progression and conclusion, are the order of the day."[2] However, as Al-Ethari's comparative analysis of Iraqi migrant women in diaspora shows, these are not new forms of attempting to reconcile fractured pasts. We obtain an interesting comparison of counter-narratives by juxtaposing Valentine Balass's Jewish Iraqi narrative in the documentary *Baghdad Twist* with Zainab Salbi's eye-opening memoir of life as the Sunni Iraqi daughter of Saddam Hussein's private pilot in *Between Two Worlds – Escape from Tyranny: Growing Up in the Shadow of Saddam*. While Balass is faced with state persecution and the post-1967 expulsion of Jews from Baghdad, Salbi lives an elite existence in the dark shadow of Hussein's personal connection to her family. Salbi is spared the loss of family members (in contrast to Balass), but at the same time her sense of terror is articulated through an insistence on retelling events through her own memories of witnessing in horror how the Mukhabarat's (Ba'athi secret service) targets were publicly executed while thousands more suffered physical, sexual, and psychological torture behind closed doors.

The Ethical Implications of Reflexive Methodology

The question of who speaks and who does not speak – or is silenced – is a tension that is central to the study of how Iraqi women make sense of "identity" and "home" through their oral histories. The greatest challenge in using this archive of 112 interviews was deciding whose voice or voices to make audible. I use my authorial power in the text to inform an analysis that speaks to both collective and individual memories and narratives. Whenever possible, I have used parts of the women's testimonies to illustrate both the form and the function of their narratives. The fragmentation and coalescing of narratives are an intrinsic part of the process of dealing with trauma, as is illuminated in Dunya Mikhail's *A Diary of a Wave Outside the Sea,* which is an Iraqi woman's narrative of escaping from the Iraqi intelligence forces. In the preface, she writes that during the period from the Iran-Iraq war through the years of the war with Kuwait, her "imagination was saturated with horror stories of imprisonment, torture, death, disappearances, massacres, and rape."[3] As an ethical stance, I have chosen not to use any material that may allow individual women – or members of their families – to be identified. Instead, I have woven many of the women's observations into the fabric of the analysis rather than resort to the frequent method of providing extended excerpts.

As a feminist researcher building a framework for a reflexive and ethical methodology, I chose not to include more excerpts from the interviews because this method, however well intentioned, implicates us, as career-minded academics, in the exploitation of migrant and refugee stories for our own purposes. It is a dangerous and misguided assumption that "giving voice" must mean that we quite literally become conduits so that our participants may commune directly with our audience. Many of the women I interviewed recoiled at the sight of the tape recorder or the official informed consent forms that are by now standard-practice institutional requirements for the completion of graduate research with living subjects. Often women agreed to speak with me only "off the record," and so I maintain their confidence by protecting sensitive material. When women refused to be recorded, I used our discussion to try to understand their fears. Significantly, most explained that they feared anonymity might not be enough to protect their families from recrimination. Using pseudonyms, I have instead informed the discussion of narratives of select women whose individual stories highlight patterns of consistencies and inconsistencies that emerged. In particular, I illustrate patterns in interviews with women of similar ethno-national/ethno-religious and/or class backgrounds.[4]

Based on my personal experience and almost a decade of interviewing Iraqi women, I believe in the need to take seriously the legacy of fear that permeates the process of memory making for Iraqis. In light of the current instability and ongoing violence in Iraq, I felt it necessary at times to consolidate the women's narratives in order to provide context and excerpts that speak to narrative form as much as to the content of the interview. The Iraqi women of my study may be living in the relative safety of Canada and the US, but their lives are not static; many do not wish to be quoted for fear of repercussions for family members who continue to live in Iraq as well as those (mostly men) who frequently "commute" to and from Iraq.[5] Kanan Makiya's *Republic of Fear*, first published in 1989, scrutinized the Iraqi state's mechanisms of silencing the population through fear. Fear largely explains why the author published the book under the pseudonym Samir al-Khalil: he wanted to protect not only himself and his family in the US, but also family members still living in Iraq. In kind, I have chosen not to include more material directly from the oral histories of women in order to maintain the anonymity and safety of my participants and their families as well as my own family members living both inside and outside of Iraq.

Memories of State

Memory is politicalized and mobilized in diaspora as part of the ongoing dialectic, even when "the politics of memory is always over-determined and unstable, the consequence of incessant human intervention."[6] When we consider Leyla's narrative, one supportive of the "narrative of state," we see how identity is being negotiated through a claim to "home" that excludes Shi'a Iraqis, who are depicted as "foreign" to Iraq. Furthermore, she frames the current turmoil as one of Shi'a perpetrators who are taking advantage of the absence of loyal Sunni Iraqis to loot and pillage their homes.[7] In seeking to account for the pro-state nationalist sentiments in the narratives of Sunni Iraqi women, this chapter examines why and how the rise of female literacy and woman-based Arab Socialist Ba'ath organizations supported and perpetuated this dominant narrative. Historically fictive ideas, such as that all Iraqi Shi'a are outsiders who threaten to "steal" Iraq from the "true" (Sunni) Iraqis, are part of the "narrative truth" that came to shape state nationalism and inform how groups and individuals made claims to the nation. This dominant collective narrative featured prominently as both a divisive and uniting concept in all my interviews with groups of women and also some of those conducted with individual women. With the nation state in disarray and the Iraqi people scattered across the globe, this fictive narrative of collective identity continues to be negotiated (and renegotiated) as individual women seek a place within new social and cultural realities.[8]

As collaborators in the research process, the Iraqi women I interviewed used their position and influence in their communities to provide me with privileged access to participants, and also the tools to understand the relationship between distinct social, ethnic, and religious locations within the diaspora. Zeynab, an Arab Sunni Muslim originally from Mosul who fled Iraq in 2006 and was resettled to Hamilton, Ontario, by the United Nations Refugee Agency in Amman was one such collaborator. Her positionality within the diaspora, and her belief and continued desire to promote Ba'ath state nationalism, provide a clearly defined historical narrative of what Eric Davis terms "memories of state."[9] Together, we have during a decade of exchange discussed how and why narrative – and in particular counter-narrative – operates as a tool of resistance for marginalized groups in Iraq. Zeynab's imaginary of home and her fierce sense of Iraqi nationalism are shaped by her belief in a history of Sunni Arab supremacy in Iraq. As part of the political elite, she belongs to a family that has fought to control the apparatus of power and the modes of production in Iraq from the period of the British Mandate to the 2003 overthrow of the Ba'ath government. As she describes to me her understanding of Iraqi identity, she subsumes other means of identification into this collective identity, and insists that all ethnic and religious women must find a way of being Iraqi in diaspora. In other words, for Zeynab, there is only one way of "being" Iraqi. With a tone that suggests annoyance, she categorically rules out all of my attempts to disrupt her narrative through reference to the persecution of ethnic and religious groups in Iraq. Zeynab demonstrates her characteristically temperamental attitude to these questions:

> Really, Nadia, what are these questions you are asking me? Of *course* we are Iraqi! We come from Iraq! The Kurds have their own ways of course, but they are still Iraqi. *We are all Iraqi because of our history and our religion.*[10]

Having developed a strong collaborative friendship with Zeynab, who was involved in my project from its inception, I feel comfortable in challenging her assumptions, but each time she unflinchingly sticks to the pro-state "script" of a collective state nationalism premised upon the ideal of Sunni ascendancy and promoted and imposed through cultural, educational, media, and political institutions. Zeynab remains steadfast that unity in Iraq goes beyond both current and historical sectarian divides, and that it is the manipulation of these divisions by outside forces that keeps Iraq in a state of conflict and despair. She has promoted, across years of ethnographic encounters together, a fastidious determination that those who have common origins in Iraq are its chosen people, and one day they will return to "inherit" and rebuild "home."

Since the creation of the modern state of Iraq in 1921, political elites have manipulated history and collective memory in an attempt to consolidate state power, shape a new collective identity, and define a coherent ideology of nationalism.[11] The articulation of historical myths and "memories of state" in many of the oral narratives of Sunni Iraqi diasporic women illustrates the success with which the state carried out its plans to inculcate an ideology of state nationalism into the lives of Iraqi women. It did so through cultural, economic, and political measures that included developing and expanding the reach of British-style educational resources to all rural and urban regions, and the "Project for the Rewriting of History," which made explicit the Arab socialist Ba'ath government's intention to manufacture an "Iraqi" past that would serve a collective national pan-Arab identity.

Educating Women: Knowledge Production and Nationalism

The nationalizing of oil revenues in Iraq between 1968 and 1980 set the stage for subsequent economic and demographic expansion.[12] The expansion of the southern oil fields increased production in the north, resulting in huge oil revenues: by 1980, they grossed 98 per cent of foreign currency earnings and 90 per cent of the state's revenues. With the help of these funds, the Iraqi Ba'ath scored many achievements over the next decade. These included the electrification of 75 per cent of the countryside, access to education for urban and rural children, a decline in infant mortality, a rise in life expectancy owing to the expansion of free health care, and a dramatic rise in construction in urban areas.[13] From 1958 to 1983, the population doubled to fourteen million, and the number of citizens employed by the state rose dramatically by the mid-1970s, when almost 40 per cent of Iraqi households held government jobs.[14]

The Ba'ath state also created a "republic of fear" through suppression of the media and opposition parties. The 1980s saw the growing expulsion and execution of suspected traitors to the party. That campaign escalated especially during the devastating war with Iran and the genocidal Anfal campaign against the Kurds, culminating in the 1991 Intifada uprisings.[15] The uprisings (or "shaking off") occurred in the Shi'a south and the Kurdish north amidst the Gulf War, following the Iraqi incursion into Kuwait. Encouraged by the US and Iran to overthrow the increasingly repressive Ba'ath party of Saddam Hussein, Iraqis rose up against the regime, only to be betrayed by their instigators. In the absence of international support, the uprisings were brutally quashed by the state.

For women, the post-1968 reforms had resulted in a steady increase in female literacy and education. Women also benefitted from a state-sponsored scheme to integrate women into all sectors of the economy. Reports suggested that by 1980 illiteracy for all Iraqis between the ages of fifteen and forty-five years had been eliminated. These same reports included statistics that supported an impressive increase in the rate of enrolment of girls in primary school, from 29 per cent in 1970 to 45 per cent by 1980.[16] Shortly after the reports went public, the state introduced its policy of compulsory education for all children (male and female) aged six to ten years. Of particular note is the expansive scope of the scheme; it did not only target urban populations, but also expanded access to primary education into rural and isolated regions. Economic gains were also significant. In 1970, female labourers, many of whom first began working as unpaid and exploited child labour, made up 50 per cent of all agricultural labourers. By contrast, women occupied only 5 per cent of professional positions. By 1976, the percentage of women in professional positions had increased to 17 per cent and by 1980 to 19 per cent.[17] After 1968, educated Iraqi women became an important part of the new program to restructure historical memory through the education system. They were also involved in the organizations that targeted the loyalty of women and attempted to teach them how to be a part of the "new" national identity.

Attempts to manipulate Iraq's history and control knowledge production began long before the Ba'ath rose to power and consolidated their hold over the Iraqi state. As the government party, the Ba'ath's initial focus was promoting pan-Arabism, with its central focus on the Arabic language and history to the exclusion of the cultural heritage of other ethnic and linguistic groups such as the Kurds and Christians. Emerging in the early 1920s, pan-Arabism was inscribed into the early framework of Iraq's modern-day education system. Modelled upon the Ottoman system, Iraq's modern (colonial) curriculum followed the French late-nineteenth-century emphasis on language and national history. Using classical Arabic grammar, Satri al-Husri (the "father of Iraqi education") eliminated local dialects in a mandatory curriculum for urban and rural children throughout Iraq. In an attempt to strengthen national consciousness, al-Husri instructed teachers that the goal of history was to present the fatherland as a cohesive state, with the focus on a national past within the broader Arab homeland.[18] The 1930s were a decade of discontent as British presence and control over the political apparatus bred in the schools a generation of disaffected youth. These youth were urged by their teachers to embrace communism as a means of strengthening the state and uniting the people against their colonial oppressors.[19] A decade later, German *volk* ideologies of a primeval ancestor nation filled the history books in Iraqi schools with nationalist hyperbole and militaristic jihad aimed at strengthening the bonds of the nation state.[20]

Following the failure of Rashid Ali's coup in 1941, British officials once again assumed control over the education system and altered the textbooks and all teaching material to reflect "Iraqi" history with a focus on the broader history of Mesopotamian antecedents. History lessons now focused on the pre-Islamic past, with a greater degree of "historical accuracy" and an attempt to synthesize the histories of all ethnic and religious groups in Iraq.[21] The political elite, largely Sunni from the period of Ottoman rule in Iraq right up to the present day, had a significant impact on how the nation state engaged with other Arab nations, as well as how Iraq's political class engaged wider political cultures developing in response to British and French mandates.[22] At the core of the Ottoman Empire was an institutional framework that privileged the employment and education of Sunnis. When the modern nation state of Iraq came into being, there continued to be significantly fewer Shi'a and Kurds who were educated at a level that enabled them to participate in the leadership of the new government. The British exploited the ethnic exclusivity of the Sunni government to maintain control over this minority political apparatus.[23] Al-Husri and other notable Sunnis set into place their political domination over the Shi'a majority and minority groups like the Kurds and the Christians by creating an education system that viewed the past through the lens of pan-Arab unity. Successive Sunni regimes used the education system to project pan-Arab and later "Iraqi" national ideologies of belonging, attempting to draw together dissenting and diverse groups into one coherent national past.[24]

"Nationalism" is a particularly problematic term for discussing the development of identity in Iraq since its precise meaning shifts over time. The term is also used to discuss overlapping but distinct ideas of "patriotism," "Iraqi nationalism," and "pan-Arab nationalism." Some historians have suggested that its multiple uses imply that the ideas and followers of these various ideologies of nationalism have a greater degree of coherence and continuity than actually exists. Pan-Arabism and Iraqi nationalism have arguably been central to a century of Sunni elite political ideology, though more coherent and unified under Saddam Hussein after 1979.[25] As politically conscious Iraqis mobilized behind ideals of social justice and an independent Iraqi state, only a small number of these can be considered "pan-Arab nationalists" since most of the Shi'a, Kurds, and Christians that did participate were fighting for the rights and demands of their ethno-religious communities.[26]

How then did this small elite of Sunni leaders impose ideas of Iraqi unity within a pan-Arab framework on such a diverse population? Hanna Batatu suggests that Iraqi identity is founded upon overlapping identities in which communal characteristics are preserved within national moulds, allowing ethnic and religious identities to exist within a united national identity. Nationalism and old loyalties co-existed in the pre-Ba'ath period, when nationalism absorbed some of the older communal identities.[27] By drawing upon these old loyalties and nationalisms, the Arab socialists were successful in fulfilling their goal of hegemony in the post-1968 period, minimizing counter-hegemonic ideologies through their manipulation of the education system and the historical memory project. Here, we need to distinguish between historical memory, a group's shared understanding about the past events that have shaped its current institutions, class/status, and identity,[28] and the use of memory by "hegemonic or counter-hegemonic elites" to achieve self-interested goals.[29] The Iraqi Ba'ath effectively manipulated historical memory to shape nationalism by focusing primarily on commemorating the pre-modern era and in particular the ancient civilizations of Mesopotamia and the Abbasid Empire.

The Project for the Rewriting of History

The Ba'ath regime revised and manipulated a politically inscribed historical memory as a means of exploiting political cleavages based on ethnic, religious, and class difference. Iraqis desired a politically stable state after decades of social and cultural changes that had destabilized the nation state.[30] Following the Qasim Revolution of 1958, the new Republic of Iraq's efforts to appropriate culture began with an attempt to reduce the barriers faced by ethnic and religious minorities who wished to enter political life. Drawing upon the legitimacy of the Iraqi intelligentsia, Qasim for the first time in Iraq's history attempted to systematically appropriate folklore and control cultural interpretations of the past in order to solidify political legitimacy. Qasim's efforts to control cultural production shifted the focus away from pan-Arab ideologies that made Iraq merely a region of a larger pan-Arab state. Instead, he used folklore to bridge the gap between Sunni and Shi'a Arabs, Kurds, and ethno-religious minorities like the Chaldeans and Assyrians by emphasizing common roots in ethnic and religious ritual, be it foods, dress, dance, or other cultural forms.[31]

The "Project for the Rewriting of History" (*Mashru' i'adat kitabat al-tarikh*) represented a significant shift away from Qasim's attempts to reappropriate a pan-Arab common past. Officially implemented by 1979, the project was not just a program of political indoctrination, but rather "an attempt to construct a new public sphere, including the reconstitution of political identity, the relationship of the citizen to the state, and public understandings of national heritage."[32] This far-reaching propaganda campaign, which sought to manipulate a new nationalism in order to control ethnic and religious cleavages within Iraq society, was implemented through the work of historians, intellectuals, and state ministries, as well as through a popular campaign using Iraqi folklore to construct notions of cultural authenticity.[33] As Eric Davis notes, the scale of the project was unprecedented anywhere in the Arab world. Moving far beyond attempts at political indoctrination or repression, it relied upon rhetoric and recognized historical symbols to control all aspects of political and cultural life.[34]

Instead of pan-Arabism, the Tikriti Ba'ath adopted "Mesopotamianism," since this was a heritage to which all Iraqis, regardless of ethnic or religious background, could relate. With a focus on Iraq's ancient civilizations, the Ba'ath socialists after 1968 made Iraq the "*primus inter pares* among Arab states in creating a pan-Arab nation."[35] Leading up to the Iran-Iraq War in 1980, the Project for the Rewriting of History increasingly marginalized Islam and gave precedence to Arabism and historical tribal ties. Under Saddam Hussein's leadership, the role of pan-Arabism in the rewriting of Iraq's history not only set Iraq apart from other Arab nations, it also strengthened the regime's tribal base by privileging Arab tribal values as the basis for Iraqi culture and society.[36]

Women's Organizations and the Project for the Rewriting of History

Saddam Hussein wrote that "history should serve the ends of pan-Arab nationalism (*al-qawmiya al-arabiya*) while simultaneously countering the dangers of regionalism (*al-qutriya*)."[37] He argued that the historian should employ symbols that promote the "Iraqi region" as part of the Arab nation or homeland, and do not invoke separatism on the part of non-Arab minorities such as the Kurds. The Iraqi women I interviewed included second-generation participants who grew up during the implementation of a project in which Iraqi women played a central role.[38] The state government was well aware that a direct attack on the Shi'a majority and the Kurdish minority groups could have produced fatal uprisings that challenged their legitimacy to rule. Instead, Hussein consolidated power through an ideological campaign aimed at compelling Iraqis to internalize a new national identity, doing so through the appropriation and restructuring of historical memory. As the state became the centre of all social action in Iraq in the 1970s, the Ba'ath increasingly sought to ensure the loyalty of women and children.[39]

Iraqi women were recruited to this national and ethnic campaign as the biological reproducers of the nation, a notion that originated in nineteenth-century Ottoman policies that sought legal control over women's bodies by restricting their marriage partners. The Ottoman legacy in Iraq is evident in all of its institutions,[40] including in the marriage laws. The Ottoman government restricted women's marital rights in an attempt to keep the bloodlines intact, which meant preventing Sunni women from marrying and bearing children with Shi'a Iranian men. Thus, being the reproducers of the nation also meant being "reproducers of ethnic, religious and national groups."[41] As the bearers of culture and identity, women helped to shape the borders of the Ottoman-Sunni state, which ultimately "subordinated women's citizenship to its needs."[42] As the Ottomans sought to pull the easternmost frontier provinces into their defined borders, they used these patriarchal structures to ensure the future of Sunni governance. Laws that prohibited marriage across ethno-religious boundaries reiterated the belief in a common blood as the basis for collective belonging, one in which Sunnis would inherit the nation of Iraq as its rightful leaders.

Making effective use of the common blood-and-belonging stance, Saddam Hussein promoted a nation of common origin in order to secure the rule of his minority government and the ascension of Sunni Muslims. This myth of common origin was "constructed across difference,"[43] so that all groups, though they were hardly equal, belonged to one Iraqi nation. The regime also promoted patriarchal gender relations as women's "honour" as the bearers of the nation became part of a larger public rhetoric.[44] Women as the symbolic reproducers of the nation were called upon to produce soldiers to fight for the glory of the nation, making them – for the purposes of the political state – both the biological and cultural reproducers of the nation.[45] As the following excerpt from one of his speeches illustrates, Hussein's exhortations that women do their part for the nation drew explicitly on the historical role that Arab women had played in the nation:

> The women of our country are the descendants of the immortal Arab women who fought valiantly side by side with their menfolk, wrote the poetry of chivalry and glory, and participated in the great Arab heritage of civilization. Thanks to their conscious commitment to the Revolution and the ideals and interests of the masses, and their correct understanding of the national characteristics of our civilization and heritage, the Arab women, together with their Kurdish sisters and all other women of Iraq, are capable of following a correct path and playing their pioneering role in the construction of the revolutionary society.[46]

Even as they called for all Iraqis to work together on behalf of the nation, the Ba'ath regime went to great lengths to highlight differences between ethnic and religious women.[47] Exploiting the political cleavages among women activists, it rewrote the history of the pre-1958 Iraqi women's movement. By officially recognizing the activist history of one group, the Iraqi Women's Union, the Ba'ath all but eliminated any opposing narratives. The "awakening" of women in Iraq[48] amid the turmoil of the 1940s and 1950s brought many community-based associations together in 1945 to form a more coherent organizational form: the Iraqi Women's Union (*al-Ittihad al-Nisa'i al-'Iraqi*). According to historian Noga Efrati, "The union sought to increase cooperation among different women's associations in Iraq and thus to strengthen women's efforts to improve their social, civil, and economic position, as well as their health and legal status."[49] In its infancy, the union also tolerated political difference and encouraged its members to rise above ethnic and religious differences. This cooperation was short lived: by 1947 the government had begun a campaign to target left-wing member organizations like the Women's League Society (WLS), a pro-Communist group composed of lower-middle-class women, forcing the WLS out of the union. The WLS later became the League for the Defense of Women's Rights (*Rabitat al-Difa"an Huquq al-Mar'a*), a largely underground organization that continued to be targeted, mostly for their political allegiances but also for their commitment to Iraqi women achieving economic independence.[50] With its leadership coming mostly from elite families, the Iraqi Women's Union instead became the sanctioned public and political arm of the women's movement.[51]

Political and ideological differences between the union and the league ultimately led to the creation of two competing narratives, or histories, of the pre-1958 women's movement in Iraq. Owing to the Ba'ath support of the Iraqi Women's Union and its concomitant restriction of the league's history, the union's account of women's activism has become part of the accepted and official history of pre-1958 Iraq.[52] This account privileges women's activities sanctioned by the regime, with a primary focus on those elite-class activists and their work with the union. The regime considered the league to be politically subversive and excluded its oppositional narrative from the official account of the past.[53] Scholars have tended to focus on the official narrative, but as Efrati suggests, "only consideration of both narratives reveals the true scope of women's contributions and the hardships they endured."[54] Attending to both master and counter narratives of the history of the women's movement in Iraq offers insight into state efforts to manipulate women's memories. Furthermore, an examination of the process by which one historical narrative was promoted at the expense of the other sheds light on how the Project for the Rewriting of History sought to infiltrate and undermine grassroots movements like the Women's League. This process has had lasting relevance to the study of Iraqi women's history, and as Efrati reminds us, will have ramifications for the political and economic status of women in Iraq for decades to come.

Zeynab: A Narrative of Arab Sunni "Official" State Nationalism

Zeynab comes from an "old" family, meaning that she is part of the former Baghdad political elite whose economic power was consolidated under the Hashemite monarchy, which accumulated massive tracts of land and resources. With the disintegration of tribal structures under the Hashemites, social status became associated with the material wealth enjoyed by a small group of families, to which Zeynab (and my own family) belonged. Elites like Zeynab's family continued to enjoy the privilege of class status during the early years of the Ba'ath state (even if they did not necessarily support Ba'ath party politics). The disparity in wealth between the upper, landholding class, who wielded considerable political strength in the state administration, and the growing new middle class, or urban educated merchants and educated tradesmen, produced significant tension in the urban centres.[55] Saddam Hussein's rise to power was attributed in part to his promises to diminish the disparities in material wealth and redistribute land to the middling and lower classes. The social and economic reforms brought about by Hussein and his party after 1979 precipitated the decline of the upper class, prompting many of these families to flee the country. Those who stayed continued to live in fear of Hussein, who abhorred their elite and historical prominence in Iraq's past even as he manipulated, through a campaign of "Sunnification," their shared roots.[56]

As Zeynab and I became comfortable in each other's company, I urged her on several different occasions to tell me more about conditions in Iraq for women from 1980 to 2003. The eight-year war with Iran followed by conflict in Kuwait and almost a decade of imposed international sanctions feature only peripherally in her recorded narrative. When asked how daily life changed for her and the other women in her social circle, she claimed that "no, sanctions did not affect us, you know, we were ok. My husband made good money and we could have a nice life. Yes, people did suffer, but not us. It would have been nice to travel, yes, I wanted to see Europe."[57] In two different interviews, she stuck to the story that life for middle-to-upper-class Sunnis did not change that much during the period of sanctions. A question that led her to discuss the restrictions on her family members' movements was the key that unlocked other parts of this story. When pressed, she admitted, "Yes, my sister was in Norway and she could not return for my father's funeral. This made me very depressed, and I could not get up for some time." In a later follow-up conversation, she offered another kernel of "truth" that helped me to connect and make sense of other vague aspects of her narrative: "Okay, yes, you could not leave Iraq during this period … Yes of course this was a problem because we were like in a cage – like an animal … it was depressing … I became too depressed. Please stop asking me these questions."

These excerpts from Zeynab's narrative demonstrate how interviewees may deflect our attempts to ask questions that will reveal traumatic moments or events. Zeynab was determined to downplay personal trauma and hardship, but I was able to piece together her more complete story by using a holistic life narrative approach in which I shared collaborative authority with my participant. Had I had only one opportunity to speak with Zeynab, we would not have made this breakthrough. It was by revisiting the same questions and returning to the same topic from different angles over the course of several years that I was able to collect, and later connect, very different parts of her life story. Indicating a difficult personal past with an untreated mental health condition, she also gave snapshots into the bleak inner lives of women who were doing their best to make sense of Iraq's growing instability and insecurity during a decade of restricted access to resources.[58]

One of the fascinating parts of recording narratives is that the process of remembering involves negotiating with the ever-changing social and political realities of the here and now. In this case, the current realities of these women range from settled multigenerational families to recent refugees and everything in between. Zeynab has amended her account of life for women during periods of instability, and even indicated an internal process that has allowed her in some sense to come to terms with the role of the Ba'ath government in contributing to the misery of the nineties for many Iraqis. In one of our last conversations on the topic, she offered the following: "You know, I think women suffer the most when there is no access to things for life, like medicine and food … of course, in Iraq we can make the medicine in factories and it's not necessary to bring from the outside. But you learn in a time like that what the government is really about … It was a bad time – they just steal from the people, that's all." Although not an outright admonition, Zeynab's story now includes a revised interpretation of these memories. Over time, and perhaps partly as a result of our collaboration, she became willing to hold the state partially responsible for the suffering caused by lack of resources and supplies during the nineties.

When we first met, the focus of my questions tended to be on the Project for the Rewriting of History and the process of "programming" an understanding of the past. Zeynab adamantly dismissed this idea outright: "no, the past is the past, you can't change that."[59] And yet as I recorded her memories of how history was taught in Iraq as well as how categories of inclusion and exclusion were created through this state-sponsored project, it was evident to some extent that ideas of national identity and historical memory *had* been altered by the Ba'ath reorientation of history. Inaccuracies in historical accounts that are retold as oral histories are certainly not unusual; however, I was interested in particular patterns of inconsistency that privileged Iraqi Sunnis. In comparison to Zeynab's narrative, for example, Leyla's account shows how the vilifying of Iraq's Shi'a characterized the legacy of "Sunnification" by the Ba'ath, for the purpose of consolidating power through a collective nationalism. Many Sunni Iraqi participants gave the same narrative of an Iraqi past engineered by Sunni Arabs, who over time accepted other groups as part of the nation. Over time, I began to see how certain women who had been most prolific in advocating this Sunnified version of Iraq's past began to amend their narratives. Sunni women participants were willing, over time, to admit that they were aware that this account omitted the claims that other groups in Iraq had to "belonging" as full citizens. And as those youths who migrated after 2003 mature into adulthood – as is discussed in greater detail in chapter 4 – they too are complicating the clamour of voices from the diaspora who are calling for new political representation in Iraq's future.

Zeynab was formerly part of the General Federation of Iraqi Women (GFIW), a predominantly Sunni arm of the regime co-opted to mobilize women. She was therefore affiliated peripherally with the Ba'ath agenda to promote the pan-Arab heritage of Iraq. Like many other Sunni Arab women interviewed, her views of the historic place of Sunnis in national collective memory and her way of defining "Iraqi" are shaped by her elevated class status as part of a prominent religiously and politically significant tribe. Her depiction of Sunni Arabs as the "true" Iraqis was a common theme in interviews with Sunni Arab women, many of whom were quick to point out the socio-economic position of their families (especially in relation to my own), which only underscores the historical importance of tribal lineages at the core of the Project for the Rewriting of History. For Zeynab, there are the "true" Iraqis who make up the old upper and middle class of Sunnis, and there are later transplants to Iraq who are not, in her view, "native Iraqi," such as the Armenians, Chaldeans, and Jews.[60]

Zeynab is always quick to distance herself from Saddam Hussein's use of violence and terror against ethnic minorities. Over years of recorded conversations, she has never been willing to disclose her exact role in the General Federation, and has even at times hinted at doing so "for my own good." The GFIW was established after the Ba'ath came to power in 1968 and was closely associated with the sanctioned Iraqi Women's Union. This association allowed the two to co-opt select activists into the "teaching" of loyalty and service to Ba'ath pan-Arab nationalism and to the nation state.[61] As a vehicle for the resocialization and mobilization of women, the GFIW leaders were appointed and funded by the Ba'ath, who coordinated their programs and mandates.[62] With a network of over 250 centres throughout Iraq, the bureaucratic structure of the organization reached women of all socio-economic and ethno-religious backgrounds in both urban and rural areas.

Zeynab admitted to her "teaching" role when we last spoke at length, on her porch in Amman. The quiet and reserved daytime activities of Iraqis in Amman during Ramadan offered a soothing and relaxed environment for exchanging intimate memories. She was initially eager – and somewhat proud – to talk about her role as educator in the General Federation. Any attempt to extract details of specific tasks or mandates from her failed, but she was willing to broadly outline her work, which was to give public talks and circulate information to women concerning health, sanitation, and family security. When I asked her about the kinds of women she worked with in the organization, she described them as being "just like her," which she elaborated to mean educated and of middle- to upper-class social status. However, she also stressed cooperation within the GFIW with Shi'a women members who shared a common goal to improve Iraqi women's conditions.

The redirection of women's allegiances to the state party coalesced around the push to increase levels of education for women. As well, the education of women was intimately associated with the expansion of certain sectors of the economy, which relied on the influx of newly trained professional women. The state attempted to demonstrate its support of women's call for legal rights by making modest changes to the personal status laws in 1978 that governed divorce and child custody cases. The increase in women's education and literacy was a significant achievement by the Ba'ath, since these changes benefitted women across the country regardless of their social class or ethno-religious background. The Ba'ath also instituted a network of daycare centres for urban working mothers. Childcare became an imperative element in women's economic engagement, since it enabled working-class women in particular to increase the family budget by pursuing work outside the home.[63]

The official Ba'ath program to support the "family" by increasing and expanding the scope of economic opportunities for women was intended to increase loyalty to the state by diminishing connections between individuals and their family/ethnic/tribal group.[64] Tribal divisions continued to order the social stratification and political affiliation of Iraqis. Organizations such as the GFIW were designed to undermine these old loyalties and include women as active participants in the restructuring of historical memory.[65] This process of female socialization benefitted from the relatively homogeneous nature of the Iraqi elite during this period, and the fact that many educated Sunni Arabs supported the ideological framework established by the regime. The state coerced women into abandoning ethnic, religious, and kinship ties to their communities, and instead imposed new loyalties that promoted state nationalism.[66]

Conclusion

> Nationalism has to be understood by aligning it, not with self-consciously held political ideologies, but with the large cultural system that preceded it, out of which, as well as against which, it came into being.
>
> – Benedict Anderson, Imagined Communities

Zeynab's ideas of "common origins" and "indigeneity" disable the promise of peace in Iraq because they depend on the premise that one group is indigenous whilst others are adopted into the nation state. In her testimony, she provides evidence in her own life of how she believes all Iraqis should embrace the Ba'ath vision of pan-Arabism wherein the Sunnis – within and beyond Iraq – inherit an Iraq free from colonial ties. Similar to other political elites that are displaced, the Sunni Iraqi women of my study largely used part of their narratives to undermine the common threads and intersections that bind ethno-national and ethno-religious histories of Chaldeans, Arabs, and Kurds in Iraq.[67] These intricate and intertwined histories are, incidentally, essential to understanding the current state of sectarian violence in Iraq and across the region. However, Zeynab's collectivized nationalism belies a long history of the origins of other ethno-national and ethno-religious groups in Iraq. Her premise for self-identification depends upon a manipulated past that was promoted at the height of "Saddamism" (the cult of Saddam) as he reconstructed Iraqi identity through the oppressive force of the state.[68]

Even having spent so much time with Zeynab over the years, I am still unclear whether she intentionally participated in shaping a historical consciousness framed by a pro-state nationalist narrative. Though she has remained consistent in supporting the belief that the Sunnis are the "real" Iraqis, her interpretations of past events and historical periods continue to reveal new and troubling inconsistencies. As I assessed Zeynab's life narrative over time, it became apparent that she reflects some consistency amongst Sunni women of elite status in telling stories that place them within a relational world, where personal memories are threaded through representational narratives that tell the history of a nation state and its people.

Vieda Skultans and others have noted that in the discursive construction of the past, narrators draw upon strategies that often symbolize more about their present situation than about what they remember.[69] Sunni women forced into the diaspora after 2003 negotiate a new belonging not just within the societies in which they settle, but also as part of their displaced communities. Attempts to recreate a sense of belonging by constructing a coherent narrative of the past are part of a common human strategy to cope with displacement and instability. These narratives are also a tool for laying claims to "home" for the future, and it is possible that part of the reason for perpetuating historical untruths such as those carried forward – consciously or unconsciously – is to protect the claims of future generations to belonging in Iraq.[70] The desire to return is ever-present in these stories; yet over time it becomes increasingly evident that the reality for Iraqi youth in diaspora is that there will be no triumphant homecoming from exile. Instead, it is by telling stories and experiencing home through inherited memories of sights and sounds and tastes shared with them by their mothers, aunts, and grandmothers that they come to understand how to "be" Iraqi.

Individual memories are not simply an "archive of lived experiences deposited somewhere in the brain," but instead a dynamic of ever-shifting moments of remembrance. Reflected in the gendered memories of Iraqi Sunni women are important clues about narrative as a source *of* memory, as well as a source *about* memory. As Luisa Passerini demonstrated in her early memory work with working-class subjectivities forged during a period of fascism in Italy, it is possible to creatively use testimony to explore the resonance of "symbolic structures" on an individual level.[71] And if we take into consideration that our brain is "fundamentally a 'technology of memory,' operating differently depending on the cognitive functions required of it," then the act of remembering alters our memory through a combination of cognitive and emotional processes.[72] With the ascendancy of the Ba'ath, Iraq's political elite was instilled with a sense of a national past in which Sunni Iraqis were invented as the new citizen subjects. It is easy to see how, as their preferential treatment by the regime continued, women like Zeynab reinforced and stabilized pro-state nationalism by promoting this historical memory across generations.[73]

Chapter Two

Resisting the State: Shi'a, Chaldean, and Kurdish Women's Counter-narratives

There are small voices which are drowned in the noise of statist commands. That is why we don't hear them. That is also why it is up to us to make the extra effort, develop the special skills and above all cultivate the disposition to hear these voices and interact with them. For they have many stories to tell – stories which for their complexity are unequalled by statist discourse and indeed opposed to its abstract and oversimplifying modes.

– Ranajit Guha, "The Small Voice of History"

Narrative always reveals in some way the identity of the speaker. In making themselves the main theme of their oral histories, the differently located Iraqi migrant and refugee women I interviewed used rhetorical strategies to shape narratives that resisted the dominant pro-state national memory normalizing and naturalizing Sunni political and cultural ascendancy. In resistance to the state's project of legitimizing this hegemonic power-knowledge complex, counter-narratives have circulated among political, cultural, and religious actors in Iraq's different ethno-religious communities. Calls for change have also come from the diaspora.[1] The focus of this chapter is on interpreting how Iraqi women whose memories did not conform to the pro-state master narrative used the space of the interview to make subjective claims that resist what Michel Foucault has called "regimes of power and knowledge."

Mapping the individual "speech acts" of political resistance through women's subjective narratives helps to explain how and why systems and processes that preceded Ba'ath socialism continued to inform a "layering" of ethno-national and ethno-religious identities and loyalties. As the previous chapter reveals, Zeynab helped me to understand the changing relationality of the subject to the self, since living "in diaspora" is itself an unstable state of being. By producing dissenting – and contradictory – life narratives, Shi'a, Chaldean, and Kurdish Iraqi women, on the other hand, tell stories that unsettle a history crafted, manipulated, and perpetuated by a political elite. By producing accounts that contradict the state-produced myth of a collectivized state memory, non-Sunni Iraqi migrant women gave voice to powerful counter-narratives. As they continue to negotiate lived experiences of displacement and integration in diaspora, the narrative form of their stories illustrates well the *instability* of identities across borders.[2]

In analysing the "positionality" of the women who recounted these counter-narratives, I will address both the source of identity claims that resist the hegemony of Ba'ath nationalism and how the women employed these claims. Just as the pro-state narrative produced by Zeynab underwent change in subsequent interviews, there were also shifts in the counter-narratives articulated by Iraqi women from different social, religious, ethnic, and class positionalities. The many examples of shifts in these stories indicated not only that counterclaims do not have a "relatively stable fixity located in the narrator's individual consciousness," but that they can be modified over time in response to opportunities for political consciousness building.[3] Iraqi women from diverse backgrounds performed a contrary identity by giving voice to histories and lived memories of the persecution they and family members suffered at the hands of Ba'ath agents. In doing so, they reveal themselves as disruptive subjects who are simultaneously "being positioned" and "positioning oneself."[4] Women outside of the Sunni elite position themselves against the master narrative and "signal to their audience how they want to be understood."[5]

As Parin Dossa notes, women's stories that do not advance patriarchal and imperialist interests do not make their way into "the national and the international corridors of power."[6] In this regard, the women's counter-narratives that I collected involve more than simply giving testimony to Iraq's persecuted and undermined ethno-religious groups. Given women's active role in community and political organizations in diaspora, the courage they show in speaking their truth to power amid the constant threat of violence and retribution can have a politically energizing impact on the wider community. If we listen carefully to these women's narratives, we can hear the role that rhetoric and metaphor play in women's efforts to translate identity across borders.[7] As Michael Benson so aptly notes, "our lives carry the imprint of what happens in our particular social world," and this is the case for Iraqi women of varying ethnic and religious backgrounds who are now displaced and are recreating lives in Toronto and Detroit.[8] Furthermore,

Anh Hua notes that "because cultural memory is political, and because different stories and representations struggle for a place in history, memory is crucial to understanding a culture as it reveals collective desires, needs, self-definitions and power struggles."[9] As individuals and groups remember, they challenge "the dynamic negotiations between past and present, the individual and the collective, the public and private, recalling and forgetting, power and powerlessness, history and myth, trauma and nostalgia, consciousness and unconsciousness, fears and desires."[10] The fragmented personal and collective experiences are all drawn together in the act of remembering.

Creating Difference: Land, Class, and Sectarianism

Before we can turn to the counter-narratives, some historical context is required. The ascension of a Sunni elite that dominated the landholding class, the state intelligentsia, and the upper ranks of the military predates the establishment of the modern nation state. Its origins date back to the fifteenth century, when settlements of Shi'i Safavids in Iran, Anatolia, and Azerbaijan increasingly threatened the consolidation of Sunni Ottoman power in Iraq. The long-standing rivalry strained Ottoman-Safavid relations, as these former powers struggled to control trade routes, access to coastal ports, and the flourishing silk trade.[11] This conflict underlies the historical development of the Muslim al-Sham region, which created an ongoing divide between the Shi'a state of Iran and the Sunni-dominated states of the former Ottoman Empire (including present-day Iraq). These differences continue to shape how ethnoreligious groups interact within the nation state in present-day Iraq, and also how the state government interacts with the governments of neighbouring nation states as well as with Iraqis in diaspora.

European colonial powers took advantage of the breakup of the Ottoman Empire in the late nineteenth century and divided the region into spheres of Western control. The modern economic and political structures of present-day Iraq began to form in concert with this emergence of shifting allegiances in the region. One of the lasting implications of the Ottoman Empire for the contemporary Sunni-Shi'a rift in Iraq was the adoption of the state-supported Sunni religious establishment, which resulted in the official legal designation of Iraq's Shi'a population as settlers. While new borders were drawn, and then redrawn, they could not dissolve the salience of religious sites such as the shrine city economies of Iraq's southern provinces that for centuries had ensured a steady flow of the observant between present-day Iran and Iraq. In Najaf, Shi'i religious families were able to capitalize on the growth in the economies of the holy cities and amass great riches, which exposed them to the growing anxieties of an immature nation state. Fearing the power and allegiance that the shrines had within the region, the colonial European powers supported a dismantling of older allegiances by targeting both access to the sites and the power of the shrines to collect wealth and fund care for their populations.[12]

During the period of British Mandate government, Iraq moved towards an imperial market system of large-scale industry, which meant control over the means of production as well as new policies that designated private property. This development led to a dramatic redistribution of land and wealth in both urban and rural areas. In cities such as Baghdad and Najaf, the already existing social stratification based on hierarchies of wealth and religion was reinforced during the period 1921–2003. As Iraq industrialized and land was increasingly concentrated within the hands of historically prominent families, nomadic tribes were forced into a sedentary existence and a new ruling elite arose whose power depended increasingly on material wealth.[13] In the 1920s and 1930s, these upper *mallaks* or landowners, most of whom were Sunni (though a few of the wealthiest were Shi'a landowners from the shrine cities),[14] emerged as a "class in itself." By the 1940s and 1950s, this class had become a distinct, politically self-conscious group.[15]

The early years of the Hashemite monarchy in Iraq brought about a closer relationship between ethno-national group identity and class, since this was a prominent theme in the rise of a distinctly Sunni-Iraqi state elite.[16] The consolidation of state power in Iraq was largely a product of colonial policy developed in conjunction with the emergence of a class-based elite that controlled economic and political power.[17] In an attempt to ameliorate the growing tensions between Sunni and non-Sunni communities, King Faysal made education more accessible for the Shi'a and Kurds on the assumption that it would allowing them to join the new middling professional classes. Although Faysal was moderately successful in this respect, the monarchy increasingly distanced itself from the nationalist movement, and instead tied its fortunes to British development in the region. In response, the old and politically powerful Sunni landholding families who, like the tribal sheiks, continued to wield considerable power in the rural regions, showed their displeasure with the monarch by joining forces with the growing urban middle and labouring classes.[18] These alliances led to a series of uprisings: one against the established colonial powers in 1941, again in the Intifada of 1952, and later as part of the July 14 coup d'etat against the monarchy. The overthrow of the Hashemites in 1958 marked the culmination of nationalist sentiments that established Iraq as an Arab nationalist and socialist state. Henceforth, promoting "nationalism" or "loyalty to nation" became an increasingly dividing exercise because the "new" nationalism after 1968 did not appeal to Iraqi Kurds, Christians, or Jews. It also failed to assimilate Iraq's Shi'a population, and lacked the intimate associations of old loyalties and tribal affiliations.[19]

In light of the current state of sectarian violence that feeds the instability across the region, we must better understand how difference has been constructed in Iraq. Steering clear of a narrow "ethno-confessional" model that reinforces the region as a violent and dangerous place,[20] I follow Suad Joseph's example of exploring how beliefs about difference are situated within the Iraqi worldview. This is important because, as Jacqueline Ismael astutely reminds us, "people can believe they are very different when they are not."[21] Competing narratives are a common point of reference for historians of Iraq concerned with the lasting effects of repression and of the subversion of political dissidents.[22] The individual narratives of the Iraqi migrant women I interviewed offer insight into how women narrate individual stories that speak to group or collective counter-narratives, and how these positions are negotiated against the "imaginary" of pro-state collective memory.

Nostalgia in the Counter-narratives of Iraqi Shi'a Women

I interviewed Ameera in 2009, shortly after she arrived in Toronto. A mother of three who was then in her late forties, Ameera is a Shi'a Iraqi refugee to Canada whose family originates from Nineveh in northern Iraq. When I first asked if I could record her story, she responded very positively, saying that "I am dying of missing my home, and I don't know so many people here."[23] She articulated a nostalgic longing for home that many other recently arrived women refugees from Iraq expressed. As we discussed her experiences, Ameera also expressed a sense of nostalgia for the same Ba'ath regime that targeted and ghettoized Iraq's Shi'a population. Her fractured and competing recollections form part of the complex process by which narratives that counter the hegemony of state nationalism are complicit in supporting the master narrative, even as they position a resistant counter-remembrance.

To illustrate the point, consider Ameera's animated response to my question regarding life before the Ba'ath were ousted from power:

> Life was better – no killing. Even though Saddam was not good, Shi'is could make a good salary ... Well at least there was peace – we could enjoy our lives – socializing, we had electricity and water, and my brothers could leave the house after 6 pm.[24]

Ameera's answer reveals how the total breakdown of security, predominantly between 2005 and 2008), engendered a nostalgic idealizing of what life was like during the regime. Other Shi'a women who lived in Baghdad before becoming refugees answered in a similar fashion. Although clear in her account that life was not good for Iraqi Shi'a under the regime, Ameera joins Iraqi women across ethnic and religious lines who in diaspora seem to perpetuate structures of state power by expressing a fond and nostalgic "collective" remembering of the Ba'ath state before 2003. It is important to keep in mind, however, that in this case "life was better" marks the difference between the more recent danger of being killed in the streets by suicide bombers or kidnapped for ransom as opposed to the "old" risk of being kidnapped at night and "disappeared" by the state.

Ameera's "memories of state" provided glimpses into how the Project for the Rewriting of History was internalized by Shi'a women who belonged to neither the rich families in the shrine cities nor the political and economic elites in metropoles like Baghdad. In one of our first conversations, I asked her to tell me the history of her "people," situating my question within the vernacular usage of common terms for group belonging. As I did with all of the women, I left it up to her to explain who she was and how she understood her group or community allegiances, both past and present. Ameera proudly relayed the long history of Shi'a in Iraq, saying at one point that "Shi'is are not originally from Iraq – yes, this is true. We came from Iran in the beginning and settled in Iraq, I think because of the shrines."[25] When I asked her to expand on how she came to know this "origin story" of her ethnic group in what is present-day Iraq, she replied: "Actually, everybody knows this. This is why we had so much trouble from the Ba'ath when the war was with Iran. Of course, Saddam thought we would fight for our homeland."[26]

Despite her pride in her Iraqi Shi'a heritage, Ameera's own narrative mirrors that of the dominant, and pathologizing, discourse that Shi'is do not originate in Iraq but are settlers, and therefore have no claim to national belonging. Ameera explains that, despite their loyalty to the Iraqi state (she calls it her "homeland") during the war with Iran (1980–88), Shi'is remained under suspicion because of state-promoted paranoia over potentially disloyal citizens. Ameera's understanding of her "Iraqiness" is shaped in part by state nationalism, and perpetuated in the act of remembering this manipulated historical account. Other Iraqi Shi'a women who were similar in age to Ameera said much the same thing, supporting this feeling of separateness from Iraq as a community even as they narrate painful experiences of exclusion from the modern nation state.

Ameera's sense of disenfranchisement from the state is remembered through a narrative of exclusion that speaks powerfully to the contemporary influence of nation state consolidation and federalization on "memory making" for diasporic citizens. The political and economic realignment of southern Iraq has reshaped the relationships of its individual members to the community at large. In the case of Iraqi Shi'a, the forced settlement of nomadic tribes and the restructuring of economic and political allegiances in the south continue to resonate in part because of the link to the education of Iraqi children through the state education curriculum.[27] Prior to the period of forced land distribution that reshaped Iraq's social and economic classes, the lucrative and expanding shrines of Najaf and Karbala encouraged the idea of a rival Shi'a state in Iraq's south that would be based on a loose alliance of fragmented old tribal confederations. The redistribution of land and the "conversion" of tribes to an organized system of agriculture also promoted a demographic shift that saw the rise of a new urban working class in the shrine cities. The proto-Shi'a state was governed by the top *mujtahids* (authorities on Islamic law) of Najaf and Karbala, who promoted an emerging identity based in Shi'a religious ritual and a centralized system of tribal loyalties.[28] Because these were sites with centuries of meaning and influence in the region, the British and Iranian military forces initially supported the uprisings of Shi'a Iraqis in Najaf from 1920 until the consolidation of the state. Even before the end of the First World War, the British were busy perpetuating distrust on both fronts by creating divisions between the most powerful actors in the emerging state. As they promoted the freedoms of Shi'a in the south, the British forces working with the central government also played on anxieties regarding the rising influence of the semiautonomous and lucrative religious sites. The British Mandate system brought about the desecration of these sites because they were politically and economically threatening to the central administration of the new state. After 1967, Najaf and Karbala were cut off from their main source of income, the *waqf* or fee that Shi'is paid to bury their dead in the shrine cities. The state first infiltrated and then banned the long-time custom of the "corpse traffic," transportation of bodies from Iran to these holy sites. This policy had transformative implications for the realignment of political and economic actors in the centralizing state, one of which was the devastating loss within a few generations of the prestigious Shi'a *madrasas* (theological training schools) as world-famous sites of learning.[29]

As the influence of the shrine cities declined, the nation state drew many Shi'a towards Iraq's largest urban centre, Baghdad, while also working through other channels to decrease the importance of Iran in the Shi'a imaginary.[30] Ameera has internalized the notion that Iraqi Shi'a are "aliens" because, as she explains, it was taught to them in school. The apparatus for developing Shi'a exclusion is rooted in the legal system established by the British when the new borders of the nation state were defined after 1921. Furthermore, the 1924 Nationality Law legalized the "foreign" status of Shi'is in Iraq by recording the names and details of all Iraqi Shi'a who held Ottoman nationality before 1924, as well as those who retained their Iranian nationality.[31]

The redistribution of political and economic influence from the South towards the centre worked in concert with amendments to the Nationality Law that disenfranchised the predominantly Iranian Shi'a *mujtahids* from the shrine cities. The 'Abd al-Muhsin al-Sa'dun government passed a clarification to the law in 1964 that designated all Shi'a who held Ottoman nationality before 1924 as "indigenous Iraqis" (*asliyyun*), whereas others had to apply for Iraqi citizenship. After 1964, the constitution was amended to block Shi'a from high-ranking positions in the state offices. During the war with Iran, it was used to legitimize a wave of deportations of Iraqi Shi'a.[32] Imperial efforts in the region, due especially to British support of the 1991 failed Intifada, escalated the paranoia latent in Saddam Hussein's rhetoric and plans to "educate" the population of Iraq. For those who could not be educated in a systematic sense, such as Baghdad's growing ghettos of urban and illiterate Shi'a, the state enforced the ideals of Arab unity and Arab nationalism through the large-scale cultural production of images and iconography. Determined to prevent Shi'a calls for political representation to ever again threaten the stability of the central state, the Ba'ath regime undermined and persecuted Shi'a individuals and organizations until its overthrow in 2003.[33]

In my conversations with Shi'a women in Amman, Detroit, and Toronto, I asked them how, in light of their experiences, they responded to the abhorrent question all migrants face: "Where do you come from?" Ameera replied by saying: "Maybe we have not been in Iraq from the beginning, but we are still Iraqis."[34] It would appear that while her understanding of the historical positionality of Shi'a in Iraq bear the marks of the state's propaganda, she believes strongly that Iraqi Shi'a are also "authentic" Iraqis. As I call into question the disparities between her accounts, she grows frustrated and tries to clarify: "We fought for Iraq during the war with Iran ... but really we are not like the people of Iran at all – we have a totally different history and language!"[35] "And how has your identity been affected by your experience of being a refugee?" I ask, in order to open up a point of entry to discussing Iraqi Shi'a living in Toronto. "Well, let me say to you that I wanted to change who I was when I left Iraq … in my heart I am always with Iraq, but now life here is good and my children every day are happy and smiling. Yes, they miss their father of course – I told you he is in the Gulf for work, yes? – really it is enough for us to say we are from Iraq but now we are part of a new place that does not treat us like dogs."[36]

In a follow-up interview, I revisit the above reply and Ameera falls silent. Her eyes begin to brim with tears as she adjusts her hijab and stares at the floor. More silence. Apologizing, she then disappears for some time into one of the bedrooms in her apartment. When she emerges, her eyes are puffy and red from crying, and I get up to comfort her. "No! Please!" she waves me away, "I am fine. It is just … okay, what I want to say to you is about my personal life or memories or whatever … can we stop the interview now and I will tell to you the reason?"[37] I am no longer surprised by this request, as most of the women I interviewed preferred to share their subjective and personal history in an "informal" space, as I will discuss further in chapter 3.

Ameera brews and serves coffee, and we go and sit with her children in the family room. Now she is willing to share with me the painful memories of losing her younger brother a decade previously: the national guard took him for questioning and he never returned. Now she tells me how her family suffered because of her husband's tribal affiliations in Iran, adding that this explains why she now questions her identity. In the process of disengaging from the "formal" interview and moving into a more intimate space of sharing, Ameera begins a jumbled and emotional account that weaves together a mix of prescriptive advice, nostalgic longing, and memories of state-induced trauma:

> You ask me if I am Iraqi, and until I die I will be this, okay, but listen to me when I tell you that when you are talking with the women for your research, don't ask them about these things. Iraqis do not know who they are any more, and now our children will never get to play in the dirt and eat from the date trees. Iraq is over. My life has been always proving I am Iraqi – in the home [Iraq], and now in Canada – and for what? What will I have to pass to my children from our home? No, I don't live like this anymore, and now I want to just focus on Canada. *Insha'allah* my husband will come soon with us … You can just be what you want here, I think, so I tell my children they will always have our history and religion, but now they can be real citizens … I never want to see a day when my daughter is spit on in school because someone called to her a *shroogi*.[38]

Ameera expresses multiple and overlapping identities through her depiction of a life fractured by displacement, persecution, and nostalgia. In the above excerpt from a much longer exchange are important clues about how she views her position in Iraq, and why she feels that Canada provides opportunities for her children to be rid of the stigma of being persecuted for both class and religious affiliation. Other Shi'a women expressed the same kind of mixed nostalgic longings for home and the relief of new opportunities that allow them – and their children – to overcome structures of exclusion and oppression they faced under the Ba'ath in Iraq. The way in which Ameera understands Canada as a place in which her children can hold full citizenship also demonstrates how Shi'a in Iraq understand their unequal citizenship and membership in the Iraqi nation state. Amal, a friend of Ameera that I interviewed twice in Detroit, gave further shape to these hopes when she stated: "Ameera may tell you she does not know who Iraqis are outside of Iraq, but I tell you that the Shi'a can never know who they are *inside* of Iraq. This is the truth – you can be Iraqi and Shi'a in America, but we cannot even have this identity in our own country!"[39] No longer having to "prove" their loyalty to a home they love or loved was an ongoing focus within Iraqi Shi'a women's narratives.

Claims to Indigeneity in Chaldean Women's Narratives

Chaldean and Kurdish Iraqi migrant women expressed more explicitly anti-state narratives of resistance than the Shi'a women I interviewed. Rita, who was at the time a very recent Chaldean refugee from Mosul to Dearborn, began her narrative by detailing at length how the Chaldeans became the "first nation in Iraq."[40] By emphasizing the long history of Christians in the region, Rita positions Muslims as the newcomers to Mesopotamia. Given her recent arrival in Detroit at the time, and under extremely difficult personal circumstances, Rita's narrative is raw and emotional and produced to be part of the record. She tells me that the world should know how the Christians in Iraq suffered the ultimate persecution by the Ba'ath on account of their religion. Unlike the Kurds, she argued, Christians were shut out of the political process under Saddam Hussein and forced to flee in order to live in safety abroad. Her anguish is palpable as she testifies that "We are killed in the country that we were born in, we were raised in, and we have sacrificed for throughout our history." With the power vacuum left behind after the state's dismantling, Islamic militias gained control of many areas outside of Baghdad, which only furthered the precarity of marginalized minorities. In Rita's heartbreaking words, "it's not fair ... no one hears us, no one can protect us ... none of us will be there to tell our story in Iraq before long."[41]

In 2009, Iraqi Christians formed less than five per cent of the total population of Iraq. Their claims to "indigeneity" in the region and as the first documented people of what is present-day Iraq are a complex entanglement of Eastern and Western rites and associations with ancient pre-Islamic empires. The origin of each present-day group (Chaldean, Assyrian, and Syriac) is still a topic of contention amongst scholars, though most agree that the ancient land of Chaldea in south Babylon governed by Nabopolassar as king of Babylonia dates back to approximately 625 BC.[42] Assyrian scholars, however, claim that all Chaldeans and Syriacs are of Assyrian ethnicity since the persecuted Nestorian people (whom they believe were the ancestors of today's Chaldeans) were driven from Basra and Baghdad, and ended up in Mosul, where a large part of the Detroit migration from Iraq originated from approximately 1921 to 1999.[43] What was interesting was how much of these histories was related to me through interviews with Chaldean and Assyrian men and women in diaspora. Furthermore, many women could accurately cite how and why they considered their community to be "indigenous" on the basis of histories that dates back centuries or millennia.[44] One of the reasons for including this potted history of early Mesopotamia is to demonstrate why and how millennia-old feuds still hold meaning; they are reframed for the sake of contemporary political manipulation and become part of a new resistance from the relative safety of the diaspora.

Despite ongoing attempts by the Ba'ath to blur the boundaries between Assyrian and Chaldean histories and traditions in Iraq, today's populations are living proof that these distinctions continue to hold significance for communities that have for long been under threat of state persecution. The main differences that continue to separate the communities are language, religious rites, and customs. However, as interviews with the prominent individuals in these communities illustrated, their differences began to take on new meaning with the breakdown of the Ottoman Empire and the promotion of Chaldean dominance over Assyrians in terms of their ability to protect and administer religious rites within Iraq. For example, the Patriarch of Babylon was established in Mosul in 1830, and later moved into a central and prominent location in Baghdad after 1950. This newly established seat of power initiated a large migration of Chaldeans from predominantly northern Iraq and into the city of Baghdad. The state's initial desire to support as well as "manage" the community meant that they were able to develop new institutional arms that helped to assist the most recent forced migrants. Seventy per cent of Iraq's remaining Christians are Chaldean, and the networks that early migrants established to support further chain migration has meant that there are now over 130 Chaldean parishes worldwide, including episcopal sees established for bishops in Detroit

(1982) and Los Angeles (2002). The largest and most politically active of Chaldean communities outside of Iraq resides in the Detroit metropolitan area.[45] Detroit became an important part of the diaspora early in the twentieth century, and it is possible to trace at least four successive waves of migrations that were precipitated by persecution in Iraq. The women I interviewed who identified as Chaldean came from across these four waves, with some three or four times removed from the initial migrants who left between 1946 and 1958. Most, however, were part of migrations that preceded the war with Iran (late 1970s) or followed the failed Intifada resistance (late 1980s to the early 1990s). Those who remained – most of whom have since migrated or died as a result of conflict – have been subject to ongoing persecution by Islamist militias. What is perhaps most notable about the Chaldean Iraqis who have settled in Detroit is that they have over four generations established an important living community of Arab Christians in the West that continues to work to support those in Iraq by fighting for their right to vote and participate as members of the nation state.[46]

I ask Rita the question that I ask most of my interviewees at the beginning of our conversation: What does "being Iraqi" mean for her? She takes her time to define her identity against the Muslim majority within the country, which she feels have been the primary reason for her misery over the years. Not without a sense of humour, Rita exaggerates by raising her voice for the benefit of the recorder in saying that "Iraqi means my blood rose up from the soil of Mesopotamia – before the Muslims even found their way there!" Driven from her home in 2004 by violent extremist Islamist groups, Rita's experiences of conflict inform the "markers" that she uses to help her keep track of the chronology of her memories. She has no training in the humanities but is intensely interested in the idea of oral history as a way of recording both memories and histories. One of the many open-ended questions that I asked women was how they learnt about their identity through histories that were taught to them, including who was responsible for passing on these narratives. Rita animatedly answers, "Well, you won't learn about Chaldeans in school! We were taught by our mothers, fathers, grandparents, aunts – all of them – they all taught us about Chaldean history."[47] Both new migrants and second- and third-generation Chaldean women strongly emphasized the role of the Chaldean church in transmitting oral knowledge about their past through their own distinctive language. Even among those who did not consider themselves to be "very religious" or who did not practise religious rituals outside of holidays and events, almost all consider the Chaldean church an important means of preserving and transmitting identity by teaching students informally about their history, language, and cultural heritage.

A long-time migration route from the region of Telkaif in northern Iraq has, in Rita's case in particular, connected her to settled communities of migrants who have lived most of their lives in the Detroit area.[48] Of interest in Rita's narrative in particular was the way she spoke of growing up "between" migrations, as families who remained lamented those they lost to the diaspora, and those in diaspora continued to send back remittances to families in Telkaif. Rita has witnessed multiple wars followed by the devastating impact of sanctions through the 1990s. It mattered to her that she was considered Iraqi, but it mattered far more – as she strongly insisted – that she was recorded in my study as Chaldean-Iraqi. As she expressed it, she was Chaldean first because that was the core of her identity, and Iraqi second as part of a new identification with a developing nation state. Rita's sense of belonging to Iraq raised interesting questions regarding how the exclusion of members from belonging as citizens also binds individuals and communities across borders. She provided a necessary comparative to most of the Christian women from Iraq that I interviewed who were part of settled communities in Amman and Detroit.[49] Exclusion and exile from the nation state as a means of consolidating identity in various forms of political resistance is a theme that runs through most of the counter-narrative histories I recorded. As the next section demonstrates, these sentiments were particularly prevalent and urgent in the narratives of Kurdish migrant women active in political and community organizing.

Kurdish Women's Resistance Narratives

I first met Saheena in 2007 in Toronto, where I was introduced to her through another Kurdish woman interviewee who was active in building political resistance for diasporic Iraqis. Saheena has since become a long-time collaborator and friend, and she remains a formative voice for Iraqi Kurdish women because of her work with the community. She is statuesque and elegant, with long, dark, henna-treated tresses shining in the sun and a charismatic way of making everyone around her feel loved and welcomed. My work with Saheena has been unique not only in helping me connect to women across ethno-religious communities, but also because I have interviewed and collaborated with her in all three sites explored in this study. She unfolded her life story for me across three different locations by telling me her story from front to back. While it took many years to unravel parts of her narrative, I distinctly remember how she began to tell her own story at what she calls "her beginning," which in this case is her most painful memory: losing her children during her divorce from her husband. In our first interview, Saheena worked back from this traumatic event chronologically to her early childhood. It was only during my subsequent attempts to gain her trust and continue to interview her that she began to unravel other parts of her life, including her experiences as a long-time migrant in Canada, where she has resided since 1988. A fascinating storyteller, Saheena paints a portrait of what many other women fondly call the "golden age" of Iraq: a period before all of the conflict began to steal lives and hope for Iraqis of all backgrounds. She remembers a childhood bathed in light and fond memories of a home she knows no longer exists. During her early life she moved to Baghdad, where she was educated in the French Catholic Institute and later attended the University of Baghdad. She claims that life was good at that time (late 1970s) because it was a period before the bloodshed began and it became necessary to be "freed" from the "murderous regime, who kept all except the political elite like undereducated dogs, waiting for scraps from their table."[50]

Saheena originates from Mosul and identifies herself as a Kurdish-Iraqi-Canadian who rejects the idea that there is one way in particular to embody "Iraqiness." The topic of identity is one that we both enjoy discussing at length and in any kind of context, and so it is with her help that I have been able to connect beyond simply familial and friend networks in these three settlement sites, since she also has an extended professional network through her work with migrants and refugees. Our relationship has evolved so that it is no longer possible to separate "formal" and "informal" interview spaces that we occupy, as I have often asked her questions for the purpose of recording her responses in the most unlikely of places. This is true of most of my relationships with key informants who were influential in helping me collect information, connect with women and their families, and interpret the stories I had recorded. It is by spending so much time with Saheena in different kinds of personal and professional spaces, and across borders of both space and time, that I have been better able to make sense of the narrative of her life.

Saheena's is perhaps the strongest narrative amongst my archive that articulates the process by which the Ba'ath Project has excluded ethnic minorities and censored the historical memory of minority groups in Iraq. Active in the Kurdish movement for self-determination through transnational organizations such as the National Kurdish Congress of North America, Saheena asserted that "Kurdish people are the first people of Iraq ever since the mountains were there – Iraq didn't even exist at that time."[51] Much like Rita, she makes claims to the indigeneity of her own ethno-national group: "the Kurds are the Iraqis, there were no Arabs in this region before a thousand years ago."[52] When I ask her how the Ba'ath were so successful in manipulating historical memory, she responded that "most Arabs are ignorant and in denial of the true history of Iraq, especially after all these years of oppression around them. There is ignorance because of the censoring of history books. This occurred long before Saddam and is a true structure of colonialism. Education has bred ignorance in the Iraqi people – this is not a chosen ignorance."[53] Once again, and like Rita, Saheena focuses on the important role of education in perpetuating the damage of the Ba'ath project across multiple generations of Iraqis.

Saheena is also active as part of a transnational diaspora movement in fighting to establish an autonomous nation state of Kurdistan in northern Iraq. When I ask her how she feels about having been forced to flee Iraq, she defiantly responds, "Thank god I came here [to Canada] ... and now I must use my new power to help those women suffering in Iraq."[54] This response, as with so many others, demonstrated the desire not to dwell on that which had forced her to flee initially, but instead on the positive impact that migration had on her life. When I asked her to elaborate on how she understands her positionality with respect to Iraq, she responds, "It's complicated – I am Kurdish-Iraqi-Canadian – who knows!"[55] Saheena, like many other Kurdish women I interviewed, made claims to belonging that are rooted geographically in Iraq but predate the significance of Iraqi citizenship at the level of the nation state. For settled migrants from Iraq like Saheena, the nation state remains a technical reality of new borders and citizenship that bears little relevance to her claims to belonging in Kurdistan. Furthermore, she believes there is a growing identity crisis in Iraq, which has deepened in recent years as Iraq has increasingly become "everyone's home and nobody's home." When I asked her to clarify the statement, she explained that "Iraq was a mosaic under the oppression and force of obligation to live together under one roof. The moment they [religious minorities] could get away, they did – now every group is asking for their own nation."[56]

An Iraqi state held together by oppression is a common theme touched upon by Iraqi migrant women from all ethno-religious backgrounds. The fine balance that the Ba'ath attempted to achieve after 1968 involved maintaining a kind of "homogenous heterogeneity" in which all groups censored their opposition to the regime and prevented their differences from drawing attention to their religious or ethnic identities. Saheena sees Iraq as a "false state, created by the British for oil … Had it been a state, really, it would not have broken apart."[57] In a poignant metaphor of the family, she addressed why Iraq has suffered such a crisis since the fall of the regime:

> If you are divided from your family for many years, when you come back together you are still a family because there is a sense of belonging – no one can come up to you and say they are your cousin, because they are not. This is the case in Iraq – they were never a family to begin with – Iraqis belong to each other because circumstances brought them together, not real ties.[58]

Straddling the borders of Iraq, Iran, Syria, and Turkey, the Kurdish people of each region have developed distinct regional and dialectic differences that have further fractured the Kurds as one community.[59] In Iraq, the Kurds are overwhelmingly Sunni Muslims although there are also remaining pockets of Jewish and Christian Kurds in the northern provinces.[60] Whereas religion is the central basis for Iraqi Chaldean identity, for Iraqi Kurds it is a confluence of territory, language, and cultural distinctiveness that sets them apart from other Iraqis.[61] The history of how the modern Kurds have been amalgamated into the nation state helps to explain their exclusion – and self-exclusion – from belonging as full members of the Iraqi nation state. Kurds have long occupied the margins of the region in many forms, providing a mercenary army (economy of export) for pay over many centuries.[62] The breaking apart of the Ottoman and Safavid empires enabled the Kurds to expand territorially and also extend their military prowess by cooperating in a system of border policing. As an economically efficient staffing source for imperial armies, Kurds existed for centuries as semi-autonomous people until in the nineteenth century they began to depend increasingly on the British to reinforce their self-governance. Following the defeat of the Ottoman Empire in 1918, the Treaty of Sevres (1920) dashed Kurdish hopes of self-determination, and in a back-handed move that has led to decades of bloodshed and forced exile, the Kurds were divided by imperial forces between four states where they are subject to four separate ethnically nationalist governments.[63] This crucial division has – much to the benefit of the states within which Kurds currently reside – exacerbated existing divisions between political factions of Kurds. Kurdish tribalism and the growth in prominence of *shaykh* families in Iraq have produced revolutionary leaders such as Jalal Talabani (PUK) and Mustafa Barzani (KDP), whose supporters have continued to fight for political dominance in the Kurdistan Regional Government.[64]

The history and diversity of the Kurdish-dominated north of Iraq made it an ongoing thorn in the side of the state regime. In particular, the Ba'ath struggled to effectively mobilize and utilize the Kurds for their own political agenda.[65] Even before the Ba'ath began a genocide against its own people later in the century, the Kurds had already suffered from decades of colonial mismanagement of ethnic and religious interests in northern Iraq that resulted in bloody massacres in 1933 and later in Kirkuk in 1959.[66] As a result of their intertwined histories and oppressions by the Ba'ath, Kurdish and Christian Iraqi women from the northern region express narratives that convey common threads of nostalgia for the millennia of coexistence that was undone in just one generation by the state-enforced consolidation attempts.[67]

On the topic of identity, there was one occasion during a group interview in Detroit when a participant confronted me about my interest in identity. At the time I was taken aback, making it difficult to react in the moment, but I realized upon listening to the recording how revealing her answers are of how the Ba'ath used fear to consolidate identity. The participant asked: "Why ask us about our identity, when this [identity] is what has made us targets of the Ba'ath? Do you really understand Iraqi history if you are asking us about what we have experienced? Do you know that what we witnessed is not connected to our history – no – this is all the Ba'ath wanting to change our history because they fear that we have the claim to Iraq?"[68]

While this was by no means the only confrontation that resulted in questions being asked about identity, there was a certain dynamic that took place in group interviews that made me – by proxy – the protagonist in the conversation. The first time I was openly confronted was jarring, and it took me a long time to build up the confidence to conduct group interviews again. However, what I began to notice after conducting a number of small (two to five people) and large (five to ten people) group interviews was that some interviewees used anger – in this case directed at me – as a means of masking the questions that made them most uncomfortable. In the example above, the participant refused to allow me to continue to ask my questions to the group by constantly interjecting that these were the exact kinds of questions she would expect from a Sunni from Baghdad. However, I also sensed in her a desire to have her narrative heard, and so I following up with her in order to conduct an individual interview. She eventually agreed, and during a somewhat hostile individual interview, she made her feelings towards me evident in her deconstruction (within earshot of anyone at the coffee shop who cared to listen) of my legitimacy as an objective researcher since, as she emphatically stated in order to end our interview, "all Sunnis are out for themselves in Iraq – this has and always will be the case. End of discussion."[69] This interviewee, who refused even to be identified by a pseudonym, believed that my identity as part of a Sunni Iraqi family made me extremely suspect as someone who would protect her narrative and help uncover histories of resistance to the Ba'ath regime.

Saheena has over the years been the kind of collaborator that I could always turn to in times of need, and upon finishing my interview with the group and then the woman mentioned above, I called her one evening to ask if I was in some way compromising my own research by revealing "too much," being careful not to unequivocally accept the answers that were given to this contentious question. In fact, the question of identity remains one that I ask *all* Iraqis I meet since it can inform a basis for entire friendships and professional relationships. It is also one that is useful to continue asking as generations of migrants – including these women and their extended families – settle outside of the homeland and integrate, thus informing new identities.

Political activism was a means by which Saheena chose to inform me about her personal and professional lives, using her advocacy work and the meaning behind it to answer questions on memory and identity. When I asked her to speak about the meaning of her work with the Kurdish Congress, she provided by phone a moving admission: "I shall deliver this voice – for people living in the diaspora, this is our duty to educate the people about the legitimate rights of our nation. Actually, this is a role I created for myself."[70] Active participation in the Kurdish movement is extremely important to her sense of being and belonging outside of the homeland, just as it is to her sense of pride in her "Kurdishness."As we debated her positionality according to how she understands the intersections as historically meaningful as well as part of the contemporary political climate of Kurdish and Iraqi identities, she offered the following reflection:

> You ask me these questions about being Iraqi ... I would turn this around and ask you, what does "Iraqi" mean to *you*? Are *you* Iraqi? Now, you did not live there for a long time, but is it something you cannot be if it is in your blood? When you were a child you put your hands into the soil in Baghdad – this is the meaning of "Iraqi"! We grow from the soil of the fertile ground as strong women! Come on, I am only joking with you, Nadia ... if you stop asking me about my identity maybe I will start to explain to you why the Kurds are the original Iraqis!

In her usually frustrating way, she had outmanoeuvred me into positioning myself as part of a growing diaspora where I was also responsible for determining who I was in relation to "Iraqiness." And for those who are born into the diaspora, this question will have continued salience and meaning as the nation state's political actors realign and stumble towards a new power compact.

Conclusion

One voice cannot speak for an entire community; however, the aim in this chapter has been to expose the impact of state control and manipulation of the national narrative on the narratives of individual Iraqi women from the diaspora. Zeynab's narrative is inscribed with elite Sunni expectations about the prominence of this group in Iraq's past, whereas Rita and Ameera counter these claims, expressing as they do a confusing confluence of accepted alienation from national belonging and also an expressed disregard for these boundaries entirely. As with all politically motivated programs designed to reinterpret history for the purpose of political ascendancy, the message from the Ba'ath project influenced all of these narratives, even if the outcome of the message has been differently interpreted.[71] The need to impose such a narrative also speaks to the fragility of the Iraqi nation state, and the fact that a power vacuum initiated by the removal of Saddam Hussein has plunged the country into a struggle to control the political apparatus (and the narrative) of Iraq's future.[72]

Shi'a, Kurdish, and Chaldean women's oral histories tended to produce narratives that counter the statist collective memory imposed on Iraqis. What differentiates non-Sunni from Sunni women's narratives is in large part the layering or overlapping accounts of identities and histories that are at odds with each other, and this is especially so in the case of Kurdish Sunni women interviewed for this study. As Ameera's narrative reminds us, the collective national identity favoured by the Ba'ath continues to feature prominently in their negotiation of an Iraqi identity.[73] Older loyalties, networks, and tribal affiliations were to some extent able to co-exist within the framework of pan-Arabism because nationalism, while corroding older loyalties over time, also absorbed some of the psychological elements of tribal loyalties.[74] By drawing upon these older nationalisms, the Ba'ath were able to create a historical memory of a united Iraq, and an Iraqi identity founded upon newly forged belongings. If "hegemony can only be successful if it finds its origins in society, not in the state apparatus,"[75] then the Project for the Rewriting of History depended as much on the use of existing differences as it did on "the large cultural system that preceded it." There are, as Benedict Anderson noted, communities that are largely held together by an imagined framework of older forms of belonging that against all odds come into being.[76]

Iraqi women "imagine" themselves as part of multiple nations, and in some cases these nations are at odds with each other and one seeks to eliminate the other, as in the case of the Kurds. The Kurds have imagined their community to be a territorial political entity that has developed in conjunction to, but separately from, the Iraqi nation. The primordialist approach to ethno-symbolism that is adopted by those who oppose the modern origin-of-nations approach perhaps best explains the Iraqi case, where modern nations (however broadly understood) have strong connections with pre-modern ethnic communities. In this sense, Iraq is an invention of modernity, a colonial creation that constructed its past around the constraints of a single *ethnie*. A community created around an idea of shared territory, the nation of Kurdistan links to its ancient history and proto-national identity to reveal the importance of language and ethnic culture to territorial belonging.[77] As Anthony Smith argues, in order to understand a nation's roots and continuing appeal, "we must trace them ... to their underlying ethnic and territorial contexts."[78] In the case of the Kurds in Iraq, ethno-nationalism trumps Iraqi nationalism, an identity from which they had until 2003 felt entirely marginalized, and with good reason.

As these more recent refugees reinvent themselves as part of a new and porous historical dialogue in which their agency in the present enables them to remember the past on their own terms, they recreate the parameters of their identity as Iraqis and as part of transnational ethno-religious communities of migrants. Alessandro Portelli reminds us that "the discrepancy between fact and memory ultimately enhances the value of oral sources as historical documents because such discrepancies reveal how ordinary people caught up in historical events make sense of their experiences. This too is worthy of historical analysis."[79] As these counter-narratives indicate, personal identity is imagined through many different metaphors and tropes, as the next part of this book will demonstrate, and also in resistance to a collective, statist remembrance of the past. As part of diverse ethnic and religious Iraqi communities, these refugee women produce narratives that also capture the multiplicity of ways in which Iraqi refugee women expressed ideas of nationalism and national belonging, including how this intersected with their personal identity.

Jan Assmann's concept of "mnemohistory" is useful here as it urges us to be "concerned not with the past as such, but only with the past as it is remembered."[80] Counternarratives can also not be considered an "innocent window into participants' interiors," as Michael Bamberg argues, since they must be analysed as "interactive social and cultural practices, which entails a close scrutiny of how such responses are put to use."[81] National identity, as promoted by the Ba'ath, is based on a "narrative template" through which women give coherence to the nation's past through their individual memories. This coherence provides what Marek Tamm considers to be one of the cornerstones of collective identity, "repetition and consistency" as vital attributes towards preserving and furthering a nation's historical consciousness.[82] As women's counter-narratives are negotiated against this "template," they too expose overlapping boundaries of their ethnic and religious "mnemonic communities" that cut across the national narrative, but in so doing also reappropriate the "nation" as the framework within which they conceive of their identity.[83] Without this framework, their memories are dislocated from the chronology of time and the location of memory within the context of specific time and place. Counternarratives in the context of Iraqi women's memories are positioned as part of a political and historical intervention that resists the oppression of the past, and in order to achieve this, women contextualize their countering of state-imposed national memory through their rejection – to varying degrees – of the master narrative.

Chapter Three

Towards an Affective Methodology: Interviewer, Translator, Participant

But without stories, *without listening to one another's stories*, there can be no recovery of the social, no overcoming of our separateness, no discovery of common ground or common cause.

– Michael Jackson, *The Politics of Storytelling*

In her work on gender and memory in post-apartheid South Africa, Annie Coombes observes that survivor testimony is often located "in the temporal and spatial detail of the quotidian – in the intimacies of domestic routine and family life – and consequently, it is here that the insidiousness of daily infringements of civil liberties and their effects on individuals is most keenly represented."[1] Iraqi women's experiences and memories are similarly shared across multiple and intersecting temporalities, spaces, and intimacies. Like Coombes, I found that it was in intimate and domestic spaces that women delivered survivor testimonies that interwove emotion, metaphor, and silence. Drawing upon new gender histories and ethnographies of emotions and the senses, this chapter engages with new ways of "layering scale and perspectives" based on the narratives that Iraqi women migrants shared.[2] Alessandro Portelli reminds us that "oral sources are *oral* sources." This means we must also listen to the unspoken – potentially, but not necessarily, silenced – transcript of the interview, since this process of "listening in stereo" to spoken and unspoken cues provides valuable clues to unlocking meaning in oral history narratives.[3] By highlighting the dual use of textural and ethnographic analysis in "reading" narratives, I listen carefully to the said and the unsaid, the use of authorial voice, and the demonstrable utility of silence.[4]

I am intimately situated in this research as both an insider and outsider within communities of Iraqis abroad. Here, I draw upon a rich tradition in attempting a more transparent ethical and embodied ethnographic method that draws upon a framework informed by historical context in order to develop a decolonized and collaborative method for working with racialized participants. I do not imagine that as "informants" the women in question do not in return study me through our conversations, seeking "knowledge" of "truth" about my own stories. In practice, sharing and exchanging stories is an important part of building trust; it also fosters a sense of relationality with the women participants. Michael Frisch's early work on "sharing authority" with participants remains salient, since this helps to diffuse the "authorial voice" in oral history interviews with racialized collaborators.[5] Feminist oral historians have long discussed the idea of sharing authority, and this connects recent feminist engagement with affective methodologies as a means of making sure we do not reproduce the clichéd "anthropological gaze" that renders informants as objects of analysis rather than as subjects of their own lives.

I am deeply connected through the work to individuals and organizations, and I would be amiss not to credit them with taking on part of the burden of the research. It would have been impossible to imagine connecting across three distinct geographic locations with Iraqi women of such diverse class, ethnic, and religious backgrounds had I not invested in organizations and people to provide whatever support that I could in return. The community and non-government-funded organizations that assisted me during the period 2003–2012 include: in Amman, UNHCR, National Center for Human Rights, Mitnaz Law Group, CARE, and Caritas; in Toronto, Arab Community Center of Toronto and Assyrian Canadian National Federation; and in Detroit, Chaldean Federation of America, Chaldean American Ladies of Charity, and American Community Center for Economic and Social Services of Detroit. I sought a range of perspectives and experiences beyond the political elite and the predominantly Sunni (both mixed Kurdish and Arab) professional class in which my family and community are located. Revisiting anthropologist Clifford Geertz's "thick description" approach to interpreting emotions, textures, and silences, this chapter explores the layers of interactions that make up "the interview." It also considers how historians should interpret the kinds of stories and rhetorical forms they encounter.[6] Drawing on the work of other feminists who, like me, are positioned as hybrid or racialized researchers, I address what it means to create space for participants by sharing authority and acknowledging that the interview is a collaborative effort.[7]

Interviewer: An Insider-Outsider Perspective

Correcting power imbalances in oral history interviews with women has been at the forefront of feminist research in ethnographic and historical methods of memory making.[8] From the rise of social history through to the "cultural turn" in history, women's historians attuned to these methodological issues have been actively involved in the creation of new archives of oral sources through which women's lives could be "read." The diversity of the women featured in these oral history archives has enabled feminist historians to write new and more inclusive histories. Early studies of racialized migrants and their communities lacked sensitivity to non-Western, decolonial, and non-secular ways of understanding womanhood, femininity, and agency.[9] Chandra Tolpady Mohanty's intervention in 1991 rejected the interpretation of postcolonial and racialized women as "victims," and called for non-Western feminists to challenge the systemic racism at the heart of the academy.[10] In continuing to answer her call, feminists have reinterpreted histories of religious and racialized women – most recently with a growing focus on Muslim women migrants – with research that moves away from the colonizer-colonized dynamic of most early participant-observation studies.[11]

Accessing the female voice is a difficult task. It is especially so in the case of groups migrating from "zones of exclusion" and into "zones of inclusion," as is the case of Iraqis migrating to North America.[12] In order to access voices across the widest possible range of class, ethnic, religious, regional, and age categories, I myself had to "be mobile." As a woman researcher interested in speaking primarily to other women (though men are included both as individual participants and as parts of group interviews in my sample), I was struck by the fact that most of the women I contacted invited me to their home for the interview. When this was not possible, I met others at coffee shops, professional offices, or at the mall. In addition, I conducted a number of interviews at an (undisclosed) UNHCR (United Nations High Commissioner for Refugees) camp in Jordan.

Some women asked if their husbands or sons could be present for the interview, and, in a few cases, I accepted the terms because to do otherwise risked not interviewing certain participants at all. There were certainly instances where the presence of men in the interview eclipsed the collaborative space I sought to nurture. Husbands tried to shape a wife's narrative so as to bring it in line with their own recollection of a given event or period. In an equal number of cases, however, male relatives were critical sources of support, helping the women to deal with the emotional fallout from disclosing details of their personal trauma. I did what I could by urging upset participants to take a break so they could recover their composure. During these breaks, the women usually found solace and courage in the arms of male and female relatives, who then usually accompanied them for the reminder of our time together. In a few cases this proved helpful, as it deflected attention away from the source of the tension and allowed the women to confer with family members regarding exact dates and places. Significantly, the woman wanted to provide an "accurate" account of their past. In one memorable example, a woman who had arrived in Jordan two months before I interviewed her wept loudly during the interview but refused to stop the recording. Finally, her husband, who had refused to leave his wife or their home during the interview, asked if he could sit with her in order to comfort her and calm her down so she could continue to speak. I was very thankful for his help. She resumed speaking as she clung to his hand, her pain visible in the seeming endless tears. The physical embodiment of her grief was evident in her shaking body and her wailing for the sad process of remembering. It was also conveyed in the cracked voice with which she said: "What can we do now, the Shi'a stole the government and now they will steal the oil, and we will lose our country. Who will save us now – who will save the Iraqis? Now we are hiding like dogs here in Amman, and waiting to go home." Raising her voice to a wail, she ended by saying "IT IS OUR HOME!"[13] Later, as I was leaving, the woman struggled to calm herself and, taking my hand, she looked at me with bloodshot eyes and "confessed" in the space of a sentence what the emotional rupture of forced migration from Iraq had meant for her: "It is a shock for the heart ... Iraq now is in pieces, just like my heart."[14]

In a historiographical review of "confession," oral historian Alexander Freund notes that "the oral history method, and in particular the interview, has a long history that deeply entangles it in the development of confession, the interview society, and the rise of a mass culture of confession."[15] One can certainly imagine the interview as a site of self-revelation through confession. However, as this chapter demonstrates, the interview is also the site at which the narrator constructs the self within the context of her interpersonal negotiations with the interviewer. Drawing upon the idea of the "halfie" researcher who belongs at once in two different imaginaries, I understand the form of confession in which I ask women to "speak about the self" in interviews within a Western form of knowledge production in which the individual subject is the focus. I often struggled, on the other hand, to explain to the women participants who the "self" was within this relationship, and why being able to "tell their stories" was so important.[16]

As oral historians, we do come into the interview with a clear understanding of what it means to "speak about the self," though the "confessional" is also changed. Furthermore, how individuals interpret "confession" and "speaking about the self" differs enormously across spaces and periods and peoples.[17] In the West, the ubiquitous use of the confessional form is influenced by the interconnected systems of power, knowledge, and mass communications that infiltrate all societal interactions in modern life. But, as Freund suggests, sociocultural expressions of confessing are not universal. Different and incongruous modes of confessing are prevalent in our daily interactions, and in how we relate to research participants. To take an example from my own fieldwork, in July 2008 I fell ill in Amman and required an urgent consultation with a gynecologist. I called all the recommended private gynecological clinics in the city, but no one agreed to see me at short notice. However, when my father tapped his network of displaced Iraqis, he found a female specialist who agreed to see me the same day so long as my father accompanied me – an unmarried daughter – to the appointment. My father and I assumed that he would remain in the waiting room, so we were both caught off-guard by the doctor's insistence that he participate in the appointment. The doctor, who referred to me only in passing, asked my father to explain how the illness had developed. Then, to our mortification, my father also had to be present during the examination. The appointment was in many ways an extremely important moment for me as I was provided with an on-the-spot diagnosis (endometriosis). The doctor then very happily reported that the ailment could be "cured" by childbirth, which she recommended highly to my father, adding portentously that "even if she doesn't change her mind, all I need is your agreement and we can begin a course of hormone therapy that will increase her chances … and get her married! Next time I see you, this is the story I want to hear!"

Narratives of the self are tailored according to their purpose. For example, when we visit the doctor, lawyer, or therapist, we tailor our story to address a material concern. We must also be aware of other social-cultural articulations of the confession. It thus follows that our readings of women's narratives must attend carefully to how our participants understand "confession" rather than take its meaning for granted. From my standpoint as a halfie researcher, I strove to remain sensitive to colonial structures of power and knowledge that have used confession to further an agenda of fear. That is, I understood that because I am a Western-raised researcher, my understanding of sharing testimony differed enormously from that of my narrators who, having escaped a paranoid and brutally repressive regime, feared that confessing, or the act of recording testimony, could serve the interests of the state. In other words, technologies of power can usurp technologies of the self. As Foucault argues, this negotiation between the two technologies forms the modern subject, and it is as a part of this ongoing internal dialectic that subjective identities are articulated in our ways of remembering.[18]

Initially, the greatest challenge I faced in conducting interviews with recent refugees in Amman was the women's perception of the interview as a site of coerced confessions.[19] When I began this research in 2007 during a particularly intense period of conflict in Iraq, many women agreed to speak with me but refused to be recorded. A continued source of anxiety for both me and the participants was obtaining a signature for the informed consent form that is required by most university ethics review boards. This official-looking document, a source of abject horror to some of the participants, generated a tense atmosphere of palpable fear. As one of the participants observed (before encouraging the other women in the group interview not to sign the form): "This is a form, and you want me to sign it, but maybe one day it will end up in the wrong hands."[20]

Translator and Facilitator: The Problematic Third Person in the Interview

Without the help of personal, familial, and professional connections in all three of my locations, I would have found it virtually impossible to contact woman willing to agree to participate in my project. I am particularly indebted to one close family member, Om-Muhammad (mother of Muhammad), for setting up many of the early interviews I conducted in Jordan.[21] The process of locating potential participants initially began in 2006 when I was conducting research for a graduate paper on the theme of racialized and immigrant women in Canada. That year, members of my extended family living in Amman and Damascus were resettled to Hamilton, Ontario, through the UNHCR program. I was fascinated by their observations of life in Canada; they were struck by how orderly all of the processes were, including the airport, immigration, and their temporary placement at an immigration facility in Toronto. As someone whose own family migration to Canada from Wales had been a relatively smooth process, I longed to understand and support my cousins as they sought to reorganize lives disrupted by forced migration from Iraq. Life had scattered many of us far from Iraq, and for the first time in a decade and a half cousins, aunts, and uncles came together under one roof in an adopted home to rebuild a family. Like many of the other Iraqi families with whom I shared time in Canada and the US, my family included transmigrants, that is, men who, like some of my uncles, had left Iraq much earlier in order to support families with wages earned in the Middle East, South and East Asia, or western Europe.

My family's happy reunion in diaspora was not a planned one, but rather the result of unforeseen events. As I spent time getting to know these relatives, other family members arrived. They not only agreed to be interviewed but also connected me to other participants. They also helped me "map" the spatial settlement – as they saw it – of Iraq's different ethno-religious families within the Toronto area, including Hamilton, Brampton, and Mississaugua. Based in Toronto as a PhD student, I took full advantage of this privileged access and interviewed women over the course of my five years (2007–12). During this period, I made summer visits to Amman in 2007 and 2008 in order to conduct interviews, and four trips to the Detroit area (2008–11). During summer 2007, I enrolled in Arabic classes at the University of Jordan, Amman, to improve my language skills while also conducting several intensive interviews with the assistance of Om-Muhammad, whose role as occasional "translator" is discussed in this chapter.[22] Om-Muhammad's insistence upon "chaperoning" me during the early interviews "for my own good" so that participants would know I was from a decent family (in her opinion) also helped me to see how participants limited their intimate sharing when she was present in comparison with when I interviewed women alone.[23]

My hybrid and insider-outsider status as an Iraqi-born woman who grew up in Wales and moved to Canada as a young adult was the reason I engaged Om-Muhammad's help when I began my research in Amman. Because I left Iraq at the age of five, my connection to the country is real in my own mind but tenuous in the imaginaries of others. Being both Welsh and Iraqi (and a naturalized Canadian) provides me with many passports that enable me to move between identities, fixed and fluid. Among the many markers of supposed cultural difference that separate us is our accents – I still maintain a slight British accent that positions me in a particular way as an Iraqi with privilege and one who has grown up predominantly outside of Iraq.[24] Scholars such as Lila Abu-Lughod and Gayatri Spivak, discussing being a halfie researcher working with postcolonial Muslim communities in the US, have spoken about the need to shape a reflexive methodology that assumes knowledge production is a form of information exchange rather than a one-way transmission. The challenges of being a halfie researcher or "wild anthropologist," they argue, demand a different kind of methodology, one that resists recolonizing the narratives of women into Western patterns of recording memories frozen in time and place. At the same time, halfie researchers, as Binaya Subeidi argues, are themselves positioned against dominant narratives, and as such they present to their participants bodies that are also hybridized and unstable.[25] That they are people who have themselves lived transnationally may help to create trust in the interview.

The presence of another Iraqi woman, Om-Muhammad, in many of my Amman interviews made clear just how much the women's perceptions of my class status and moral reputation mattered to their willingness to participate in the research. As others have observed, the still strong relationship *to* class and *between* classes in Iraqi culture informs all social interactions, including perceptions of a woman's sexual and familial reputation.[26] In Amman, I did not initially realize that Om-Muhammad's presence as my chaperone also served to corroborate my "good" standing in the community. When I entered the interview with her, I was met with affection and familiarity as a member of the respected Al-Gailani family. One participant verified this by stating, even before she had started answering my questions: "I know who you are, my dear. You come from an old family. You are a *good* girl."[27] References to my modesty and reputation reflected the respect and social standing enjoyed by my family members both within their community in Iraq and across other social groups in Canada. On the other hand, Om-Muhammad's involvement also affected my ability to maintain what control I could over the interview process. It similarly meant that I had to cede authority in interviews where she took liberties to shape women's stories and direct them to talk about happier times during Iraq's "golden age."[28]

My hybrid status conferred a dual identity that acted like a passport allowing me to move between categories and realities with relative ease. I could not, however, circumvent the efforts of women to enlist me into their hierarchy of moral regulation, where those of higher class standing feel entitled to police and regulate those in less fortunate economic circumstances. The term "good" was used often throughout the interview, often accompanied by a knowing nod, a pause, or even at times a pat on the shoulder or knee. One participant made me feel very uncomfortable when, clasping my hand between hers so as to "read" my secrets through the lines on my palm, she commented: "You are not married? Why not, are you not a good girl? Your father should marry you as soon as possible – you are beautiful now, but this will not last!" She then added: "My son is young for you, but we are from a good family – I am the mother, so my job is to find him a good wife who will have many babies!"[29] I would receive other marriage proposals over the course of the research, and what began as amusing anecdotes over time became invasive and unpleasant. The interview just described demonstrated how women's use of shaming tactics to regulate other women also makes them complicit in policing other bodies to ensure conformity to the universally acknowledged but equally diffuse ideal of a "good" woman.[30] In the presence of Om-Muhammad, a woman of good standing in the community with a reputation that commanded a certain respect, the women were even more emboldened to ask me, often through teasing, intrusive questions, about the state of my "intactness" (virginity) and my history of relationships with non-Iraqi men. In her aptly titled article "Fieldwork of a Dutiful Daughter," Lila Abu-Lughod similarly recalls how her female participants from "home" asked pointed questions about her marital status. In her case, she admits to resorting to lies as a self-protective measure, that is, to protect her standing in both home and research community:

> I was asking them to be honest and was trying to find out what their lives were like, but was unwilling to reveal much about myself. I was presenting them with a persona. They knew nothing of my life in the US – my friends, family, university, apartment – in short, much of what I considered part of my identity. I felt compelled to lie to them about some aspects of this life, simply because they could not have helped judging it and me in their own terms. In that scheme, my reputation as a young woman would have suffered. So I doctored my descriptions, and changed the subject when they asked about me, but I felt uncomfortable doing so.[31]

Her frank reflections on how she chose not to divulge personal information encouraged me to develop strategies for handling invasive questions without necessarily lying to my participants.

As Abu-Lughod notes, there is a process of "editing" that occurs from both perspectives that we also much account for as we read back through our interview material. When I returned home from Amman in 2008 and started transcribing the interviews, I realized that I had prepared a pre-emptive narrative for explaining my marital status, believing that I could deflect the focus on me by claiming to be previously engaged. The women waved away my claims, making similar comments to that of a Kurdish friend of Om-Muhammad:

> What is this engagement you are speaking of – this is not a real Muslim engagement, it is just you say this, he says this, maybe you plan a wedding. If you are Iraqi, you are not engaged before the *mahar* – no! No, Nadia!

> Don't worry, there is still time for you, and you can just throw away this American boy and marry my stepson. Yes! Wait – he is very handsome – let me get the picture![32]

As I continued to attempt to negotiate a comfortable space of sharing, but not sharing too much, about my past and present circumstances, I eventually came to understand their comments as part of an interesting power dynamic by which women's modesty is the central focus.

The added risk and security concerns associated with interviewing Iraqi refugees during that troubling time in Jordan also helped me to better understand the spatial and temporal boundaries of the oral history interview. I have always struggled with how the space of exchange within the interview is imagined, and when in fact we consider the interview to begin and end. In the case of interviews that were arranged by a facilitator, or by email, text, or phone, I did not always meet the person prior to arriving at the interview. According to oral history guides, this makes me a "bad" researcher, though that assumption ignores the challenge of interviewing in dangerous places. Furthermore, these interviews were nevertheless meaningful ones that provided valuable information. It bears noting, too, that, even when we make preliminary contact, we still go into an interview not knowing everything about that participant. This raises the question: when is the interview really an interview at all?

The many handbooks and guidebooks that address oral history research with women participants tend to say little about why it is important to consider what interactions have preceded the interview.[33] In Amman, Om-Muhammad contacted the women by phoning them at home, and then accompanied me for the interview. I was largely unprepared for what happened, especially in those cases when Om-Muhammad had not only facilitated the interview but also translated certain portions of the discussion. In fact, my energy had been so focused on maintaining authority within the interview with her present that it was not until later, when we sat down together to transcribe the interview, that I realized just how much she had shaped the information exchanged and recorded. Om-Muhammad had in many cases pre-engineered a template for participants' confessions, guiding the women through the parameters of the research questions (as she understood them) and offering them "suggestions" of stories they could share. Since Om-Muhammad did not disclose her tactics to me in advance, it took time and careful scrutiny of the transcript to determine that she, the facilitator and sometimes translator, had undermined my questions and position in the interview by indicating to the women what she thought would be helpful for them to share with me.

Om-Muhammad was at her most interventionist when she actively regulated the women's stories in order to conceal certain experiences. With such a diverse and multilingual group of participants, it was not easy to decide how to structure the interview, or how best to convey the information. My English was much better than my conversational Arabic. I understand some Kurdish but could not communicate effectively in it or the many other languages and dialects of the participants. I conducted the interviews primarily in English as most of my participants spoke it reasonably fluently. I also provided the opportunity for participants to be interviewed in Arabic and Kurdish by recruiting a translator (a neutral third party not associated with Om-Muhammad). Equally important, at some point I had to let go of the idea of producing nice, neat transcriptions of my exchanges with the women. After all, our conversations were a jumble of interactions that shifted easily from one language to the next, and there was a sense of fluidity and emotional movement in the exchanges I recorded. However, this did make the task of untangling the threads of Arabic, Kurdish, Chaldean, and Armenian from the tapes laborious!

As we continued our collaborative work together, I began to realize how Om-Muhammad had used language to manipulate and "protect" women from sharing certain memories. She advised those within her close personal networks not to share experiences of living conditions during the 1990s in Iraq. We know from Nadje Al-Ali's extensive research of the period of international sanctions in the nineties that the opportunities women had enjoyed during the golden years of Iraq's economic boom were abruptly reversed. Travel became increasingly difficult. Women were forced back into the home due to crippling cuts in childcare programs, and many families found their fortunes significantly altered.[34] In English, many of my upper- and middle-class Sunni (both Arab and Kurdish) participants responded to my questions about this period by saying they hardly felt the strain since they continued to be able to access higher education, health care, and travel. There was one memorable slip, however, when a participant joked with Om-Muhammad about the irony of their situation. For the first time in decades, she said, they were able to travel, but only to be transported as *shroogi* refugees.[35] As we discussed these inconsistencies in the transcriptions over many cups of coffee, Om-Muhammad confessed that the difficult times were a source of shame for Iraqis, especially since Iraq's economy had shown such promise in the preceding decades. She recalled that, as Iraq fell in the eyes of the world, so too did the situation of well-to-do Sunnis like her family. For the first time, she displayed a kind of wounded pride instead of the dark humour with which she normally discussed the Ba'ath state. Moreover, she removed herself – and the women – from the experience by referring to the impact of the difficult times on families and on men's experiences. "It is not nice for you to know these things, I think," she told me, adding: "and I don't want your father to be angry that I told you. Yes, it was hard to get medications and things like this, but your father travelled to Amman, so for us we were fine. For my father it was a depressing time because the world started to see Iraq like a desert with just oil and Bedouins. *We* are the cradle of the civilization!"[36] Refusing to allow me to interview her officially, Om-Muhammad nevertheless provided interesting ways of framing narrative when attempting to tell the stories of others.

In a few of the Amman interviews that were set up by a third party or organization, Om-Muhammad also accompanied me as a translator. CARE Jordan helped connect me to pockets of Shi'a Iraqi refugees who could find affordable shelter only in Amman's bustling and crowded old city. One afternoon, we set out together in a taxi to visit the home of a woman the CARE community workers described as a widow from Baghdad whose husband had recently been killed. They also said she was struggling to sustain her family with support (including a housing allowance) from local agencies. Communicating mostly in Arabic, the woman, speaking excitedly, disclosed why she had been forced to leave Iraq and described her experience as a refugee in Amman. When I asked Om-Muhammad to translate what the woman had said, and to ask her where she hoped to be relocated, Om-Muhammad's translation provoked an outburst of fury. Heated words almost led to a physical altercation. Suddenly, Om-Muhammad and I were thrown out of the living room and were practically running down the street to get away from the screaming woman.[37] Since I had not understood much of what had transpired in a mere matter of minutes, the woman's white-hot anger came as a shock to me. Om-Muhammad was shocked as well. Drawing on her own stereotypes, she later tried to pass off the incident with a glib comment about Shi'a being uneducated "invaders." The participant had interpreted the question not as part of the interview, but as a slight against her as a Shi'a for not being a "real" Iraqi. Confused, I wondered why this would trigger such an extreme response. Over many cups of coffee, I kept pushing Om-Muhammad to explain what had happened. Finally, she said that it was not my question that triggered the emotional response, but rather the short exchange between the women that had followed the woman's initial outburst. Om-Muhammad criticized the participant's plans to stay in Amman and wait for the war to end. As Om-Muhammad revealed her own plans for resettlement in Canada, the participant conveyed her disgust with the "old" Sunni class for abandoning Iraq in its time of need. I also then learned that what she had screamed at us in Arabic as we fled was that my "Britishness" was a mark of my father's failure to raise an Iraqi daughter.

In the emotional space of this interview, the historic divide between Sunni and Shi'a played out through the participant's interpretation of my personal family history. I was an Iraqi with a foreign accent that did not meet the participant's expectations of an Iraqi daughter.[38] Using language as part of her argument, the participant excluded me from belonging within the imaginary of Iraq, arguing that she and her family were far more Iraqi since they had remained true to the nation, unlike "traitors" such as my father who had not fulfilled his duties as a good citizen. Language increasingly becomes important in territorial and identity struggles for the modern nation state, as young Iraqis in the diaspora speak less of their native languages over time.[39]

Collective Memory as a Site of Identity Negotiation

For some participants, the topic of religion enabled them to articulate their subjectivities in the interview space. Muslim participants who were hesitant to discuss religion during the taped interview seemed to attempt to appeal to more secular sensibilities of womanhood and belonging. Informal discussions after the recorded interview opened up more comfortable spaces for discussing faith and how women's participation in religion was changing in diaspora. I rarely asked directly about religion; however, it did become the focus of a 2008 group interview in Detroit with eight women participants of mixed Sunni, Shi'a, and Christian backgrounds. Zeynab had helped me to draw together a group of women from mixed Iraqi backgrounds who were willing to join me for a group interview. Following an interesting but subdued discussion of the changing role of religion in Iraqi politics, we stayed seated around the dining table while I explained the consent forms. As they began to talk amongst themselves about issues I had raised, one of the Kurdish Muslim women said they actually rarely thought about women and religion. She started questioning the Christian women, asking why they revered Mary, the mother of Christ, since she was a "whore." As the conversation developed before me and I sat there speechless, silently wishing I was recording, I realized this off-the-record debate spoke clearly to the daily realities – at least since 2003 – of interpersonal conflict fuelled by religious and ethnic divisions in Iraq. And, indeed, as I thanked each of them individually for signing the forms, they covertly communicated what they considered to be the primary causes of internal strife in Iraq. We found, in flashes after the formal interview was over, ways to share how the sectarian divides have come to structure so much of daily life in Iraq.[40]

In the group discussion, this mixed group of women for the most part adhered to a typical "myth of state" in which the collective held to the story of a collaborative past. Using terms such as "civilized" to describe Iraq in relation to the surrounding region, the women solidified their position in relation to me within the interview space.[41] As Iraqi refugees who have preceded a vast number of significant migrations from Syria in particular, the women strongly endorsed the "civility" of Iraqis compared to other Arab Muslims.[42] This idea of being "civilized" is a strong underlying theme binding various expressions of their collective past. On the record, the group interview reflected a common fieldwork problem that I faced – a hesitation to discuss any topic related to sectarianism.[43] Still, in the informal space, the women broke down the barriers of their supposed civility and divulged personal opinions and experiences of sectarianism and violence that continued to contradict the official narrative.[44]

The hesitancy that individuals and groups showed towards discussing the changing practices of religion in Iraq and in the diaspora was most notable in group interviews with other women, and especially so in family interviews with multigenerational participants. In group or family interviews, younger second-generation women did not tend to challenge the opinions of first-generation women until after the interview was over. Group interviews made for challenging procedural decisions, as it was always evident that someone did not feel as though they had the space to tell you their story. Similarly, women felt confined in certain group gatherings when they had felt pressured to attend, as they could not tell their stories before the others in the group. For example, during the winter of 2008, a close acquaintance of mine in Toronto invited all of her closest friends – all Kurds originating from Sulemaniyah – to a dinner party so that I might explain my project and interview them in an informal setting. Over coffee, music, and seemingly infinite amounts of food, I engaged the group in conversations about living in the Kurdish north and what part the Kurds played in the myth of Iraqi Ba'ath nationalism. Feeling secure amongst their closest friends and relatives, most women easily discussed their experiences as a result of the Ba'ath campaigns to rid the north of political opponents.[45]

After many hours of enjoyable conversation and endless eating, the gathering began to dissipate; one woman lingered behind the rest and asked if she could talk to me privately. She wanted to tell me *her* story and experiences of trauma and loss. An activist in Iraqi Kurdistan, she fled in the early nineties to the Iranian border on foot with her brothers, where she was captured and held in a detention camp for many months. Having endured sustained physical and sexual abuse, she eventually made her way to Canada. She explained that during her captivity in Iran, she was informed that her parents had been murdered by Ba'ath soldiers. Her tragedy did not end when she arrived in Canada, as her younger brother mysteriously died from a gunshot wound (potentially self-inflicted), and her other brother had to be institutionalized in a provincial mental health facility for many years. She told me in confidence that she was an atheist, making it very clear that this was not an opinion she could share with others:

> How can they believe in God? What God would do this? God is dead. He will never exist to me again. My heart is broken because of my brother. They are hypocrites, making me feel like an outcast because of my hair, my clothes, the way I act, [the fact that] I am not married. Who are they to tell me how to feel?[46]

Others in the group had pre-empted what they feared she might reveal by sharing gossip about the participant's so-called wayward lifestyle and strange beliefs. As the participant had correctly predicted, not one of the women acknowledged her recent engagement because her fiancé is deemed unsuitable, being a Shi'a Muslim of lower socio-economic class. Eric Davis's notion of the "dialectic of memory and counter memory" rings true here, for all historical memory is negotiated against hierarchies, belongings, and identities that shift and are remade in the diaspora.[47] Ultimately, as Shahnaz Khan reminds us, the dichotomy between the official narrative and counter-narratives of Iraqi women suggests that it is imperative to offer women an alternative space where they can articulate lived experiences of subjective pasts.[48]

Location and Dislocation

Leyla's narrative is shared in the opening anecdote of chapter 1 as a means of illustrating the fears that women face in diaspora as they continue to worry about the safety of friends and family who have remained in Iraq. In particular, Leyla fears hearing the phone ring late at night, connecting this with notification of her father's death. In moving between my three sites of interviews, I came to understand how the stretching of the passage of time distorts the process of remembering. Not only did the waiting and longing make the chronology of their lives at times hazy; it also illustrated how proximity to the site of trauma/site of longing shaped the way in which participants responded to questions about safety. In Amman, these fears were acute and could be felt in the tension of the interview, as I will discuss below. The threat of loss has led many second-generation Iraqi young adults to develop anxiety disorders, and many of the women openly confessed to suffering from insomnia, eating disorders, generalized anxiety disorders, and depression since arriving in Canada. Like Leyla, these young women are often intimately tied to the homeland through technologies (Skype, WhatsApp, etc.,) that connect them with family and friends in Iraq on a daily basis.[49] What further exacerbated their worry and also isolated them from friends and colleagues from different backgrounds is that many women participants have fathers or husbands who continue to live in Iraq or a neighbouring country and send back funds to support families in diaspora. There was a noticeably lesser degree of anxiety over family relationships amongst Chaldean women I interviewed in Detroit who were not born in Iraq and are not waiting anxiously of news from close family members who live between Iraq and the diaspora.

As the next anecdote demonstrates, fear of retribution was not simply used as a rhetoric but also to illustrate the dangers that Iraqis in diaspora continued (and continue) to face. In the first summer of my fieldwork in Amman (2007), I was quickly initiated into the unsettling reality that oral history interviews can be perceived as dangerous. With its proximity to Iraq, Jordan became the expected first site of settlement for Iraqis, as many had previously travelled back and forth between Amman and Baghdad for work and to fly outside of the region. Its proximity also made it one of the first sites of migration (Syria being the other) for those who fled Ba'ath persecution. There were some participants, like the Sabean Mandean family of this anecdote, who were virtual prisoners in their homes because of the influence militant groups have across the region.[50] This interview also serves as a reminder of the ongoing realities of religious persecution in Iraq, and the nefarious connections (both implicit and explicit) that transcend national borders.[51]

Despite having ready access to networks of Muslim Arab and Kurdish Iraqi women in Amman, I found it an ongoing struggle to gain the trust and consent of Chaldean, Assyrian, and Sabean families. Having worked with several community agencies (including CARE and Mitnaz Law Group, Amman), I was eventually granted a meeting with a Sabean family living in Amman's bustling city centre. To protect the safety of the family, the community worker who assisted me in setting up the interview asked that I keep the interview a secret, and she would not provide a phone number or let me contact the family in advance. In the apartment, the shades were drawn, the air was stale, and the atmosphere was tense. The mother sat with her sons and spoke at a muted but level monotone of the family members lost over the past thirty years. Her official narrative differed significantly from that of the majority of Arab and Kurdish interviewees in Amman, who spoke of the unity between ethno-religious groups and the freedoms and protections afforded to these groups by the state prior to the US invasion in 2003. This woman openly detailed the persecution of minority groups such as the Sabeans by Saddam Hussein's Ba'ath government.[52]

In preparation for the interview, I had met with counsellors at CARE as well as a lawyer at Mitnaz, who informed me of the family's precarious situation. As much as possible, I tried not to disrupt the mother's narrative and allowed the interview to be a free-form narrative of her experiences and memories. Having been informed of the dangers, we kept the interview short. I had brought along Om-Muhammad to help with translation and as some protection; in her usual fashion, she heeded nothing of these warnings, and as soon as the recorded interview was over she engaged the participant in a heated debate. Their disagreement over the place of non-Muslims in collective memory quickly spiralled into an argument, as the sons who had previously sat silently began to interject on their mother's behalf. The recorded narrative focused on a history of fear and loss within Iraq. In the aftermath of the argument, the mother began to weave new threads into her story, admitting that they were forced from Iraq due to death threats. She informed us that her sons had been unable to leave the apartment for months because of the threats. Breaking the tense silence, she motioned towards one of the sons and exclaimed, "Look at him, he hasn't had a decent haircut in so long he will soon be like a girl!" And with that she returned to detailing how her brother had been murdered in his home shortly before they decided to flee to a refugee camp on the border between Jordan and Iraq. Although in this case the recorded interview contained a much different official account of ethno-religious divides in Iraq's past, the counter-narrative of trauma veiled the participant's personal loss, excluding it from the formal record.[53] In this particular case, proximity to the homeland was certainly a factor in the construction of narrative because of the imminent threat of physical violence and the very recent loss of family members in the homeland. This interview illustrates the impact of fear in shaping narrative and memory. In such cases, fear and the threat of violence prevent Iraqi women in diaspora from providing a complete account of their lives and memories during the recorded portion of the interview.

Women's stories of the past, their identity, and their place in the Iraqi diaspora did shift over time and in relation to their location within the diaspora. In several cases, I was able to carry out follow-up interviews with women interviewed in Amman after they arrived as refugees in Toronto before relocating to Windsor.[54] Miriam, a Sunni woman I interviewed with her three daughters in Amman in 2008, openly expressed her dislike of Iraq's Shi'a population, blaming them for the disintegration of a once great nation. She stressed that the Sunnis alone had created the great civilization of Mesopotamia. Several times, she referred to the Iraqis as the "only civilized people in the world" and said she hated the thought of migrating to Canada where there "is no history and no culture, only snow."[55] In 2008, she had been in Amman for three years, and her narrative expressed her strong emotional connection to the homeland and to remaining physically close to Iraq. Conveying her adherence to the official "myth of nation," she spoke of returning home soon to help in the rebuilding of a "greater Iraq."

During a follow-up interview in Toronto in 2011, she confessed even during the formal interview to liking Canada very much and being impressed with "the opportunities, so many different foods – my God, everywhere you turn there is Thai or Sushi or Indian [food]. You can really do anything you want here and no one can tell you what to do."[56] When I reminded of her previous hesitancy and views of Canada she replied, "My eyes have been opened! Once I came here I saw so many different people and they are all living together and no one is being killed. What more can you ask for? Only that it is hard for us to find jobs, but in time, *Insha'Allah*, this will change."[57] Over time and distance, her Canadian experiences had also changed her views on Iraq. In conversations and by meeting Chaldeans in Windsor and Detroit she was impressed that "they are all very successful because they are helping each other," whereas Iraqi Muslims were not, but "only seeing it as what can you do to help me." Moreover, she attributed the Chaldeans' success to the fact that they had "kept the old ways alive more than us,"[58] ascribing to this minority group what she considered were the "traditional" Iraqi characteristics of mutual support as the indigenous Iraqis.

There was an even greater transition in how her daughters had shifted their views of Canada. When I interviewed the group in Amman in 2008, the eldest daughter was married with two small children, and the other two daughters were attending private colleges in Amman. Unlike her mother, the eldest married daughter considered moving to Canada as positive, since her children "will never have to experience what it is like to live in a war. What it is like not to know if your family will be alive the next day. Who can live like this?"[59] In Amman, the two unmarried daughters lamented leaving their home in Iraq and refused to entertain the notion of settling in Canada, explaining that they would never be able to find an Iraqi husband and raise their children "like in Iraq." Now settled in the Windsor area, the eldest married daughter was far more negative about life in Canada, commenting that "it makes good Muslims bad, and Iraqis forget who they are here."[60] Her unmarried sisters were, on the other hand, far more positive about the opportunities for women: "you can do anything you want here in the university. They have courses for everything. Women can do more jobs in Canada."[61] As for finding a potential husband, both agreed there were many "good" families in the area and far more Iraqis in Canada than they had expected. Moreover, marriage was no longer their foremost concern; as one sister noted, "I am not worried about marriage now, I just want to study and be a doctor."[62] They explained that the opportunity to be a working mother in Canada without the stigma experienced in Iraq encouraged them to choose a higher education before a marriage partner.

Time and distance, then, has in different ways shifted the longing of these four women to return to Iraq. With time, and another relocation (this time more permanent), the pressing homesickness and ties to expected homeland roles for women in Iraqi society had altered considerably. On living in Windsor, all four women discussed a newfound sense of independence, more explicitly in the case of the younger daughters, who no longer focused on marriage exclusively and instead considered choices that gave them a sense of independence. What was also fascinating about this particular group interview was how the mother's focus returned to other Iraqi groups in Windsor and Detroit. She continued to cite examples of "successful" Iraqis and, in her mind, the "most" successful community outside of Iraq, which were the Chaldeans in Detroit. The married daughter remained optimistic about the prospect of returning to work after having children, remarking that "in Iraq this would not have been possible for me, people will talk and my husband will not like this."[63] Even though her financial situation in Canada was the primary reason for returning to the workforce, she nevertheless embraced it as a new opportunity to meet people outside of her Iraqi social networks. Interestingly, none of the family members (including the father) consider themselves part of the "Iraqi community" in Windsor; instead they embraced their independence from "the old ways, you know, where everyone is watching what you are doing, what you are buying, who are you eating with, who does your daughter marry."[64] This shift from the "old" ways to "new" ways embodies both a physical and imagined transition, and has at least in this small case prompted these Iraqi migrant women to revisit preconceived notions of other ethnic groups in diaspora.

Of course, not all women produced conflicting narratives, though most provided different ways of communicating their story on and off the record. In my interviews with Chaldean and Kurdish Iraqis residing in Toronto and Detroit since the early 1990s, there was less resistance to speaking critically of Iraq's colonial and Socialist Ba'ath past on the record, and a greater degree of consistency between formal and informal narratives. Women who had fled Iraq during this period of upheaval tended to be far more critical of the state's violent policies against its people. Kurdish women who left Iraq during its crackdown on political enemies in the north were particularly vocal about their experiences at the hands of the Ba'ath army, and their painful memories of the occupations of Kirkuk and Suleimaniyah. When asked about religious minorities in Iraq, one of these women boldly declared:

> Iraq was a mosaic under the oppression and force of obligation living together under one roof. The moment they [religious minorities] could get away, they did – now every group is asking for their own nation.[65]

Yet even in these cases, loss and trauma were noticeably absent from their formal narratives. Even in informal discussions, Kurdish women discussed loss without emotion and in the third person, suggesting that, like other survivors, in order to cope in the present they felt the need to disassociate from this traumatic past.[66] Also absent from Kurdish women's narratives in advance of the US invasion were tropes of nation and national unity so prevalent in the narratives of Sunni and Shi'a Arab Iraqi women. This undoubtedly reflects their political affiliations, as many such women freely admitted a desire to see a sovereign Kurdistan restored after the fall of the Ba'ath Party. They did, however, conform to the view that religious groups in Iraq had lived in relative harmony for millennia before the present sectarian divisions, indicating their partiality as Muslims to the foundational notions imbedded in the "myth of nation" that Iraq was founded on Islamic principles that predate the spread of Islam through this region of ancient Mesopotamia.[67]

There was an interesting paradox between the constructions of loss and trauma in the narratives of Kurdish women who migrated to Toronto in the 1990s and those of second-generation, US-born Chaldean-American women in Detroit. Whereas Kurdish women tended to distance themselves from discussions of personal loss and trauma, Chaldean-American women embraced narratives of trauma and persecution passed down through their families and communities. Despite their having lived in the US their whole lives, their Chaldean-American identity has formed around community-led commemorations of past traumas and the ongoing persecution of Chaldeans in Iraq. Second-generation women constructed their identity in relation to these past persecutions of Chaldeans, connecting the past traumas of their families with the plight of current Chaldean refugees fleeing Iraq. Through settlement and refugee aid work in organizations such as the Chaldean American Ladies of Charity, these women remain connected to the Chaldean community in Iraq and continue to reconfigure their identity as hyphenated Chaldeans in America. In helping to counsel refugees through their experiences of war and trauma, second-generation women often adopt refugee narratives of displacement and loss as their own, claiming "*we* are still suffering in Iraq" and "even though *we* have lived in Iraq since the dawn of time, they are still killing *us* and saying we are not Iraqi."[68] These inherited or adopted traumas of the second and third generations of Iraqis who are now living in the diaspora is the focus of the next chapter.

Conclusion

The differences in the construction and delivery of narratives in interviews conducted with women in Amman, Toronto, and Detroit suggest that time and distance alter the relationship between the individual and their ethno-religious group, as well as their connection to the homeland. In diaspora, the women's perspectives on the place of religious groups in Iraq's collective past shift as the threat of loss is displaced by more pressing daily concerns like education, marriage, employment, and acculturation. New identities are forged as communities reconvene (as in the case of Chaldeans in Detroit) and nationalisms are reconsidered and reconstructed in the aftermath of life after persecution. As Saskia Witteborn notes, "the diasporic imaginations of Iraqis are characterized by resistance and survival and transcend national, social and political spaces."[69] Over time, Iraqi women find new ways to express lived histories and to understand their place in Iraq's past. Second-generation Chaldean-American women in Detroit are an active part of reimagining Chaldean identity and the history of this community in Iraq, while many of the Kurdish women I interviewed were invested in the political and legal process of reclaiming autonomy in northern Iraq. And as the next chapter will explore, Toronto's second-generation Iraqi migrant women who are now coming of age are following suit to become part of the process of redefining the identity of this diasporic community through their own experiences of war and trauma, and collective memories commemorated through the oral retelling of family histories.

If hybridity is at once physical, psychological, geographic, and cultural, then we as ethnographers who occupy these hybridized and overlapping spaces are shape-shifters between these worlds.[70] Part of this ethos of "shape-shifting" became an intrinsic aspect of my developing feminist method in interviewing Iraqi women, and negotiating between the familiar and the unfamiliar, all the time knowing that finding the absolute was an exercise in futility. There is no one way of being Iraqi, much as there is no one way of being an oral historian, and the method should very much follow the research and adapt to the context of the case study or situation at hand. There is an importance to Ruth Behar's notion of "listening vulnerably" that is imbued within every part of how this research was designed, conducted, and communicated. And yet even now I hesitate to ask if I have in fact succeeded – even in some small way – in fulfilling the mission of a postcolonial researcher to disrupt "notions of power and difference that are typical of debates about Self and Other in traditional ethnographies wherein the Self is the White, Western academic."[71] What I do offer in this chapter are honest reflections and difficulties I faced in an attempt to design and produce ethical research. Part of the importance of developing an oral history feminist method is to highlight the necessity – not present in all feminist case studies of refuges and migrants (men or women) – of becoming embedded in the research and in the people, and of not considering the task of the ethnographer as to observe and make notes and then return to a desk to analyse and publish the findings.

Over the course of developing this methodology, I sought advice from many community members and organizations who helped me consider how to approach women from backgrounds with which I was unfamiliar. Clifford Geertz's "thick description" remains one of the most salient ways to inform an ethic for a feminist methodology of this kind.[72] It is impossible to conduct this kind of research without becoming invested, and it is especially hard not to make personal connections and allow those to guide your research. I listened and observed vulnerably, and had I not bored a hole through the intersecting histories, migrations, and experiences of different individuals, I could not have understood how the roots to many of the central questions this book seeks to answer are indelibly interconnected.

Chapter Four

Qahwa and *Kleiche*: Cookbooks, Coffee, and Conversation

I remember our garden in Baghdad. Rose bushes lined the walls and orange trees hung over the blossoms and dark leaves. A date palm stretched high over the foliage, intermingled with a few fronds from the palms in the large garden that backed onto ours. We had a pomegranate tree that bore small fruit that my younger sister liked to eat. We grew mint and parley for salads and my mother even nurtured a loofah plant that she harvested for household sponges. A grapevine crept over a trellis on a patio behind the house, giving us shade in the heat of summer. The grapevine reminded my father of his home village in Syria but the vine didn't produce grapes. The climate wasn't right for them to ripen. But my mother wrapped fresh *dolma* in the leaves.

– Leilah Nadir, *The Orange Trees of Baghdad*

As Leila Nadir so beautifully describes, sensory memory is a powerful tool for remembering home. Interviews with Iraqi women always involved the presence, physically or in memory, of food and drink. Women remembered home through sensory memories of their past lives; olives fresh from the trees, sweet *dibys* (date syrup) on bread in the morning, and the intoxicating scent of night-blooming jasmine. Not only are food and drink a large part of Iraqi social culture, but they also played an important role in the interview, designating official and unofficial spaces within which women shared different (and frequently conflicting) memories. Coffee – its presence, presentation, and accompaniment – provided me with signals that cannot be recorded on a transcript, but that were nevertheless integral to my understanding of the fluid intimacy implied in its offering. Iraqi women in diaspora are also starting to share their knowledge and history of food and drink with a broader audience in North America; the cookbooks they publish make them cultural public ambassadors for the entire community. Through these cookbooks and a "thick description" of interview etiquette (in this case the offering and consumption of food and drink), this chapter explores the power of foodways and sensory experiences to evoke memories and create metaphors that resist the hegemony of collective national narratives.

The study of food as the culture of everyday life goes well beyond merely exploring food as sustenance. Food is not only survival; it is intimately connected to all other aspects of our lives in both public and private spaces. Food informs our self-identification, and also shapes the ways in which we understand social, political, and cultural contexts and hierarchies in the world around us.[1] As Mary Douglas's foundational work has shown, food is a "code" that can be seen to express patterns about social relationships, and as such is a language of its own. Directly linked to both ritual and culture, food and drink have become a form of communication employed by anthropologists, sociologists and, more recently, cultural historians as a means of exploring how we create cultures. In viewing food as a means of communication, we can conclude that "through its absences and presences in everyday life, food and foodways highlight the moral, aesthetic, and ethical concerns of a given cultural milieu."[2] Foodways also have special meanings for those who long for home. As food memoir authors such as Claudia Roden, a Sephardic Jewish migrant from Egypt, remind us, cooking and cookbook writing can be the direct result of the experience of being in exile, as migrants desire the "fruit of nostalgic longing" for the food of a world they left behind.[3] Food, and drink can in this way come to occupy the very centre of longing, as migrants seek comfort in the act of consuming, savouring the nostalgic memories evoked by foods they associate with home. As Sidney Mintz notes, "eating is never a purely biological activity" but instead holds social meaning(s) that are symbolic, or at least are communicated symbolically.[4] Food and drink have histories. Certainly, Iraqi women's individual and collective memory is deeply embedded in, and communicated through, an engagement with food.

Cathartic Consumption: Food and Memory

Mesopotamia has long been recognized as the seat of ancient cultural and culinary heritage in the Middle East.[5] This illustrious history of cuisine has recently been the source of multiple cookbook and food memoir publications in North America by Iraqi women who arrived as part of earlier forced migrations (as in the case of Chaldeans in Detroit), those who fled the recent conflict as refugees (and settled in the Toronto region), or foreign journalists living in Iraq.[6] The recent proliferation of "nostalgia cookbooks"[7] tells the story of Iraqis who have been in diaspora for one or more generations. With the recent influx of Iraqi refugees into centres like Detroit, Los Angeles, Toronto, and Montreal, and as communities continue to grow, authors are capitalizing on the increased interest among North Americans in Iraqi culture. Between 2007 and 2013 there was a noticeable increase in Iraqi cookbooks published from the diaspora, all of which in their own way narrate a version of Iraq's past through sensory histories of Iraqi cuisine and its ingredients. Furthermore, in the case of cookbooks marketed as Iraqi, there is an effort to highlight ethno-religious methods of food production and ritual in nation-centred texts. In fact, as the best examples of these food histories illustrate, sensory histories of Iraq have their own historical tradition that date back to the first recipes recorded in Sumerian tablets. They also speak to the ways in which different ethnic traditions have shaped what is now considered to be Iraqi cuisine. Below I consider the cathartic nature of food and food memories, focusing in particular on the lens through which Iraqi women from different backgrounds remember and depict the "nation," and their place in it, through food.

In *Delights from the Garden of Eden: A Cookbook and a History of the Iraqi Cuisine*, Nawal Nasrallah paints a vivid and textural portrait of the infusion of Iraqi cuisine with methods handed down unchanged through thousands of years of families gathering to prepare and eat together, emulating – as she describes it – ancient Babylonian and Assyrian traditions. Though modern Iraqi cuisine arguably shares culinary traditions with the rest of the region, there are distinct characteristics that reveal the diversity of its roots and the refinement that has developed across millennia. In her remarkably rich food history, Nawallah reaches back as far as the codes of Hammurabi and the *Epic of Gilgamesh*, where archeological records show that the Mesopotamians were refining over twenty kinds of cheese, and a hundred kinds of soup, along with over three hundred varieties of bread. Her text stylistically harkens back to the first documented cookbook in human history, which dates back to 1700 BCE and can now be found in the Yale University Archives. As she notes, this first text is sophisticated in that it documents meat and vegetable stews and complex ways to cook domestic and wild game birds, even though what remains is thought to be only a small fraction of the vast catalogue of Babylonian food science.[8]

Studies of Iraqi cookbooks have documented the remarkable consistency and continuity of the cuisine across a thousand years. Medieval Baghdadi cookbooks contain cooking methods that closely mirror present-day culinary practices. The myth of Baghdad as "navel of the earth" and the site of culinary power and luxury arose in the medieval period, following the rebuilding of the capital by the Abbasids. The city emerged as the marketplace of the world, its important trading highways carrying caravans of foods and spices from all over the globe. Indications of the cosmopolitan shopping experience that could be had on the streets of medieval Baghdad are contained in the *Arabian Nights* story "The Porter and the Three Ladies of Baghdad." The porter follows the lady as she proceeds to buy Syrian apples, Osmani (Ottoman) quinces, Omani peaches, cucumbers from the Nile region, Egyptian limes, Sultani oranges, Aleppine jasmine, Syrian cheese, perfumes from Alexandria, as well as sweets and dried herbs and flowers from across the region.[9] The beloved cuisine from the period has been passed down not only through popular texts like the *Arabian Nights*, but also cookbooks such as Ibn Sayyar al-Warraq's *Kitab al-Tabih* (Book of Dishes) of Baghdad and the later, similarly titled Ibn al-Khateeb al-Baghdadi's later work, *Kitab al-Tabeekh* (Book of Cookery).[10]

Al-Baghdadi's cookbook lives on in the imagination of food historians and food memoir authors who reference the text and the modern-day usage of many of the methods explained in the text. This ancient book has a living presence in the oral methods that are passed down through families. What we learn from these food histories and food memories of migrant women is the desire to bring the old into the new, and to amend those beloved recipes to the daily realties of working mothers. Furthermore, the advancing of food memoires has opened up a conversation about how foodways and food-centred activities provide a lens through which to explore gender relations and identities across cultures.[11] Control over food production, distribution, and consumption shapes not only gender roles within the family, but also the social position of men and women, as differential control over and access to food ensures that class, race, and gender hierarchies are maintained.[12] Women (and men) play an important role not only in transplanting and modifying familiar foodways, but also in adapting ritual food methods to fit into new ways of life in a transnational context.[13]

The negotiation of a cathartic nostalgia and a desire to establish a place of belonging through food reinforces elements of "Iraqiness" and a growing "North Americanness" in interesting ways. In Annia Ciezadlo's *Day of Honey: A Memoir of Food, Love, and War*, she tells of her early marriage amidst the carnage of the 20003 US invasion of Iraq. From her vantage point as a foreign journalist living in Baghdad, she talks about food and cooking as the guiding force in her experience through war, and a way to create a sense of belonging in an unknown place. The title of the book is taken from an Arabic proverb, "day of honey, day of onions," signifying the life cycle of sweetness and grief. Winner of numerous awards, *Day of Honey* is rich with Middle Eastern history and the tactile experiences of Iraq's cafes, gardens, markets, and kitchens. She captures the essence of cooking as a way to both create a material connection to her surroundings and also combat the isolation of being outside the homeland, of being the "other" in a place that is not your home, a sentiment expressed by numerous Iraqi migrant women who have compiled cookbooks of familiar foods and national dishes.[14] Herself a migrant when she wrote the book, she deftly captures expressions of diasporic Iraqis:

> I cook to comprehend the place I've landed in, to touch and feel and take in the raw materials of my new surroundings. I cook foods that seem familiar and foods that seem strange. I cook because eating has always been my most reliable way of understanding the world. I cook because I am always, always hungry. And I cook for that oldest of reasons: to banish loneliness, homesickness, the persistent feeling that I don't belong in a place. If you can conjure something of substance from the flux of your life – if you can anchor yourself in the earth, like Antaeus, the mythical giant who grew stronger every time his feet touched the ground – you are at home in the world, at least for that meal.[15]

Reconstructing identity and belonging is a strong theme that winds through most studies of food history and memory in diasporic communities.[16] Food as a shared substance in all cultures is often examined as a potent source of kinship symbolism, where "food creates both persons in a physical sense and the substance – blood – by which they are related to each other."[17] Food has a means of transforming the outside to the inside, thus giving it a potency in creating identity markers for individuals who want to be physically a part of the homeland through the consumption of dishes that have a living historical memory both in communal and national terms. The very act of consumption is a "boundary marker" in which class, gender, and ethnicity clearly intersect to form patterns of memory through the act of preparing, preserving, and producing Iraqi dishes.[18] In reading the stunningly beautiful lyrical prose of *Day of Honey*, I also wondered to what extent this exposed a form of "cultural food colonialism," in which foods coded as exotic replicate the logic of Western colonial dominance, reiterating colonial practices by relying on the unacknowledged collaboration between colonial and colonized actors/cooks.[19] The book is extremely careful to point out the origins of Iraqi dishes, and so the extent to which methods employed have been modified over time remains opaque to the reader, part of the charm and fragility of national foodways.

The offering of food and drink, or the act of "breaking bread," invites shared intimacies. Interviews conducted in the homes of Iraqi women often involved food and drink as part of the process of sharing and exchanging stories about the past. In my work with Iraqi migrant women there was never a dull moment, and often the interactions were animated, loud, and boisterous affairs. Partaking in a meal prepared by the host holds an important place in the historical imaginary of Iraqis, where the act of sharing bread and salt establishes an unbreakable bond or covenant. As this book's opening anecdote of Sahena and the bowl of *bamieh* suggests, food can also help us to understand the complexities of "being Iraqi." Drawing upon the ideal of a communal and collective memory of Iraqi past, women often stressed their dissatisfaction with Iraqis outside of Iraq by referencing food and food etiquette to show that Iraqis are like the disparate and scattered ingredients of a global diaspora, unable and often unwilling to coexist as one community.

In a 2009 conversation with a Sabean woman in Detroit, I asked her why she thought there were such divisions between ethno-religious and ethno-national groups from Iraq living in the US. She perfectly demonstrated in her response the power of a food metaphor to tell a story of complex historical divisions and their relevance in contemporary animosities:

> Iraq is a dish that has been poisoned, and we are forced like dogs to eat from this dish. Saddam has forced us to take in his poison and carry it with us. You think we are free here to be like one community – no, we are not free, actually, because we always remember the things that they forced us to believe. That the Sunnis are the chosen people, that we are not Iraqis, that we are from somewhere else, that we must worship Saddam the dictator. *That* is why ethnic groups cannot come together in America. This hatred follows us and eats at us inside.[20]

Far from the complex but intertwined food histories of other diasporic cookbooks, this analogy draws upon food and its constituents to brazenly (and with beauty) uncover the root cause of the poison that continues to corrupt Iraqis even in the diaspora. In being forced to eat from the poisoned dish, all minority groups are compelled to bend to the hegemonic will of the regime, carrying forward this poison with them as they scatter across the globe. The description of non-Sunni groups as forced to feed "like dogs" also captures the dehumanization of ethnic and religious minorities during Saddam's regime, and documents histories of genocide and ethnic cleansing as the regime forged ahead with its construction of a new national ideal. As well, the metaphor incisively describes the act of consuming a lie, of being conscious of the state's manipulation of Iraq's history, its people, and their place in the nation.

As Angela Little suggests, "eating constitutes the most intimate act of our existence. In this regard, I put eating ahead of sex – usually considered the most intimate act – because the substance of food, and food alone, becomes transformed into our very own substance."[21] The connection between identity and consumption is blurred, giving food a central role in the creation of not only a self-identity but a communal or ethnic identity as both a public and a private marker. In the food metaphor, Iraqis as a community are forced to consume a lie that results in the formation of a constructed and enforced identity. Her experience of being forced to consume a history that represents neither her ethno-national past nor her individual experience was echoed in the oral histories of many other Iraqi women, who similarly claimed that the present situation of Iraqis in diaspora renders them unable to form a cohesive community along national alliances.

As Peter Farb and George Armelagos point out, "Eating is symbolically associated with the most deeply felt human experiences, and thus expresses things that are sometimes difficult to articulate in everyday language."[22] Food provides a means by which to discuss the past, a common basis to speak metaphorically about a people divided by forced participation in a collective national history. The idea of being forced to consume a poisoned dish vividly portrays how the "myth of nation" is integrated into – imposed within – the sensory memories of women from Iraq's ethnic groups. Sahena's analogy above of Iraqis as a dish told through the lens of the Sunni experience required diversity to make the dish delicious, and the inclusion of ethno-religious and ethno-national Iraqis of all backgrounds. But when the dish is imagined from the minority perspective, it is tainted, and the state's opponents are dehumanized and forced to consume the lie of a harmonious collective past. The "boundary markers" created in the very different imaginations of Iraq as a dish frame the ways in which class, religion, and ethnicity shape how Iraqi women remember.

Sensing the Past through Inherited Memories

Studies of communal identities and nationalisms naturally intersect with memory studies, allowing us to shed light on the ways that publicly memorialized and official writing sources are constructed and how we can uncover subjective pasts and marginalized voices. Since counternarratives are frequently omitted from official histories, and in order to give voice to gendered subjectivities, it is necessary to listen in stereo and uncover the connections between historical memories and official histories. Postcolonial studies of memory tend to focus on "event-centred memory" in which subaltern memories can be accessed as a means of challenging colonial histories during specific moments in the past; less attention has been paid to the form of memories – often non-narrative and focused on sensory experience – that help us paint a more nuanced picture of *how* rather than *what* is remembered.[23]

Attention to the form of memories is central to understanding differently culturally constructed memory sites such as landscapes or the use of religious ceremonies or personal objects. Food is one such site where memory practices blur the boundaries between what is actually remembered and what is imagined. Indeed, the grey area between the passive process of receiving cultural materials and the active appropriation of said materials can confuse "the actual acts of transfer that make remembering in common possible."[24] Beyond the characteristics of Western memory production that "freeze words and images ... [and] put frames around them," cultural memory production makes possible a memory that is created *between people*.[25] Shared or inherited memories thus give rise to multigenerational means of remembering that occur across time and place, and are a way in which diasporic migrants can participate in the memory of home.

In the opening vignette of *The Orange Trees of Baghdad*,[26] Leilah Nadir illustrates the processes of sensory inherited memories, evoking living histories of loss and displacement. Drawing upon inherited memories from her father's past to piece together not just a family history, this sensory journey goes back and forth in time to a place Nadir has never physically set foot but one she can nevertheless smell, taste, touch, and imagine. Born to an Iraqi father and an English mother, Nadir imagines home through memories that are not her own but have been shaped communally by her natal family. In lyrical prose she recaptures the human side of war, its impact on families and communities but most of all on the bonds between individuals as they struggle to reclaim a life in diaspora through memories of the past. Her Proustian analogy of the scent of orange blossom transporting her back and forward through dimensions of reality, forgotten memories, and dreams is a compelling example of the confusingly non-linear "sharing" or "inheriting" of memories.

Nadir carries us back through her memory of the sights and smells of the family garden, painting such a vivid image that the reader can almost feel at one with the scene, experiencing it through the author's performance of its textural and sensory elements: we can almost taste the ripe pomegranates and feel the breeze as it ripples through the date palms overhead. And yet, as Nadir reveals, "This is not my recollection. The picture is hidden inside my father's memory. Like all our mythical origins, his beginnings are in a garden."[27] Nadir, like many other Iraqis in diaspora, has never had the chance to physically taste, touch, smell, and hear the sensations of Iraq. And yet she emphatically states, "I feel Iraq in my bones, though I have never been there."[28] This again was a common trope in conversations with Iraqi women, many of whom expressed the desire to "feel the air and the ground" of Iraq, and in other ways to consume it in a physical sense. For those who had never set foot in Iraq, the longing to belong was a guiding force in shaping their construction of sensory memories based on the recollections of family members. In another interviewee's words, she wished to "return to the place where we first opened our eyes,"[29] using the communal "we" to signify a shared memory, since it was not her eyes but the eyes of her mother that first opened in Iraq. She wanted to return to the site where life emanated, and in this case the geographic site was Iraq even if the memory itself was her own. Nadir also draws upon this communal experience over the course of the novel, leaving the reader unclear in many cases on which individual experienced the scent of the orange blossom. Her book is perhaps the best example from Iraqi diasporic literature of how the sharing or inheriting of memories confuses the chronology of time and consciousness in the narration of the past.

Invoking inherited memories also allows fractured families to thread back together the broken pieces of their pasts into a discernable family narrative. My own family has served throughout my research as a living blueprint of Iraqi diaspora and transnational connections, and they continue to drive me to seek answers to questions of belonging and identity. The transnational web that has kept us connected across borders for the last three decades began when my father and uncles left Iraq for the UK and Germany as part of a Ba'ath-funded initiative to educate and train a new professional class who were to modernize and expand Iraq's infrastructure. My parents met at the University of Cardiff, and they left for Iraq together in 1978. On the eve of the Iran-Iraq War, as tensions rose in Iraq, my uncle was forced to leave Iraq, as was the case in the families of many of the women I encountered: a great number had family members leave – or had themselves left – for the UK, the Netherlands, Germany, the UAE, India, or Australia as the conflict with Kuwait began to escalate.

Before I moved away from Ontario in 2013, my sister and I shared family photos over tea and *kleiche* (Iraqi date cookies). My father had recently returned from Baghdad, and managed to bring back with him pictures from the old house that included cherished mementos of my sister's childhood. My sister and I both remember a family history lived through the backyard of our grandparent's home in Baghdad. There are date palms overhead, a barbeque in the foreground, and a score of smiling faces enjoying the warm night over cool drinks and grilled kebab. And yet we are experiencing shared memories through pictures of different periods of time in the history of our family. My pictures reveal a scene from circa 1980 with a young newlywed and conspicuously pale-skinned Welsh bride (my mother) smiling into the camera next to my father, who is young and slim and full of life. My sister's pictures, taken circa 1996 from almost exactly the same spot in the garden, reveal an older, not-so-slim, and less jovial version of my father with my stepmother and young siblings. We imagine together the warm night with the intermingling scents of jasmine and grilled meat swimming through our senses as we envision being surrounded by the familiar laughter and chatter of the family. I experience these memories through my mother's retelling of her time in Iraq over the years and in reading her letters, kept in their original envelopes in the back of my grandmother's closet. My sister remembers through the pictures and the vague memories she has of being a young child in that same garden. And yet when we look at the past through these pictures, we both feel connected to that place, that family home, that centre of the past so important to every Iraqi family that has been forced to migrate.

Food Fights!

Inherited or shared pasts can also be a source of tension or division in the context of ethnic or religious group histories. An interview I conducted with a mixed group of eight Iraqi women in Rochester in 2009 remains one of the richest highlights of my oral history research that involved food. Towards the end of a three-hour discussion that threaded through family history, Iraqi politics, personal memories, and diasporic experiences, the host, a first-generation Kurdish migrant, leant forward to pick up one of the sweets on the table. She was growing frustrated with my questions about Iraqi identity and ethnic communities, and the individual women began to recount divided pasts and counteract the account of a harmonious past she was so anxious for me to record. Brandishing the *kleiche* cookie in her hand, she waved it in my direction and loudly proclaimed, "Look – this *kleiche* is Iraq! It is something that we all have in common; we have been making it since the beginning of time. This is what it means to be Iraqi!" The group erupted in gales of laughter and loud exchanges of "*alhamdull allah*!" with all hands waving in the air, until one of the Christian women seated next to me combated this claim by shouting across the room at the host: "*Kleiche* aren't part of your past, they are Chaldean! My people were making *kleiche* before your people found their way out of the dessert."[30] Though she said it with a smile on her face, it only added fuel to the fire of an already raucous group that were increasingly becoming agitated by each other's conflicting accounts of the Iraqi past.

Ownership of national foods like *kleiche* cookies in Iraq is an ongoing tension between ethnic groups across global foodways as local and global links reframe traditional foods in the diaspora. A simple modification from ancient Mesopotamian "*qullupu*" cookies, *kleiche* have over time become associated with religious holidays and especially *Eid*, though it is now common to find them in Iraqi homes at all times of the year.[31] There are many examples of the invention of such national traditions, where the stakes are high in the struggle to "own" a dish or a cuisine that has national import for the collective identity (real or imagined) of a people.[32] For refugees and migrants in North America, foodways are an important means by which to protect and preserve cultural customs that carry markers of identity, memory, and tradition. This can for some groups be a challenge, since key ingredients or preparatory methods are not available in the US and Canada.[33] However, *kleiche* (a simple dough with dried nuts, dates, and cardamom) can be replicated without any significant variation to the cookie in its traditional or ancient form.

The dietary acculturation process for Iraqis, as with many other ethnic and religious groups, depends largely upon where they settle in the Middle East, North America, Europe, or Australia.[34] Iraqi women shopping for ingredients in Toronto and Detroit, for example, where an already well established network of Arabic stores exist, were happy to find that they could purchase nearly all of the ingredients required for everyday meals, although many of the recent refugee women claimed to find them too expensive for everyday meals. The limitations and adaptations of the Iraqi diet in metropoles centring around Toronto and Detroit are largely guided by food costs in comparison to wages earned. That is, it is not so much a matter of access as it is the funds available to purchase items such as *labne* (heavy yoghurt), *dibys* (date jam), and premade *kibbeh* (meat pouches made with bulgur). These items typically form the basis of a breakfast or lunch and remain far more costly in North America and western Europe than they are in most parts of Iraq and the surrounding region.

Food is a means of power; it can be used to control supply and availability as well as create cooperation and the mutual assistance of community members through complex rules and rituals.[35] New food encounters in diaspora are often shaped by lack of familiarity as well as lack of trust, and confusion – none of which were noticeable in my encounters with Iraqi women who have relocated to sites of large Muslim populations, thus granting them access to food and drink ingredients that mirror those used in the homeland. Being able to replicate, albeit with some substitutions, the daily meals of home provides a sense of continuity in the lives of Iraqi migrants. It also puts women, who are primarily in charge of food production in the home, in a position of power as facilitators of stability, offering some reassurance that not everything in life has changed immeasurably because of their dislocation.[36] Through food, women become the connection that links the family from the past to the present. In their narratives, women draw upon the important place of food and food rituals to inform how they tell their past. In one informal conversation I had with a friend whose son refuses to keep up his Arabic classes, she exclaimed to him (in front of me), "Fine, then the only food you will eat in this house is Iraqi food, and it shall make you Iraqi from the inside out. Let's hope it also shapes your tongue!"[37] Shared or inherited sensory memories can also offer a means of understanding the limitations of a linearity imposed on young Iraqis in the diaspora. Accessing these memories allows the new generation of Iraqis outside the homeland to participate in negotiations across ethno-national groups for their collective identity.

Etiquette and Intimacy: Drinking Coffee in the Interview

Anthropological studies of food and memory trace the comparative context of identity in which individuals interact with one another and produce interlinked narratives of collective forms of belonging.[38] What these studies reveal is that memory is produced when individual and group performances of culture and identity intersect, setting out the cultural constructions of various manifestations of the social, the historical, and the political.[39] This kind of identity politics allows those on the periphery of belonging (as in second- and third-generation Iraqis) to experience the homeland through inherited memories. In bringing culture into a conversation with ethnicity and global processes of change, Arjun Appadurai positions it as a tool to understand ethnic groups and national identities, in which ethno-national values, actions, and organizations are the processes of nationalism.[40] When we consider "invented traditions," "imagined communities," and "*ethnies*," we are demonstrating that culture and identity are not windows on the nation; rather, they *are* the nation. In this sense, national and ethnic identity are dynamic states of being and becoming, and the values, actions, and institutions that make these identities material are differentiating practices that should be of paramount concern to social scientists.[41]

Drinking is such a practice; it is a historical and contemporary process of identity formation, maintenance, reproduction, and transformation.[42] The study of drink and drinking has wide-reaching important to scholars of identity and ethnicity since, as Thomas Wilson notes, "drinking is the stuff of everyday life, quotidian culture which at the end of the day may be as important to the lifeblood of the nation as are its origin myths, heroes and grand narratives."[43] Pre-Islamic hosts were praised in poetry for their ability to honour a guest based on their ability to provide a respectable meal: "And many a time … I have called for the arrows to choose a barren or bearing camel whose flesh was distributed to the poor relations of all and the guest and the poor stranger must have thought themselves / come down upon Tabâla, whose valleys are ever green."[44] This pre-Islamic tradition was also recommended by the Prophet, who encouraged his followers to lavish their guests with hospitality, but only to provide to the best of their ability and to give forth what they could in the good name of the family/tribe.[45]

As far back as the Sumerians, codes of hospitality mirrored ideas of plenty and the importance of preparing for guests: "Let it be plentiful – lest there be too little! Let it be more than enough – lest it have to be added to! Let it be boiling hot – lest it get cold!"[46] These encoded rituals of being a good host are still widely recognized as a means to command a good reputation across all classes within the Arab world. Historically, hospitality was foremost the task of noblemen or *emir,* who were expected to host guests for a series of days, which included providing sufficient food, drink, and shelter. In common lore, a visit from a guest symbolizes a visit of the Prophet, thus intricately linking hospitality to religious performance and observance. As Peter Heine explains, there continues to be in Iraq, as throughout the region, a code of expected behaviour as a host that has to be followed. In this sense, the social aspects of the rules of hospitality are arguably more important than the culinary ones.[47] In Bedouin culture, for example, there is a tendency to separate the male from the female quarters. In the men's part, where guests would be entertained, it is typical to find a metal basin with a glowing fire for the preparation of coffee: "Somewhere there is also storage for the cups and the sugar bowl. Often water is also available in a jar. So the coffee for a guest can be prepared without the appearance of a woman of the family. Often, especially in the tents of the important persons and families of a tribe, there is a big collection of the typical coffeepots and cans to make sure that the host will not be embarrassed by a greater number of unexpected guests."[48]

The growing literature on drink and drinking cultures often omits non-alcoholic drink and practice in which the social fields and political arenas that define and shape drinking places and spaces (whether they be regularized or spontaneous drinking practices and occasions) are considered to be different from those of non-alcoholic drinking. In fact, there is an underlying Eurocentrism that shapes the rationale that alcoholic drinks and drinking culture form the building blocks of networks of friendship, work, business, and politics, and are elements in these differentiating processes of culture and identity.[49] Can we, then, think about non-alcoholic drinking as the same act of identification, of differentiation and integration, and part of a projection of homogeneity and heterogeneity? And in particular, should we consider it with reference to the social arenas of ethnicity and national identity in the same way as alcohol is often theorized?[50] Perhaps not to the same degree, but there is certainly much in the literature on drinking in the Middle East that suggests non-alcoholic drinking practices tell us about the medium of hospitality and the attendant implications of shared substance and identity markers that are expressed through the medium of drinking tea and coffee.[51]

Coffee acquired its name from the Arabic *qahwah* (or *kahwa*), and was originally the poetic name for wine; the word was transferred towards the end of the thirteenth century in Yemen to a drink made from the berry of the coffee tree. The method of serving coffee in the Levant region underscores the ideal of a life that prizes *kayf,* or peace of mind. It is perhaps the early religious use of coffee as an elixir to fuel evenings of religious devotion that has given it a ceremonial character. Though these religious rituals no longer employ coffee, the ritualistic practice and method of serving coffee can still be observed in this most deliberate act of hospitality. Coffee is a symbol of both hospitality and respect on the part of the host, and to refuse as a guest is a perceived insult.[52]

The ritual and performance of serving coffee in the interview opened up an intimate space to share oral histories and memories. A visit to an Iraqi home will commence with the serving of tea, followed in some cases by Arabic coffee as well as baked Iraqi sweets and delicacies. Regardless of time constraints, failing to provide coffee is considered a direct insult to the family of the guest. In cases where there are time limits on a visit, coffee will typically be served upon arrival, without the preceding tea courses. Tea is served formally in *stikan,* which are tall, slender, delicate clear glasses. Traditionally, coffee is brewed on the stove and steeped with cardamom and sometimes sugar, then served in small cups and saucers similar to those used for espresso. Both courses are ceremoniously served and are carefully planned to coincide with the arrival of additional guests and the serving of food or, as I began to notice, to signify the division between formal and intimate spaces.

Most of my interviews were conducted in the homes of Iraqi women, which gave me ample opportunity to observe the ways in which I was received and regarded by each participant. I came to realize that the improper serving of coffee immediately upon my arrival signalled that the participant was only interested in a short interview; there was no invitation to linger and exchange stories after the interview was over. In some cases, there were practical reasons for serving a cup of coffee at the beginning of the interview – in cases where interviews were conducted in places of business, social aid facilities, and coffee shops. But in the homes of participants these rituals became an important indication of how the interview would unfold and whether the women intended to offer narratives that contested the hegemonic Iraqi national myth.

Upon arriving at the home of an Iraqi Jewish participant in the fall of 2010, I was immediately served instant coffee in a mug.[53] Aware that this was a potential snub that indicated she was not interested in sharing information, or that she may be sensitive about sharing her past with someone from a Sunni family, I was very careful in the ways that I approached discussions of religion and identity. It was clear from the moment we sat down to talk that she wanted the interview to be over as quickly as possible, giving abbreviated answers to complex questions, and dismissing the importance of her personal account as a Jewish refugee to Israel in 1948 before emigrating to Canada many years later. As we finished the interview, and I gathered my things, she politely asked me about my family background and how I had come to research Iraqi migration. Once she realized that my family was from Iraq, she became both agitated and animated, apologizing profusely for her reception of me. Confused, it took me a few minutes to realize she had assumed from our initial phone contact that I was not Iraqi, and so had served me instant coffee in a mug with no intention of revealing stories from her past. Substantiating my suspicions, she quickly confessed: "Had I known that you are Iraqi, I would have served you good coffee in a proper cup!"[54] Relieved and somewhat amused, I accepted her offer of *kleiche* and other sweets, followed by an informal conversation.

As Carol Bardenstein and others have noted, "national" foods often carry with them a strong unifying tendency that "accentuates discourses of univocality and traditional authenticity,"[55] subsuming as they do factors such as gender, class, and ethnicity that might complicate these. If we consider our identities as rhetorical performances in which we utilize language, commodities, and aesthetics in order to present ourselves to others depending upon the social situation, then it is telling that in this interviewee's initial "performance," she was unconcerned about what she clearly recognized as transgressive social behaviour that only an "insider" would recognize.[56] Once the participant realized I was part of what she constructed as a similar social class grouping, her behaviour immediately changed to adhere to accepted rituals of offering Arabic coffee after tea, accompanied by Iraqi sweets. Such drinking practices marks the ways in which Iraqi women construct socially meaningful identities and identifications. The proper serving of coffee for Iraqi women suggests that drinking is itself a cultural ritual, offering a performance that "runs deeper than national or ethnic makeup, as much as it is itself a bedrock of national and ethnic culture."[57]

Accessing subjectivities using feminist oral history methods can only correct the power imbalance in the interview space to a certain degree.[58] Interviewing Iraqi women as a female researcher was a privilege, and similar invitations to exchange intimacies over coffee would likely not have occurred had I been a male researcher. In fact, it is unlikely that I would have had access to women on their own in private spaces like the family home had I not been a woman. And yet I wanted to take the research a step further; as Ruth Behar best describes it, I flirted with "the ultimate taboo in academia" by listening vulnerably and inviting emotion into an academic setting.[59] This helped me blur the boundaries between personal and private within these intimate exchanges that made me implicit in the exchange, forcing me to open up and share parts of my past in exchange for being invited into interviewees' painful pasts and unsure present. Discussions of ethno-national difference and religious persecution were often initiated through the serving of coffee, where the very act of consumption interlaced past and present, weaving intimate exchanges with the recollections of the past, and making me a part of the narrative.

In Amman, my stepmother helped me set up an interview with a fortune teller, a woman of great fame in the Sunni refugee community. We spent a lazy afternoon sitting on her porch with the smell of jasmine thick in the summer air and branches of ripe figs overhead. The fortune teller was an Armenian refugee who had been forced to flee Iraq over twenty years earlier. When I attempted to ask her about this experience and her thoughts on sectarian divisions, she abruptly shifted focus, picking up my coffee cup to tell my fortune. As she delivered promises of future wealth and happiness, she also carefully wove into the "reading" threads of her personal experiences and memories of Iraq. She revealed the history of Armenian persecution in Iraq as well as her own experiences of displacement, confiding in me about the recent disappearance of her brother in Baghdad. And as she spoke of religious sectarianism in Iraq's past, she participated in a much-loved extra-religious ritual. Commonly considered "*haram*" or against Islam, reading a fortune from the remains of Arabic coffee is an old and frequently practised ritual in Iraqi families. As she held my cup and gazed into my future, she told her story through the grounds, weaving her past and present with my future. This part of our exchange initiated an almost ethereal intimacy in which I was drawn into and made a part of the painful narrative that she shared.

The interview discussed in chapter 3 with the Sabean woman and her family in Amman's old city highlighted the importance of ethnonational difference in shaping oral narratives as well as the realities of religious persecution and ongoing turmoil in the homeland.[60] Only after she watched me pack away my recorder, and I showed her sons that the recording on my phone had been terminated, did she go into the kitchen and refuse to let us leave without having coffee. I return to this anecdote since it is so rich for an oral historian, demonstrating not only the intersections of historical conflicts and traumas, but also indicating how the framework of social class in Iraq still has meaning in the diaspora: Om-Muhammad reached across as we waited for the coffee to be served and told me to pretend to sip, or else I would get an upset stomach since poor people never wash things well. I ignored her offensive remarks and indicated that she too should take the proffered coffee; we sat in silence sipping our cups until a heated exchange broke out, for even having listened to the participant's account of death and loss, Om-Muhammad did not believe that such trauma could befall one family. In her usual fashion, she policed the boundaries of our exchanges, and it was clear she wanted to leave immediately after this exchange when she whispered to me: "Nadia, she is making this [up] for you. It is exaggerating; now come on, let's go." Even without hearing the words that she whispered, the participant caught the exchange and its meaning. Shouting to her sons, she demanded that they bring us proof of the death threats, which they explored with us over the next hours.[61]

The story of their forced migration that was revealed over coffee and by way of a heated argument shone light onto a complex current web of militia groups across Iraq. In order to document the mercenary executions of many of his friends, the youngest son had produced a film and posted it online; the film contained first-hand footage of the 2004 execution of Sabean Mandeans in Nasiriya by a radical Arab Sunni group. The family provided material proof of death threats left at the door of the apartment in Amman by members of this same radical militia group. As we left the interview, our taxi driver informed us that we were being followed, which highlighted the imminent danger this family faced in Jordan. Although we were fortunate to escape unscathed, this interview was a formative and frightening brush with the real danger many Iraqi refugees face as they await resettlement or, as has increasingly been the case, are forced to return to Iraq because they have exhausted their resources.[62] I have included this participant's story and narrative within two chapters for its formative role in solidifying my commitment to all of the participants that I would keep their identities as safe as I possibly could – and in this case I have removed all possible identifying elements, since she refused to be named even under a pseudonym.

In truth, I have struggled to give voice to some of the participants for whom I was the most concerned about safety. This relates in particular to fieldwork I conducted in UNHCR-affiliated receiving camps in Jordan's desert, and close to the border with Iraq. As an intern for the National Center for Human Rights, I accompanied coordinators visiting refugee camps that housed some of the most vulnerable Iraqis who had fled across the border on foot, often with no money or resources. On one occasion, my supervisor received permission from the United Nations High Commission on Refugees (UNHCR) refugee camp we visited for me to speak with interested participants, and the administrative staff set up a small room in the main building where I conducted interviews. In the corner of the room, someone had prepared a *dallah* (urn with a large spout) of coffee with small cups for sharing. I'm sure that this was done out of respect and consideration for the "foreign" visitor; however, in a place where food resources are scarce, it was significant. Women who had expressed interest in participating were ushered into this formal space in the main building by the administrators. Once they were inside the room, I realized that the women were not necessarily there to share or even to engage in conversation. Instead many took advantage of the silence to sit and drink coffee, every so often smiling, and communicating with me through small talk about the coffee and how they missed the comfort of enjoying coffee. Even in cases where coffee did not open up a sharing of memories or of the women's experiences of fleeing Iraq, the offering and sharing of coffee with the women put them at ease and relieved the tension by inserting a normalizing practice into a very abnormal and dehumanized space.[63]

Of course, as in any fieldwork of this kind, not all of my exchanges with Iraqi women were intimate or powerful. In many cases coffee was served in order to discontinue what the participants felt was a tedious or pointless discussion, and to initiate instead a pastime beloved amongst groups of Iraqi women – gossip! To be sure, their desire to move group discussions towards gossip was also a signal that these women led busy lives and did not often have the chance to see each other and to chat informally. Group interviews in particular commonly involved women trying to use me as a source of information about what was going on in various families in their communities. In one such interview in Detroit, we ended as usual with coffee and sweets, and the women soon moved the conversation to the topic of an unmarried girl from the community who had become pregnant. This was one of many instances – in this case a rather tame example – where I struggled to reign in the discussion or in fact to withdraw from participating. Participants felt I had been allowed to ask them to share information they normally would not divulge, and my "payment" in kind was to share any tidbits that shed light on the inner lives of those in their networks. It was evident in many cases, however, that these informal exchanges were not based in good intentions, and I found myself increasingly resistant to being party to them. Sometimes this meant excusing myself when I felt that I would hear information I should not, since it put either myself or other research participants in legal jeopardy. More often, I simply did not wish to participate in the character assassination of other women. I was, however, greatly intrigued by the exchange of information that related to marriage and marriageability. On this occasion, one participant began to gleefully inform the others of a young women outside of her immediate circle (and not of the same ethno-religious background) who was pregnant out of wedlock. I listened as the women picked apart the girl's reputation, blaming the mother's moral standards and inability to actively police her daughter's behaviour. They lamented together how this cast shame on the father and the unfortunate sons who would never marry "well" because of this black mark on the family's honour. This was neither a happy nor fruitful exchange, but instead a reminder that in the intimate space created by the serving of coffee, the informal information exchange was often uncomfortable.

Conclusion

The central and ceremonial role of food and drink in negotiating memory is an important part of understanding how Iraqi women in diaspora shape narrative, and share information informally. The articulation of multiple narratives suggests that the repressive role of the state has instilled fear in generations of Iraqis who remain unwilling to tell their stories on the record. Using the ritual of coffee to divide the interview space helped women create a site of resistance within which subjective narratives could be shared, taking on different forms: some as a deliberate counter-narrative to Iraq's official history, others as fortunes threaded with trauma, and still others as claims to ownership over national foods like *kleiche* as a means of owning a voice in the construction of a collective past. Food and drink thus play an important part not just in the process of remembering and shaping narratives, but in the gendering of formal and intimate spaces, opening up access for the women to share hidden pasts and traumas.

Food, drink, and foodways create and contest group identity, once again highlighting Geertz's "thick description" approach to uncovering meaning in social behaviour and the shared significance of cultural interactions.[64] Ethno-religious and ethno-national cultures are dynamic, whereby remembering through food or using ritual ceremonies of serving coffee act as a means to construct counter-narratives in informal and intimate spaces. As ethnographers, we can read meaning in food metaphors and analogies that are "encoded in a group's patterned food system," where transnational flows of food and people open up spaces in which food memory practices and shared memories can be reinvented and reimagined in diaspora.[65] In the case of Iraqi women, what is noticeable in their patterns of communal food memories and the transplanting of ritual and ceremonial traditions is that there is a great degree of continuity structure. To a certain degree, however, "following tradition" in terms of food preparation, the ritual serving of coffee, and the use of intimate spaces initiated by food and drink shows the extent to which these practices involve choice, reflection, and variation, especially when sensory memories are inherited or shared across generations.[66] Past and present are integrated as Iraqi women remember through food, or use the serving of coffee to open up conversations that filter their life narratives through that ritual process.

Foodways or food memories are a means to negotiate, subvert, and challenge existing power structures, thereby inserting gendered subjectivities into the male-centred collective memory of Iraq's past. Systems of food and drink offer different discourses of power that compete for hegemony, enabling these women to produce new knowledge that in turn produces new power relations within the interview space. The act of eating and remembering is itself an act of resistance, where women use the centrality of food and drink in the social rituals of Iraqi culture to draw metaphors and make claims to national symbols or modes of remembering and belonging. Negotiating memory through food reveals contrasting and often competing facets of national, regional, ethnic, and gendered identities that are triggered through different sensory recollections.[67] Food metaphors were used to make claims to belonging in Iraq, whereas the role of coffee in the interview offered a way to blur boundaries and invite shared confidences, thus uncovering difficult memories of lost loved ones and lives intersected by conflict and trauma. For those generations of Iraqis living in the diaspora, unable to taste, smell, touch, and hear the sensations of home, inherited or shared memories offer a way to experience the homeland, revealing in equal parts the potency of the sensory imagination and the internal struggle of existing in one place whilst longing to be physically in another.

Chapter Five

Policing Women's Bodies in Diaspora: Toronto and Detroit in Comparative Context

Interviews with Chaldean and Sunni Muslim women between eighteen and twenty-nine years of age revealed much about the ways in which female modesty and family reputation – especially as it relates to marriage – is mediated in diaspora. Reflecting what may be part of a larger pattern of anxiety among young Arab women in North America regarding pressures to marry men within their communities, young Iraqi women's narratives speak to their struggle to negotiate between cultures, as they create and recreate new ways of expressing ethno-religious and ethno-national identity on their own terms. This chapter focuses on the influence homeland politics and the internal policing of women from within the migrant communities exert over expressions of appropriate behaviour. It also examines how the women themselves have sought to achieve sexual and political autonomy. Continued links to the homeland for Sunni Arab Iraqi women in Toronto complicate the intersections of religious and class identities in the diaspora. A different struggle emerges for Chaldean women born in the US as they negotiate their relationship to the homeland (imagined or otherwise) and what it means to be a hyphenated woman living between traditional and (perceived) Western ideals of "proper" female behaviour. Finally, as I demonstrate below, these women find in the principles of feminism a narrative of agency that they use at times to differentiate their sense of self from the ways in which their family and kin perceived them.

The attitude towards female modesty in Arab culture suggests that the conflation of female sexuality (and promiscuity) originating in pre-Islamic nomadic Bedouin culture is still very much present in contemporary attitudes towards female modesty in Muslim and Christian Arab culture. Men and women participate in the figurative and physical protection of the modesty and reputation of unmarried female family members as a means by which to uphold the social and class status of the kin group. As Sana Al-Khayyat notes, "the phenomenon of 'honor and shame' bears a direct relation to family ties, and to the complex interrelation of social organization and conduct in Arab society."[1] Unmarried Iraqi women are expected to maintain their *adhra* (virginity, a feminine term for which there is no masculine equivalent) regardless of their faith or ethnic origin. Female conduct and female sexuality are policed within the family compact, as men and women stake their claim in upholding the reputation of the family. A consideration of women's active role in maintaining reputation and protecting female modesty demonstrates that homeland ideals continue to be emulated in the diaspora. In the case of Iraqi Muslim refugees who have arrived more recently to Toronto, these ideals are conveyed through the homeland, that is, through friends and family in Iraq with whom they remain in daily contact. By contrast, among Chaldean-American women, who are further removed from their point of origin in the imaginary of their communal identity, we can trace women's changing relationship to these ideals across generations. Young Iraqi migrant women in diaspora are influenced by their mothers' ideals of womanhood and modesty but also their exposure to North American ideas about women and their bodies. In addressing the public and private performance of religiosity and female modesty, I compare and try to account for these different patterns, namely the break with tradition in Detroit's Chaldean community and the conservative shift towards adopting the veil amongst Toronto's young Sunni Muslim women. I ask as well whether these different patterns reflect competing ways of dealing with cultural perceptions of the female body in North America.

Cross-border comparison of generational differences is challenging because Iraqi ethno-religious communities in Detroit and Toronto, the two largest concentration of Iraqis in North America, took shape during different periods. As well, Chaldean-Americans in Detroit and Sunni Muslims in Toronto represent very different urban communities. Despite these challenges, a comparison offers a means to explore how women in these ethno-national groups engage with the broader Iraqi/Muslim/Arab communities. I was interested, in particular, in determining how the connections shift as each new generation of migrants reformulates multiple meanings of being Iraqi. The purpose of providing side-by-side case studies here is to demonstrate the unique challenges each generation of women migrants faces. It also demonstrates how multigenerational narratives and the policing of women in migrant communities affect each generation of women in significantly different ways.

Detroit's Chaldean community dates back to the early 1900s, with the early migrants assimilated into the broader and growing Arab-American community. After 1958, a new wave of Chaldean migration vastly increased the size and settlement area of the community. This wave produced two different generational interview groups, one comprised mostly of second- and third-generation Chaldeans/Chaldean-Americans aged eighteen to twenty-nine years who were born in America, and another of young women aged thirty to fifty-five years of age who were born in Iraq and migrated to Detroit with their families.[2] By contrast, Toronto's Muslim Iraqi community, formed much later when Kurds and Shi'a Iraqis began arriving in response to state persecution, to be joined by the predominantly Sunni Arab Muslim migrants who arrived mainly after 2003. The young women I interviewed in the Greater Toronto Area (including Hamilton, Mississauga, and Burlington) were first generation (aged thirty to fifty-five years) and second generation (aged eighteen to twenty-nine years) Sunni women, most of whom were born in Iraq.[3] Even allowing for the different profiles of young women in these two locales, the comparison sheds critical light on the prevalence of anxieties regarding women's modesty, marriage, and female bodies across three generations of women in two distinct sites of Iraqi diasporic settlement. Each case study focuses attention on the practise of religion and the role of religiosity in women's identity building across generations, and on actors who contribute in formal and informal ways to policing women's modesty and behaviour.

Chaldean-American Women: A Detroit Case Study

The Chaldean community in Detroit consists of approximately 120,000 people living in the Detroit metropolitan area.[4] Spanning several generations, the main waves of settlement have established three generations of adult Chaldeans, now estimated as one of the largest populations of Christian Iraqis outside Iraq.[5] With a view to determining the relationship between this Christian Middle Eastern community and the larger Arab Muslim community in Detroit, this section focuses on second-generation Chaldeans (both foreign and American born) and third-generation (all American born) Chaldeans living in the Dearborn, Southfield, and Sterling Heights districts of Detroit. As the population of the Arab community in Dearborn has increased over the past three decades, this community of Christian Arabs has tried to emphasize its distinctiveness so as to avoid being subsumed into the wider "Arab" community. Dearborn holds an important place within the Arab and Muslim communities of Detroit for many reasons, but in particular for Iraqis it features prominently as the most central of districts where migrations of Christians, Jews, and Muslims from Iraq have settled over the past half century.

When Chaldean migration from Iraq began over a century ago, the process was mired in US state regulations, and men typically came alone to work and then returned home to family in Iraq. After 1945, as the number of Chaldeans migrating from Iraq to Detroit increased, the Mother of God Chaldean Church was established to cater to their religious needs and to assist the developing community.[6] Communal identity has developed under the important influence of the highly active church. The community's core membership arrived mainly in the fifties and sixties, when families settled close to the church and many began their own corner stores and groceries in the Highland Park area. As the population grew and moved into the Southfield and Sterling Heights districts of Detroit, the Mother of God Church also relocated to accommodate its congregation.[7]

Having settled in Detroit with the assistance of the church and through a chain-migration of family members, first-generation postwar Chaldean migrants secured financial security for their families by working long hours in family-run corner stores.[8] The second generation, on the other hand, have been largely educated in the US and are able to access professional and better-paid positions. These better educated and more wealthy second-generation Chaldeans have developed strong community institutions and created organizations that encourage the next generation to maintain ties to the community and develop professional networks.[9] In a 2006 address honouring community elders at the Chaldean-Iraqi American Association of Michigan, the president spoke of what "the pioneer generation of the community" had provided for their children, claiming that "without the sacrifices they made and the services they provided, we would not have the building blocks that we have today to success as a community."[10] The financial success of the community is further illustrated by the purchase of the Shenandoah Country Club and Gold Course – worth US$3.5 million at the time of purchase – by the Chaldean-American Federation as a revenue property and venue to hold community functions.

The celebratory accounts of such achievements overlook the internal divisions and class cleavages that women in Detroit addressed in their interviews with me. In the informal space following the taped interview, women often spoke out against the public claims of the main Chaldean-American community organizations, of which the Chaldean Federation of America is the largest and most influential. In fact, some recent Chaldean and Sabean women told me in confidence that they believed the federation discouraged migrants from seeking government assistance and saw this as a form of moral regulation.[11] These recent migrants also claim to have little in common with second- and third-generation women who, with the help of extensive family networks and a Western education in the US, have professional jobs. The socio-economic divisions between first-generation women and second- and third-generation women in this community highlight the fact that not all members of the community enjoy the financial stability and achievements promoted by these community organizations.

As members of the Chaldean Ladies of Charity, a supporting arm of the Chaldean Federation, second-generation Chaldean women assume the benevolent roles their mothers formerly occupied and continue the tradition of connecting with families in the community through women-based charitable networks. As many of the women active in the organization remembered, their mothers who arrived first from Iraq instilled in them the duty to donate their time and money to helping other women in the community.[12] For similar reasons, second-generation mothers have attempted to continue this tradition by founding and fostering female-led youth organizations for third-generation Chaldean women, such as the Chaldean Angels, who, in addition to their charitable work, provide Chaldean teens with a social outlet.[13] Second- and third-generation Chaldean women take an active part in this inherited benevolent tradition of redistributing wealth within the community, taking donations from the wealthier members of the community and donating these to recent Iraqi (Chaldean and Muslim) refugees. These second-generation middle-class women organizers are the driving force behind political and economic organizations within the community. For them, participation in community organizations highlights their desire to promote the family unit and the nurturing qualities of women as mothers of the community. In interviews, young women involved in the Chaldean Angels spoke about the importance of religion and of maintaining a "good" reputation in the community by staying true to their past and to the ideals of virtue upheld by the Catholic Church. This means no premarital sex and no divorce. In a group interview, several members of the Chaldean Angels expressed concern that, as they put it, many young women in the community were becoming more "American" in their behaviour outside of the home, a reference to their interests in music, clothes, and socializing with the opposite sex. By contrast, the Angels are upholding the values of the "past" by being "good" Chaldean women who help members in the community, marry within the community, and raise their children to understand their heritage as Chaldean-Americans.[14]

Through their participation in the Ladies of Charity and the Chaldean Angels, women claimed to not only maintain their connection to a Chaldean past and heritage but also participate in creating a new Chaldean-American presence in Detroit. Although most of these second- and third-generation migrants have never physically set foot in Iraq, they made frequent reference to their "homeland" and their history. They talked about how they were helping to maintain this connection to Iraq by educating the community, and in particular the next generation (the fourth generation) of Chaldean-Americans. Through annual Chaldean festivals as well as ethnic "cultural nights," the Ladies of Charity work behind the scenes to foster community participation. Having interviewed and spent time with Federation and Ladies of Charity executive members, I would argue that, although the women's community organizing and aid distribution fulfils the Chaldean Federation's core mandate, the women take a back seat in community politics and business development. Second-generation Chaldean women continue to occupy a supporting role in community leadership, which is dominated by male leaders of the Chaldean-American Federation and the Chaldean-American Chamber of Commerce. In fact, the benevolent but certainly secondary role women play in the community has changed very little since the establishment of the Chaldean American Ladies of Charity in the 1950s.[15]

Traditional ideas about female conduct and modesty for women are a particular source of tension for second-generation women who have moved from the home into the workforce. Philanthropic work featured prominently in how leaders in the community positioned their Chaldean-American identity in the Detroit community in relation to the city's growing Arab population. Most second-generation women refused to consider themselves as Arabs because they equate Arabs with Muslims, and Chaldeans are Catholic. As Middle Eastern Christians,[16] Chaldean community leaders have gone to great lengths to disassociate their community from the Iraqi Arab population in Detroit, with significant consequences. While clearly a reaction to the growing anti-Muslim sentiment brought about by the "war on terror," this negative identification has become an important rallying point among Chaldeans remaking their identity in a post-9/11 America.[17]

In fact, this shift in self-identification began as early as the 1970s, when the first large influx of Arab Muslims (of mixed origin, including Iraqi) settled in and around Dearborn. Sociologist Mary Key Sengstock's work with the Chaldean community began in the 1980s, and her informative studies offer insight into the first-generation settlers. In particular, her interviews with first- and second-generation Chaldean men and women who settled in Dearborn and neighbouring regions revealed that the first-generations identified almost exclusively as Iraqi, whereas the second generation identified as Chaldean or as Chaldean-Americans. As the Arab community in Dearborn grew, Muslim organizations were established to help settle and integrate these new members. Sengstock has also noted how second-generation Chaldeans responded to this new perceived threat by focusing on ethnic difference and promoting what they considered their "distinct" heritage as Chaldeans. These tensions are highlighted in a 1986 interview with Arabic teacher M. Al-Harp of Fordson High School in Dearborn, who said of the Chaldean community, "I feel that [the] second and third generation is very much frustrated … they're not sure about their values. They are caught between cultures. It's created a lot of tension."[18] A community newsletter similarly observed that "there is definitely a cultural gap between our first generation of Chaldean adult immigrants who brought with them a distinct set of values and behavior, and a second-generation of Chaldeans bred in America with American morals and values."[19] The changing nature of the community in the 1970s and 1980s suggests that as second-generation Chaldeans came of age they were caught between homeland traditions, American customs, and the threat of being subsumed into "Arab" or "Muslim" categories of identity.

The similarities between Chaldean and Arab ideas of honour and female modesty may help to explain why Chaldeans felt at risk of being subsumed into the growing Arab community in Detroit. Here, local newspapers are an important source of information on past community activities. In 1983, young Chaldean women were included as part of an exposé on "'Arabs' in Detroit," in a section somewhat tellingly entitled "Keeping Their Respect." In this section, second-generation Chaldean women, then in their middle to late teens, were asked how life changed for Arab women living in America. Hana Jaber, then seventeen, commented that "some of us don't want to go out. We want to keep our respect. I like my culture. I am proud of where I come from. If we went out with a boy, you know what they would say about us? They would say we are loose. We would get a bad reputation even though we have done nothing."[20] Another Chaldean teen quoted anonymously said, "There is pressure from cousins to be more conservative. They think I should stick to my own kind."[21] In this ongoing debate about the integration and assimilation of Arab Americans in the 1970s and 1980s, Chaldeans were included in the media as part of this "Arab" community: on the topic of reputation and modesty, the article compared Chaldean women with Arab Muslim women from a range of national and ethnic backgrounds. Situating their narratives within this dichotomy helps us understand part of the reason why the Chaldean community felt their identity was under threat. It also helps to explain why fear of the disintegration of their ethnic distinctiveness became the motivation for community involvement and mobilization aimed at saving their community from being assimilated into American (or perhaps Arab-American) society.

In articulating their ethnic distinctness, Chaldean-American women continue to rely on religion as a factor that separates them indelibly from the recent refugee flows of Muslims. The second-generation community organizers that I interviewed were eager to explain what they meant by "teaching" the next generation about their ethnic identity. Ann Antone, chairperson of the Chaldean Community Cultural Center, captured this shared understanding in the following comments:

> We will teach that we are not Arab. Chaldeans have their distinct identity. It is not just religion. We follow Christianity. However, in the early days we were pagan. The church is our core. It is how we maintain identity and survived in an Arab land because we are Christians. We stayed who we are. We did not fight and make a scene. We did not get swallowed up in the land. Even though we are only 3 to 5 per cent in an Arab Muslim land, we stayed true to our faith.[22]

Significantly, this emphasis on being non-Arab based in a common Catholic rite for all Chaldeans is misleading, since many are by now Protestant. The diocese was overseen by Bishop Sarhad, a Chaldean from Iraq, who was the first prelate of the diocese from its inception in 2002 until he retired in 2016. Of those who had converted to Protestantism, Bishop Sarhad noted that "ethnically for sure they are Chaldean. However, they don't belong to the Chaldean Church."[23] But if membership in the Chaldean church is the cornerstone of belonging to the Chaldean community, then this is one more indication that there are lines of exclusivity that divide Chaldeans into those who belong to the original church and those who have deviated.[24]

Beyond those women who have carried on their mothers' traditions to remain active in community organizing and support, there are others who have publicly rejected the Federation and other central organizations who claim the community is cohesive and united as non-Arabs. One such example is second-generation college lecturer Deborah Alkamano, who has spoken out against the increasingly Islamophobic views expressed by Chaldean-Americans after the 9/11 bombings. Challenging the notion that Chaldeans are non-Arabs from the Arab world just because they practise Catholicism and speak Aramaic, she argues that the non-Arab definition is historically inaccurate and that Chaldeans are engaging in Islamophobia as a means to widen the gap between Middle Eastern Christians and Arab Muslims.[25] In a conference paper presented before a mixed audience of academics and community members, Alkamano claimed that there is a distinct prejudice against Chaldeans who identify with Arabs or are working with other ethnic groups rather than solely within the Chaldean community, most notably with Arab-Americans.[26] Presented at an international conference sponsored by the Center for Arab-American Studies in 2006, her paper opened up a charged conversation in the "Comments" section of *The Chaldean News*. In a letter entitled "Filled with Fallacy," Alkamano was attacked for being "part of the problem which threatens to engulf the community in larger religions and ethnic communities."[27]

Alkamano's criticism of the increasingly "Chaldean" nature of community identity, and the personal attacks launched against her in *The Chaldean News,* have been addressed by the newspaper's editor, Vanessa Denha-Garmo, also a second-generation Chaldean. Resisting the pressure to promote unity within the community, Denha-Garmo highlights the plight of women attempting to break with the acceptable models of womanhood and ethnic identity in the community. In an interview with Mark Kay Sengstock, she noted that it is because of the influx of Arab Muslims in the 1970s that Chaldeans cling to ethnic identity as part of a determined effort to protect their distinct ethnicity. However, interviews with notable community members suggested that many opposed this shift towards exclusivity in the Chaldean community. Another bishop commented that "we are not static or paralyzed, we are a dynamic community. We do not want to be stones; we are a living community. It's like a tree – it cannot stay the same every year, it grows and produces new fruits."[28] On the dangers of excluding all but Chaldeans from the community, lawyer and activist Jumhana Judeh stated: "The average American does not care whether I am Palestinian or Chaldean. In their eyes, there is no difference. In our eyes, we create a difference. We need to stop falling into the trap set by our European colonists of divide and conquer. Unless we as Middle Easterners unite, at least based on racial lines, the discrimination will continue."[29]

Alkamano's attack on what she considers to be a constructed Chaldean-American identity is in part also a counter-attack against critics within the community. Unwilling to conform to the expected role of getting married, going to church, and having children – as she claims the men of the community continue to promote – Alkamano argues that there is a much stronger link between the Chaldean and Arab ideas of a woman's place in the community than they might like to consider.[30] The changing roles of women in the second generation are the source of much debate in the *Chaldean News*, highlighting the latent anxiety concerning changes to the traditional family roles. On the issue of second-generation women turning to nannies to help them cope with the increasing demands of working full time and raising children, Jennifer Korail, a second-generation Chaldean, wrote that "Chaldeans are by nature traditionalists. Women are raised to be especially family and culture oriented. In the past it might have been unheard of for a Chaldean woman to pursue both a career and a family."[31] But the author of an article printed more than two decades earlier suggested that some first-generation parents went "against the grain" in urging their daughters to break with tradition and explore their potential. For example, Oafa Eadeh urged her daughter to leave home and attend the University of Michigan so the daughter could have the choices she never had.[32] Sue Loussia, who moved with her family from Telkaif when she was very young, grew up working in her father's grocery store in Franklin, Detroit. After establishing their business over many years, her parents put up the money for Loussia to open her own fashion boutique in Dearborn.[33] Despite resisting what might be considered the traditional path for women in the community, both second-generation women argued that their ambition and drive were "much rooted in Chaldean ways."[34]

Third-generation women have benefitted greatly from the social and economic networks established by earlier generations in the community.[35] Unlike second-generation women who struggled to break with tradition and become professionally trained and employed, the young women I interviewed in Southfield claimed that Chaldean-American parents now expect their daughters to attain a university education and work outside the home.[36] Although attitudes in the community on the education of women have changed dramatically, there still remains a stigma associated with living/studying away from home before marriage. It is a common element of Arab culture, and a core Chaldean value, that young unmarried women live with their families until they are married, or, if they do not marry, remain in the family home and help with the care of elderly relatives and young nieces and nephews. However, as young women explore educational options outside of Michigan, the controversy over modesty and reputation once again becomes a key component in discussions about maintaining ethnic identity and values. Janelle Franso, who left for New York's American Musical and Dramatic Academy, claimed that "it is common today for Chaldean kids to go away to college. I love our community and I love being part of it, but how could I pass up an opportunity like this? My family is very supportive of what I do."[37] Channelle Kizy, who went away to law school in Chicago, said "there is no reason for your lifestyle to change because you are away from home ... my parents always knew what was going on in my life, not because they demanded it, but because I wanted them to be close to me even though I was away. I felt I owed that kind of respect to my family."[38]

Nonetheless, young women who break with the tradition of remaining at home until marriage remain under suspicion regardless of their attempts to "prove" their modesty. A woman interviewed by the *Chaldean News* captured this tension when she stated: "men treat these women as if they are exotic 'wild girls' who have parties and entertain men in their homes – this is of course not true because the women are working to pay a mortgage."[39] As single women gain a sense of independence from their families, third-generation women interviewed for the article all commented on the social stigma that follows those who leave their home before they are married. It is not only the women who are judged since, as community member Mary Kalou noted, "There is also a lot of judgment on the parents for 'letting' them leave."[40] Of this newfound independence, Renee Antoon, who bought her own condo at twenty-three years old, commented that "Chaldean girls are so sheltered, and our parents give us everything. We're not taught to be independent. So many girls think the only way out of the house is to get married."[41] Her comments suggest a cultural shift towards an ideal of female independence more commonly associated with the values of individualism and self-sufficiency. And yet, even though third-generation Chaldean-American women have synthesized the traditional values of female behaviour with narratives of individuality and independence so prevalent in US culture, they continue to be judged and policed from within the community according to concepts of family reputation and female modesty conveyed from the homeland more than half a century earlier, reinforced by the constant influx of new migrants from Iraq.[42]

Third-generation Chaldean-American women show a somewhat different pattern of integration and adaptation in the US than do women in their mother's generation. Second-generation Chaldeans, and especially those active in community organizations, have followed what Min Zhou and Alessandro Portes call the "rapid economic advancement with deliberate preservation of the immigrant community's values and tight solidarity" model of segmented assimilation.[43] Third-generation youth from this community, by contrast, follow a pattern of "growing acculturation and parallel integration into the white middle-class,"[44] although they attempt to retain ethnic exclusivity even when it competes with their acculturated lives and daily realities.[45] Religious activism is another means by which those central to the community are appealing to young Chaldeans – yet another indication of the ongoing effort to tie ethnic identity with membership in the Chaldean church. The Eastern Catholic Re-Evangelization Center (ECRC), an outreach program that targets young Chaldeans in Detroit, reported some success in appealing to Chaldean youth through extra-curricular social programs.[46] In addition, the Chaldean-American Student Association (CASA) was established as a non-profit organization dedicated to preserving Chaldean culture, history, and language on campuses throughout Michigan, with branches at Wayne State, Oakland University, the University of Michigan Dearborn, the University of Detroit Mercy, Michigan State, and the University of Michigan. In an interview, one executive member commented that CASA was established at Michigan State as "a means to encourage more parents to promote their children to attend MSU by creating a significant Chaldean present that is truly here to cultivate generations of well-rounded loving and *Christ-like* Chaldean men and women."[47] This kind of religious rhetoric echoes the claims made by second- and third-generation members of the Ladies of Charity and Chaldean Angels concerning the upholding of traditional values of modesty and charity for women.[48]

Second- and third-generation women have followed patterns in terms of education, marriage, and family planning that are similar to those of other Arab-American groups who settled in Detroit in the post-war period. Findings from the 1990 census data indicate that Arab-American women were more successful and affluent than other Asian immigrant groups. A study of Arab-American women living in the US for between ten and twenty years also suggests that the women have smaller families over time, potentially indicating a greater degree of family planning.[49] Their high levels of education and labour force participation in comparison to other immigrant groups indicate a greater degree of assimilation into American society. Labour force participation is made more difficult by the responsibilities women carry in the home, coupled with the expectation that they adhere to the norms of an Arab wife and mother.[50] This is certainly true of second-generation Chaldean women I interviewed, who spoke frequently about the struggles of juggling home life and the expectations of their Chaldean spouse. These trends are beginning to change in the third generation, as Chaldean women marry at a later age and are beginning to establish financial independence from their families. Although the trend towards homogamy continues, over time as women move away from the Detroit community, these high levels of intermarriage may begin to decline.[51]

This section has traced the limits of ethnic exclusivity in the second generation, noting the break that occurs as third-generation Chaldean youth move away from home and establish financial and emotional independence from networks of family in the Detroit region. The US invasion of Iraq in 2003 reinforced the Chaldean community's desire to differentiate as Iraqis (versus Arabs), and in particular from the new wave of Iraqi Muslim refugees settling in Detroit. Just as the frequency of attacks against Chaldean-owned businesses rose during the 1991 Gulf War, so too have racist attacks on Arabs and Muslims in the US since 9/11.[52] This negative attention directed towards the Chaldean community, in addition to the new wave of Arab Muslim immigrants into Detroit from Iraq, has reignited the community's defences and revived its emphasis on ethnic difference. Third-generation Chaldeans increasingly identify as Americans, or hyphenated Americans, in an effort to distinguish themselves from Arab Muslims in Detroit.

Iraqi Sunni Arab Women: A Toronto Case Study

Transgenerational ideals of womanhood, modesty, and reputation in Toronto's first- and second-generation Sunni Iraqi women expose how these women negotiate female reputation in Canada, and how internal and external influences play out on the corporal site of their bodies. "Living transnationally" forces recent migrant and refugee Iraqi women to reconcile the traditions and expectations of family and friends in the homeland with the realities of living in North American society. Linked to global networks of Iraqis, second-generation unmarried Iraqi women face the pressures of protecting their reputation from the threat of discrediting rumours and gossip in the homeland and in diaspora, in many cases to safeguard their marriage prospects in Iraq. Most notably, I observed a growing trend in veiling amongst second-generation unmarried women who had resettled in Toronto and chosen to wear the hijab as a means of defending their modesty and reputation. These women revealed in interviews with me that they believed performing their modesty by veiling increased their chances of securing a good match with an Iraqi man.

First-generation Iraqi-born Sunni women participants form a distinct "ethclass" whose values and behavioural patterns were shaped as members of former aristocratic families who later became Iraq's professional middle class.[53] These first-generation Kurdish and Arab Iraqi women shared key cultural markers (class, education, professional experience), and most had spent a significant portion of their adult lives living and working in Baghdad before migrating to Canada. In addition, over two-thirds of the first-generation participants interviewed in Toronto, ranging in age from thirty to fifty-nine years, left Iraq as students to study in Western nations during Iraq's "golden years," when the government funded thousands of students to study abroad on the understanding that upon completion of their studies they would return to Iraq. The program was designed primarily for educating men, but women often took advantage of it by accompanying husbands or brothers in their studies abroad.[54] This moment in the lives of young Iraqis permitted freedom of movement, intellectual pursuits, and even a loosening of the rigid boundaries of male-female intimacies. It is important to note that this period of relative freedom was enjoyed by a very small group of young adults, from predominantly Sunni backgrounds, who were not considered to be a political threat to the regime.[55] This encounter with Western societies as young adults profoundly influenced the religious, cultural, and ethnic ideals of first-generation Sunni Iraqi women migrants.

The forced exile of the professional class as a result of the growing violence in Iraq has brought this group of women back into the West. Now they face the stigma of being refugees, in sharp contrast with the positive welcome they received when they were foreign students in the 1970s. Many of these first-generation women commented that Islamophobia was an uneasy part of everyday life in Canada. A recent refugee noted that "when I lived with my husband in Indianapolis in the late sixties we had Christian, Jewish, communist friends – no one cared. Now I feel like I have to hide my faith or people will think I'm a terrorist."[56] When questioned regarding their faith or religious affiliation, most were hesitant to articulate their religious beliefs, simply stating that they were Iraqi. Expressing a self-conscious awareness of Western notions of Islam, first-generation women were largely unwilling to discuss their relationship with other Muslim groups from Iraq, although they were adamant that they not be categorized simply as "Muslim" because this did not adequately distinguish them from other racial groups of Muslims. One first-generation interviewee went so far as to suggest that Canadians considered Muslims to be "uncivilized" and refused to be categorized as anything other than "Iraqi."[57]

Many of the first-generation Sunni Iraqi Arab women of my study were born into a period of prosperity and change in Iraq, as the country capitalized on the growing price of oil to develop its infrastructure, workforce, and an increasingly secular system of government. Whereas other countries in the region looked outside the nation to expand their workforce, the Ba'ath administration looked within, drawing upon the growing number of university-educated women graduates.[58] By the 1980s, Iraqi women were some of the most educated women in the region, encouraged by the government to participate in the public sphere and in the development of the nation. During the golden years of the 1970s and 1980s, this generation of women travelled to study abroad, participated in public life, and embraced the state's attempts to modernize by reforming female dress codes and extending women's legal rights. However, after so many years of warfare and sanctions and the ensuing inflation, the state infrastructure – which had included funding for daycare services – went into rapid decline. Many participants commented that this period was difficult because of the growing anger and frustration of male family members as their professional conditions, wages, and quality of life rapidly deteriorated.[59]

These first-generation migrant women, then, have experienced periods of both expansion of women's legal rights and professional opportunities (1970s to the late 1980s in Iraq) and of rapid decline of their rights and freedoms during conflict and sanctions (1990s until the present day). Kurdish women have to some extent been more successful in their public role, especially in their political involvement, but these gains are increasingly under threat from conservative members of the government. Women from old and established upper-middle-class Muslim families in the nineties were matched by the growing nouveau riche, a group of social climbers profiting from black market dealings during the sanctions period.[60] As financial conditions continued to worsen from 1995 onwards, growing numbers of men left Iraq for jobs in Syria, Jordan, and the United Arab Emirates. In so doing, they transferred the burden of responsibility to their wives as head of household in their stead.

This trend of "women without men" is also present in diaspora, as men continue to work in the Middle East, providing remittances to families living in Toronto. In interviews conducted in the Toronto area, women highlighted the difficulties of living without either their husbands or their extended families as support networks, leading to their increasing isolation from the Iraqi Muslim community in Toronto. Cases where husbands were living abroad are not infrequent, and these women tend not to join the Canadian workforce, focusing instead on helping their children integrate into the education system and participate in extracurricular activities such as sports or cultural clubs organized through local mosques.[61] By contrast, first-generation women who move to Canada with their husbands or as unmarried women express a much stronger connection to networks of Sunni Iraqi women in Toronto, Hamilton, and Mississauga. In most cases, these women worked outside of the home in some capacity and were able to connect much more easily with other Iraqis. Chain migration to specific locales such Hamilton and Mississauga in particular have created enclaves of Sunni Iraqis, recreating old-world social and kin networks. As Iraqis continue to arrive in the Greater Toronto Area, these networks are an essential source of support and comfort for immigrants attempting to recreate their lives in diaspora. Unlike the growth of Detroit's Chaldean community around the church, the mixed Iraqi community of Arabs and Muslims in Toronto is spatially diverse and lacks central community organizations. This community is connected nonetheless by ethno-religious and class hierarchies transposed from Iraq and recreated in Canada. The women I interviewed pointed out that as the concentration of Iraqis grows in regions such as Mississauga, so too do the divisions within the community. Some suggested that these divisions were present in the homeland, but more apparent in diaspora because there Iraqis had a choice of living close to or far away from each other. There are also interesting trends in smaller relocations of families away from large concentrations of Iraqis in Mississauga and Hamilton, perhaps indicating those families' desire to break away from the old-world feuds and divisions.

Many of the first-generation Sunni women I interviewed viewed the hijab as a symbol of more recent conservative Islamic trends in Iraq. During the 1940s and 1950s, reforms to female dress codes were introduced, urging women to stop wearing the traditional floor-length black *abaya* over their clothes in public.[62] By the late 1960s, first-generation women claimed, it was common to see young women sporting miniskirts in public.[63] Only a few women from the first-generation participant group wore the hijab; these explained that Sunni women often began to wear the hijab later in life after they were married with children. Salwa, who began to wear the veil following her husband's death, confided that "I didn't want to remarry, so I started to wear hijab. Then the men, they left me alone."[64] She explained that wearing hijab is an expression of the biological stage in a woman's life, and a sign that she is no longer fertile. Nour explained that after her husband went to work in Germany, she felt more secure living alone with the children when she began to wear the hijab. She commented, "if you wear the hijab there is no question that you will have a good reputation."[65] In addition to the clear religious symbolism of the hijab, it functioned as a deterrent to unwanted male advances and, more importantly, a means to protect reputation and honour in the absence of a male head of household.

When I asked these same first-generation Sunni women in Toronto if they would like their daughters to wear the headscarf, they all responded emphatically that professional Sunni women should not be veiled until they are married with children. They said that one day their daughters might choose to wear the hijab, but this should not happen while they are still young and unmarried. As they explained the logic of this dichotomy, those women wearing hijab underscored the importance of beauty in securing a good marriage match with a partner from Iraq. When I asked Salwa (a *hijabi,* or hijab wearer) what she considered to be the key factors in securing a suitable marriage partner, she responded, "you must be beautiful, of course, and come from a good family and have a good reputation. My daughter is very beautiful and we come from a good family, so *ensha'Allah* we will be successful in getting her a good husband even though now our situation is not so good in Canada."[66] Based on the responses from the first-generation group and especially those women in hijab, it is clear that the women believe wearing the headscarf limits marriage prospects in this ethno-religious group, and that young women are encouraged to appreciate their beauty as an asset.

The trend in both the age and marital situation of second-generation Iraqi women in Canada who adopt the veil is significantly different. Second-generation participants aged from eighteen to thirty-five years were all born and partly socialized in Iraq. Over two-thirds of this group comprised unmarried women when the interviews took place.[67] Having experienced traumatic disruption during their formative years of development, these women did not follow a pattern of distinct "ethclass" in a traditional sense, mainly due to their varying degrees of education and employment. The devastating effects of sanctions throughout the 1990s and the invasion of Iraq in 2003 interrupted the high school and university education of many women, owing to the growing threats to security at educational institutions and the high mobility rates for middle-class Iraqi families. Many young women were forced to delay their education by two to three years as families fled the unrest, relocating temporarily to Syria and Jordan before being resettled through the UNHCR to Canada and the US.

Most of those women who ended up in Toronto complained about the difficulties they faced having their education credentials recognized by Canadian institutions and employers. Those still in their high school years fare the best in some respects, because once they earn a degree from a Canadian institution, their integration into the workforce is easier than if they used foreign university credentials. Accessing postsecondary education is difficult because of the many TOEFL upgrades and additional courses required to satisfy the admissions requirements of most Canadian universities, and Iraqi graduates arriving in Canada with equivalency papers are more often than not required to rewrite the exams in order to receive certification for their degree or training in Iraq. Women also complained that Canadian universities often required additional documentation to be sent from institutions in Iraq – a process that often takes twelve to eighteen months, further delaying their access to professional work.[68]

Education and employment are among the most important and often cited problems that young Iraqi Sunni women (and indeed most immigrants) initially face, and are formative issues in shaping the experiences of second-generation Iraqi women. In addition to the more tangible problems of credentials and employment, young women struggle to understand where they belong in diaspora, and how to negotiate Western ideals of female bodies versus their own cultural codes of conduct. These women live within transnational social fields where they maintain transnational families with transmigrants – often fathers, brothers, and in some cases mothers – who move between Iraq, Canada, and regions of the Middle East in order to support their families. Uprooted during their formative teenage years, their connections to the homeland are heightened in diaspora as they struggle to understand divided loyalties and hyphenated identities.

As a distinct in-between group, these young women have "sociocultural characteristics and psychological experiences ... [that] are distinct" from those of first- and second-generation Canadian immigrants. These women are best described as the "1.5 generation," neither fully Iraqi nor fully Canadian. The "transnational" second generation is able to move between different identities and develop a sense of self "shaped by personal, familial and organizational connections to people 'back home' and at the same time in terms of race, ethnicity and nation are part of a political process that extends transnationally."[69] Without the strong internal network of a community organization, as is present in the Chaldean community in Detroit, this in-between generation is vulnerable to a lack of "access to mobility ladders," resulting in their professional stagnation and inability to maintain the socio-economic status of their parents' generation.[70]

The position of this generation of women is further complicated by the fact that they are of an age where one of their primary concerns – as they related to me – is to find a husband and start a family. Typically, in Iraq, endogamous marriages are arranged through families from similar backgrounds in an effort to ensure a suitable match for the marriage partners and their extended networks of kin. Families tend to settle in close proximity to each other, with several generations often living in old family homes, providing support networks for professional women with young children, as well as unmarried or widowed family members. Although men and women from several generations typically participate in the matchmaking process, it is the senior male family members who have the final say in their sons' or daughters' choice of partner.[71] This patrilineal organization of Arab society means that older male relatives are charged with supporting the extended family financially while women are the embodiment of family honour.[72] In diaspora, families cut off from these transgenerational support networks shift the burden to younger male relatives entrusted with moderating marriage proposals and upholding the family's reputation and social standing in both diaspora and Iraq. Due to the meagre supply of available partners in the Toronto community, young women in Canada look to Iraq for a suitable marriage partner, relying on family networks to match them with appropriate men.

Young unmarried women living in the West are considered to be "at risk" from the corrupting influences of loose morals and open sexuality. In marriage negotiations, the modesty and reputation of these women and their families are frequently called into question, as friends and family of their potential suitors inquire into the conduct of young Iraqi women in Canada. The growing religious conservatism in Iraq since the 2003 US invasion and its aftermath has once again focused attention on women's bodies. Since 2005, head coverings have become increasingly popular in urban centres in Iraq, and on the streets of Baghdad Iraqi women are wearing hijab to avoid their bodies becoming the focus of jeers and taunts from American soldiers and Iraqi men.[73] The young women that I interviewed in Toronto reported that this growing conservatism has affected their lives mainly through the increase in malicious gossip regarding their conduct both in the homeland and in Iraqi communities in Toronto. Gossip has become a potent force of female policing: young women frequently mentioned that the threat of "bad" gossip about them controlled what they wore, who they made friends with, how they spent their weekends, and what studies they chose at university.

In a reaction I consider to be a form of "defensive modesty," many young second-generation women have responded to this policing via female gossip and male family members' increased control over their bodies by adopting the hijab. Eight women from my second-generation participant group wore the hijab, of whom six had adopted the headscarf upon arriving in Canada.[74] When I asked them why, all six expressed their dissatisfaction with what they considered to be "loose Western morals" and the way in which women in Canada dressed and behaved in public. They all began wearing the headscarf in their late teens as a personal expression of their faith. Conversations with unmarried second-generation veiled women revealed that they were more overtly conservative in their religious beliefs than their parents. As one participant, Salima, commented, "I am proud to be a Muslim, so I would like to wear hijab to show people that I am not afraid to be a Muslim."[75] They were also deeply concerned about protecting their modesty in diaspora, as it becomes increasingly difficult to arrange endogamous marriages for Iraqi women living outside the homeland. The perceived "freedoms" that their mother's generation enjoyed are being replaced with a growing concern about female reputation and marriage prospects. Second-generation participant Amina commented on the prospects of marrying men from the homeland: "if we wear hijab then they will know we are good, and we will get the good men from Iraq." Female bodies thus become the cultural terrain used "to demarcate boundaries between 'us' and 'them,'"[76] in this case virtuous women of intact reputation versus Iraqi women in diaspora who may have fallen prey to Western temptations and are no longer considered modest and "pure."

The families of these six women responded to this form of religious expression in a number of interesting ways. Given the increase in policing of female conduct in diaspora, I expected that families would readily welcome their daughters' decisions to veil, thus silencing any rumours regarding her sexual conduct and protecting the reputation of the family. This was, however, not the case. All of the other families expressed concern that wearing the hijab would attract negative responses from the Canadian public; this was especially so where the women had finished university and were searching for employment.[77] In one case, despite the fact that two of her aunts wore hijab, a participant mentioned that when she first made the decision to veil she endured her cousins' ridicule and her father's anger for ostensibly portraying the family as backwards and conservative.[78] First-generation Sunni perceptions of the hijab were informed by campaigns in Iraq during the Qasim and Ba'ath regimes to separate religion from the state. The campaigns of course did not sanction a shift towards greater sexual freedoms, although many women privately suggested that this was a result. Their early encounters with Western societies did, however, inform how they negotiated between racialized and religious ideals versus Western secular ideals of sexuality and the female body.

Despite fearing for their daughters' reputation and prospects in marriage, first-generation mothers opposed the idea that veiling was a suitable expression of female religiosity for unmarried women. Even in families such as the one mentioned above where first-generation family members wore the hijab, it appears that the standards for acceptable female religious performance depend upon the age and marital situation of the woman in question. Being "too religious" suggests that the family is more traditional, a label very few "non-traditional" middle-class families wish to bear, especially now that they are settled in Canada. One husband casually remarked during a group interview that he wished his wife would stop wearing hijab so that she could more easily mix with other Iraqi and Canadian women. This casual remark was met with a strong response from his wife, who quickly (and sharply) replied: "I won't take this scarf off for anyone. Not even you."[79] This exchange illustrates the deep-seated belief in this generation that conservative expressions of religiosity effectively amount to a rejection of modernity and a more westernized way of life. And in general, although religion was clearly a central component of life for many if not most of the Sunni Muslims in this participant group, there was also an emphasis on private devotion rather than the very public expression of religiosity favoured by young second-generation Iraqi-born Sunni Arab women.

Given the absence of a hijab-wearing tradition in the families of second-generation participants, and the families' concerns over or hostility towards the hijab, I asked the women how they decided on this course of religious expression. Three of the women said they had followed the example of female friends at school who wore the hijab. The women in this sample looked primarily for Muslim immigrant woman friends rather than specifically other Iraqi women (in contrast with young men: in family interviews, young men seemed to place a higher degree of importance on retaining an Iraqi circle of friends in Canada). Though they found solace in these groups, there was also an element of peer pressure concerning acting as a "good Muslim woman, and follow[ing] the true words of Allah the merciful."[80] One area in which they did need the help of their friends was in providing a forum within which to discuss both the physical and the spiritual change they had undertaken in donning the hijab. As one of the interviewees commented jokingly, "I didn't know how to put on a hijab at the beginning – it was so hard! My friend, she laughed at me, and tried to show me, but really I had to practise a lot on my own!"[81] Another interviewee suggested that it was a very personal decision for her based on what she felt was her calling – although again, supported by her female friends who also wore hijab.[82] In these cases, other Muslim women migrants seem to have influenced the decisions of young Iraqi Muslim refugee and migrant women in Toronto; a broad exploration of the influences on young migrant women would prove a fruitful area of future research.

The responses of second-generation women in hijab suggest that they consider veiling to be a feminist act. I was reluctant to discuss or raise the issue of feminism because of what I feared might be its perceived emphasis on secular Western ideals of women's agency. But it did come up in conversations with women of all ages, and one participant, Salima, spoke openly about being a feminist. I was most intrigued with her ideas about freedom through faith for women in Islam, and the degree of safety and agency she felt in covering her body. Her ideas of feminism reflect ideas about individual choice, most notably the notion that she had chosen this course of action, and by wearing hijab and traditional dress she reclaimed control over her sexuality, thus liberating herself as a woman. For Salima, feminism was about the right to choose, and she made it abundantly clear that it was her choice to cover her body. She commented that "you see, it is not about safety really because in Canada you can wear what you want. But I want you to look at me, at my eyes, and listen to my mouth when I am talking."[83] Her rationale behind veiling, then, was that controlling her sexuality meant almost desexualizing her body so that her voice and mind became the focus, as opposed to the physical display of the body. It is this idea of agency, and of liberating by refusing, as she described it, to participate in Western culture's obsession with sexualizing the female body, that underlies what has come to be known as Islamic or Muslim feminism.[84]

Young second-generation migrant women are also responding to an increase between 2004 and 2012 in conservative Islamic practice in everyday life for Sunni Iraqis. Since the invasion of US forces and the emergence of Islamic fundamentalist militias, female dress and behaviour are increasingly the subject of scrutiny. Living transnationally also means that these ideas are being communicated and internalized by young women in diaspora. Maintaining a "good" reputation and adhering to normative homeland ideas of female behaviour means conforming to more conservative expressions of religiosity in order to "prove" their purity. It is also important to see these shifts as part of broader trends in religious practices amongst young Muslims in the West. Haideh Moghissi, Saeed Rahnema, and Mark Goodman suggest that there is a tendency among the younger generation to identify with an idealized Islam that is much more conservative and intolerant than the Islam actually practised by most Muslims. Experiences of social and cultural exclusion and of being "othered" play a large part in this more political turn to global trends of political Islam and a "distorted Islam" that is projected as young people's own identity. This heightened identification with Islam does not represent a growth in religiosity as a means of fulfilling spiritual needs; rather, it is the use of "Islam as a powerful ideological tool of resistance – indeed, in the absence of a viable, antiracist, and leftist movement, it is practically the only force that appears to effectively challenge global power structures and systems of domination."[85] As Muslims are increasingly racialized in Canada and the U.S., Moghissi and others suggest that this has increased the appeal of political Islam.[86] Conversations with Iraqi women suggested that their increasingly conservative Islamic observances were being "taught" by Muslim friends. They experience a desire to be openly Muslim and to challenge the stereotypes of Islamic fundamentalism by being part of an open dialogue that includes people of all religious backgrounds. Some, like the cookbook author Samira Cholagh, mentioned above, are becoming more public in their desires to distribute material to Canadians and to "teach" people about the message of Islam.

Conclusion

These case studies provide a microcosm of the challenges young Iraqi women from different backgrounds face as they negotiate living between two worlds. Avoiding malicious gossip that could tarnish their reputation featured prominently in the anxious reflections of Chaldean and Sunni-Arab Iraqi women in Detroit and Toronto. Traditional expectations of reputation and the behaviour of women continue, to a varying extent, to inform the role of women both within the family and within the community in both groups of Iraqis. In the case of Chaldean-American third-generation women, they are beginning to break away from close family networks in order to pursue education and lives outside of Michigan. As female modesty comes into question, so too does the reputation of the family within Middle Eastern communities. Due to their ongoing close connection to the homeland, second-generation Sunni-Iraqi women in Toronto are increasingly affected by the changes in religious movements in Iraq, which has led to a new trend of unmarried women wearing the hijab in Toronto. As Sunni migrant women grow increasingly concerned with maintaining modesty and securing a marriage partner given the small and fractured nature of their communities in Canada, they use the female body as a means to negotiate sexuality and physically represent their modesty.

Conclusion

With the historic rise in global migrations, the predicted effects of cultural homogenization have served instead to heighten awareness as well as promotion of ethnic diasporas living outside the homeland. In the aftermath of the general ethnic revivalism that has spanned the past four decades, ethnic and ethno-national minorities have gained greater legitimacy and also been more successful in their attempts to assert their interests within Western pluralistic and multi-ethnic states.[1] But while multicultural and polyethnic states tolerate these efforts to a point, there are also forces within these societies that oppose these thriving ethnic communities on the grounds that they pose threats to national security and to the coherence of dominant ethnicities, however imagined these might be. In some cases, that opposition can turn violent, as occurred in the post-9/11 backlash against Arabs and Muslims. Iraqi ethno-national and ethno-religious migrant communities are formed as a result of both voluntary and forced migrations to North America, although arguably all of the groups involved expressed narratives of exile as a result of past and present religious, cultural, and ethnic persecutions. This is especially true for the Chaldean, Assyrian, and Kurdish Iraqis, who "remain minorities in their host countries and thus are potentially faced with possible expulsion, social, political and economic hardships, and alienation."[2]

Diasporic imagination takes on many different forms in the lives of multigenerational, ethno-religious, and ethno-national Iraqi women. In the case of Detroit's Chaldeans, women's active participation in the Chaldean church and community organizations protects against the assimilation of Chaldeans into Detroit's extensive Arab communities. Settled in this region for over three generations, Chaldeans are an example of how "diasporic solidarity is not solely based on ties to the homeland" but "fully emerges in the host country and reflects conditions there. Based on such solidarity, there emerges a degree of cohesion within such groups."[3] Some might consider this process to be one of ethnicization; however, I argue that the Chaldeans continue to live in diaspora especially because the second, third, and fourth generations cannot return to Iraq because their communities have been decimated by oppression and war. It might also be helpful to reflect upon what "return" really means here, since most American-born Chaldeans likely do not wish to migrate back to Iraq. Despite the somewhat ambiguous connections to "home," group identity for Chaldean-Americans continues to be premised upon a history of exile that began with earlier migrants and is now entirely connected to their ethno-religious identity. In recent years, as they face the struggles of overcoming generational, class, educational, social, and ideological differences within the community, institutional leaders and Iraqi female gatekeepers encourage the younger generation to participate in community organizations and activities, reaching out to the youth through recreational clubs and associations meant to draw young Chaldean-Americans back into the fold.

The integrative force of education in the US, however, enables Chaldean-American women to break with traditional customs and to move away from their families in search of better employment opportunities. In addition, the community faces the difficulty of uniting an increasingly geographically dispersed community, as affluence and better job prospects in the second and third generation have allowed Chaldeans to move from the inner city into the middle-class suburbs of Sterling Heights, Southfield, and Rochester. Chaldeans born in the US are increasingly invested in their rights as American citizens, and as a result community organizations cater to the social, political, and cultural needs of the community through funds and services offered by the host government. Ideally, the establishment of these diasporic organizations creates the possibility for "dual authority and, consequently, of dual, divided, and ambiguous loyalty vis-à-vis the host country."[4] In my time working with members of this community, various female members indicated to me that there is a growing apathy among Chaldean young adults about participating in Iraqi politics. With some exceptions, over successive generations Chaldeans increasingly identify as Chaldean-Americans, and they are gradually loosening their ties to Iraq.

By contrast, the Kurds as a politicized group committed to independence are deeply invested in homeland and transnational politics, with consequences for women. The diasporic solidarity of Kurdish Iraqis living in North America is evident in the work of women, some of whom

I have interviewed, who use their transnational networks to fight for the rights of Kurdish migrants and for an independent Kurdish nation state. Gabriel Sheffer argues that "identity and solidarity serve as the twin bases for maintaining and promoting constant contact among the diasporas' elites and grassroots activists," and that "these relations are of major social, political, economic, and cultural significance for diasporas, their host countries, homelands and other interested actors."[5] All of which raises the question: do ethno-religious and ethno-national Iraqi diasporic groups actually form cohesive and consensual communities? Sunni, Shi'a, and Kurdish communities of Iraqis in Toronto show a high degree of solidarity and cohesion, though in terms of activism, their respective communities range from strong (the Kurds) to weak (Sunni Arabs). In contrast to the Chaldeans in Detroit, these new diasporas have not yet had time to coalesce and organize as ethno-religious groups and community organizations in diaspora. Perhaps these groups are still in the process of determining whether their stay in North America will be permanent or temporary. Ties to the homeland through transnational exchanges of money, communication, ideological beliefs, and people force these migrants to constantly renegotiate their diasporic citizenship as well as their imagined and real connections to the homeland.

The generational negotiations that shape the ways in which refugee and migrant women imagine and construct the past in relation to their present has been the focus of much of my research on the different communities of Iraqis in diaspora, particularly their female members. The different life experiences of foreign-born first- and second-generation women, as well as those born into the diaspora, inform such women's retelling of the past and the ways in which they negotiate the pressures and policing of ethno-religious communities in the present. The narratives of Iraqi women reveal the complex process of negotiating between the official history of Iraq as promoted by the Project for the Rewriting of History, the communal histories passed down orally through their ethno-religious kin networks, and their own subjective experiences of war, loss, and migration. Recent migrations of Sunni, Shi'i, and Kurdish refugees who have settled in communities in Toronto, and who are intimately tied to each other through their shared traumas of the recent past as well as through ties of family and friendship, continue to feel the repercussions of Iraq's civil unrest. For Chaldeans settled in Detroit over successive generations, traumatic pasts are communicated through communal memories in which ethno-religious identity in diaspora is tied to the continued victimization of this group in Iraq. Even though third- and fourth-generation Chaldean-Americans are disconnected from the horrors of war and violence in Iraq, they nonetheless perpetuate an identity based upon victimhood and marginalization, which feeds their agenda of ethnic exclusivity in the US.

Second- and third-generation Iraqi women are "growing up transnational" in situations very different from that of their parents. As young Chaldean women born in Detroit and young Sunni women born in Iraq come to terms with the complex boundaries of performing identity in North America, they negotiate expected religious behaviour with their own ideas of feminism and agency, projecting these onto racialized and religious bodies. Young second-generation Iraqi women in Toronto develop a sense of self that is both shaped by "personal, familial, and organizational connections to people 'back home'" and, with respect to issues of race, ethnicity, and nation, is "part of a political process that extends transnationally."[6] This is especially true of young Sunni women choosing to veil, who in engaging in the conservative practises of a political Islam are distinguishing themselves from their communities and from the Canadian population at large. The multiple meanings that the hijab holds for these young women makes it difficult to say precisely why they choose to perform identity in this way, their motives reflecting a mix of anxiety, identity politics, political awareness, ideological beliefs and, in many cases, fear about the future. As growing numbers of young Muslim migrants in Canada choose to veil while discrimination against Arabs and Muslims in the US continues to increase amid the ongoing war on terror, the subject is sorely in need of further investigation.

A focus on national categories such as "Iraqi" glosses over the important ethnic, religious, and class differences between these migrant groups, their differing migration processes, and the different ways in which they interact with host countries. Similarly, attempts in academic studies to define the boundaries of a North American "Muslim" diaspora or an Arab-American community have a tendency to conflate cultural traditions with more specific ethno-national identities and politicized ethnic identities.[7] As this book argues, we must deconstruct the imagined and imposed Iraqi communal identity shaped by authoritarian regimes in Iraq, in order to understand instead how these diverse groups have come to be a part of modern-day Iraq, as well as parts of divided diasporas. We need more "thick" ethnographies that examine the lives and lived experiences of diverse groups of Middle Eastern migrant women who make North America "home." Marginalized from participating in the political processes in Iraq, these women in diaspora are emerging as community activists, mentors, counsellors, and professionals. Their transnational participation in global Iraqi networks links them to worlds outside of North America while it increasingly roots them in Canada and the US. As they become settled, ethnic identities are negotiated within the frameworks of multiculturalism, as they look inwards to carve out a place in North America. For the more recent migrants, transnational connections remain strong and the homeland is ever-present in their diasporic imagination, as they continue to define their future as part of the rebuilding of Iraq.

The adoption of a feminist historical approach to understanding how ethno-religious and ethno-national identities were integrated into the modern Iraqi state provides an important foundation from which to understand how Iraqi women transplant and reinvent identity in diaspora. The purpose of this book was not only to un-silence Iraqi women's words, but also to understand how Iraqis, including women, replicate historical differences that predate the sectarian conflicts of the present, and also how, in diaspora, Iraqis forge communities around these distinctions, using difference as a platform from which to assert their place in Iraq's future. Initially, my main concern was to bring studies of Iraqi communities into North American scholarship on migrant and diasporic women, taking up the call of other feminist migration scholars to decentre the male elites that are more visible in these diasporic communities. I wanted also to access the complex ways in which women resist power structures both within their communities and as individual actors in multicultural and polyethnic states. Drawing from a rich body of scholarship on Third World, racialized, and non-Western women, I initially positioned myself uncomfortably between the colonial and the colonized as I struggled with how in postcolonial discourses we distinguish between these unstable categories.[8] As Daphne Patai reminds us, there is an inherent danger that the researcher will interview "down" when speaking to women who belong to less powerful groups. Recent Sunni refugee women, however, are cosmopolitan and well educated, and they are acutely aware of the ways in which they are racialized and marginalized in North America. One of the most important lessons I learned from my research is that references to "First" and "Third" World women that assume such women encountered identical forces no matter their geographic locations are reductive and ignore the multiplicity of ways in which class, nation, ethnicity, and religion influence individual and group experiences across the Middle East. While their histories are shaped in significant ways by colonialism and imperialism, the voices and experiences of Iraqi women, including the diverse women interviewed for this book, defy the essentialism embedded in these broad categories.[9]

To return to Gayatri Spivak's central question about how the "subaltern [can] speak,"[10] I recognize that, despite my best attempts to conduct research with women from a variety of different backgrounds – a goal I share with others scholars of Iraqi diasporic women – this book has in many respects privileged the voices of middle- and upper-class Iraqi migrant women. Still, my research and analysis sheds important light on the differences among women in the various ethno-religious and ethno-national groups, and also makes clear that there are many different subalterns to study. A central concern of this book has been to illuminate the manifold ways in which Iraqi women remember and retell their narratives, and how, by doing so, they provide a counter-narrative to the patriarchal collective narrative nurtured by the former Ba'ath state. A related critical object was to un-silence the individual voice of these marginalized or heavily misunderstood women. Many of my female participants noted that "you cannot find Iraqi women in the history books" and that "women in Iraq do not fight the wars." Even the minority of participants who said that "women have always been the ones behind the men in power"[11] similarly observed that we still know too little about the history of Iraqi women. Such comments underscore the value of oral histories in capturing women's voices and in offering leads and clues into how female diaspora identity is shaped by class, ethnicity, race, sexuality, politics, and other social categories.

Themes of food and intimacy complicate discussions of women's ethno-religious and ethno-national identity in diaspora. In one of my group interviews, as we have seen, so-called national foods such as *kleiche* became the focus of a particularly raucous exchange among women of different ethnic and religious backgrounds, with each claiming the food as their own. By contrast, the cookbooks published by Iraqi-American and Iraqi-Canadian women suggest a far greater degree of sharing across different cultural histories than the women themselves acknowledged. The value of inviting collaboration and giving voice to the similarities as well as differences among Iraqis is well documented in Chaldean cookbooks by Samira Cholagh, which feature several recipe submissions for each of the Iraqi dishes, indicating a degree of cultural sharing that takes place between different Iraqi groups living in the Detroit region.[12] As Cholagh's daughter, Valerie, recalled in an interview, the cookbooks made her mother something of a local celebrity, featured on morning talk shows and in local newspapers. Valerie noted as well that her mother's objectives changed over time. Whereas her goal in promoting the original cookbook was to highlight the importance of the Chaldean community to the Detroit area, by the time of the second edition she claimed to be more interested in educating Americans about the many different ways of being Iraqi. She also wanted to facilitate understanding of the long-terms connections between Chaldean culture and history and the national history of Iraq.

One way in which women can critique the masculinist character of nationalism is to adopt gender as an avenue of "internal decolonization." Analyses of the constructions of Third World nationalisms have tended to emphasize the forms of "internal colonialism" generated by regional, ethnic, and religious divisions. By un-silencing women's voices, however, we can place them into conversation with the male-dominated and elite-dominated national narrative of Iraq's past and, moreover, assess and validate the contrary narratives that often emerge.[13] Talking to women, recording their voices, listening critically to the ways in which they connect themselves to Iraq both in the past and in the present helps us to move from an important but general concern with class and gender and towards a postcolonial framework that focuses attention on the shifting centre of postcolonial identity. Such reflection is especially important today, given the many women forced to flee conflict in Syria as well as Iraq, and who need as well to find new ways of connecting as refugees to multigenerational "settled" communities composed of their kin in locales throughout the diaspora.

As this book demonstrates, within the intimate – and safe – spaces of the interview, social relations not only can be carefully analysed, but the attentive and respectful listener attuned to the alternative or contradictory narratives of some or many women can also correct the trend in scholarship whereby nationalism is viewed solely as a cultural contest between self and other, colonizing and colonized cultures. My analysis here has both drawn on and contributed to the feminist literature and ethnographic work that has promoted the notion of a deep-listening interviewer who seeks to engage in the research holistically. This means paying attention to tone, words, facial expressions, gestures, and body language as well as the narrative structures and patterns of the stories that women (and men) tell. It means as well listening for stories that are told and retold, constructed and reconstructed. As oral historians, our close interactions with our research subjects help us understand the relationship between the individual and the state, the individual and his or her ethnic group, and the individual's connection to both "home" and "host" land. Within these social interactions are implicit moral codes that police the bodies and behaviours of young women in diaspora.

Finally, this study also suggests avenues for new research, one of which is the study of intimacy within recent and current diasporic communities. Building on and also moving beyond the insights and contributions of this book and the scholarship it has engaged, I plan next to engage the body of work dealing with intimacies across borders by exploring the new modes of communication that link individuals virtually to Iraq but also to each other in intricate ways.[14] The new global reality of living in the digital age heightens the interconnectedness between countries and people. The ability of people in diaspora to communicate so regularly with kin via Skype and thus to feel as though they are physically connected to home complicates the ability of diasporic Iraqis to "become" Canadian or American.[15] Through these technological modes, Iraqis remain virtually connected to the homeland – they can "see" the homeland and virtually interact with the people and spaces of their past in the present. This line of inquiry may generate new insights into how intimacy is maintained across borders. My long-term research plans include as well a full-length study of the extent to which virtual intimacies and communities inform the activisms of young Iraqi women, including how they craft a "religiously constituted political consciousness."[16] I hope, too, that the findings discussed in this book, as well as the new scholarship by such important feminists as Minoo Moallem, Nadine Naber, and Pnina Werbner, will encourage others to interrogate the spaces that Iraqi migrant women create for themselves in both real and virtual worlds. There are exciting and important ongoing discourses that explore "Muslim spaces" online, drawing upon Islam as a framework for contending with patriarchy, empire, racism, and war. Engaging the new frameworks established to examine the creation of these new religious politicized identities, this new research will contribute to the important scholarship on the role of women – including those Iraqi women of this book – in the resistance of "globalization from below."[17]

Notes

Introduction: Narrative, Memory, and Identity

1 See "Medieval Guide to Party Crashing in Iraq Reveals 'Different' Islam," BBC, http://www.bbc.co.uk/news/uk-england-manchester-20509649.
2 *Bamieh* is a Middle Eastern lamb and okra stew.
3 Interview with author, Toronto, 23 January 2010.
4 Among the vast body of work, see Terrence Des Pres, "Holocaust Laughter?" in *Writing and the Holocaust*, ed. Berel Lang (New York: Holmes and Meier, 1988), 216–34; Paul Draper, "Surviving Their Survival: Women, Memory and the Holocaust," in *Sisters or Strangers? Immigrant, Ethnic, and Racialized Women in Canadian History*, ed. Marlene Epp, Franca Iacovetta, and Frances Swyripa (Toronto: University of Toronto Press, 2004), 399–414; Henry Greenspan, *On Listening to Holocaust Survivors: Recounting the Life History* (Westport: Praeger, 1998); Luisa Passerini, *Fascism in Popular Memory: The Cultural Experience of the Turin Working Class*, trans. Robert Lumley and Jude Bloomfeld (Cambridge: Cambridge University Press, 1987); Alexander Freund and Laura Quilici, "Exploring Myths in Women's Narratives: Italian and German Immigrant Women in Vancouver, 1947–1961," *BC Studies* 105–6 (1995): 159–82; Luise White, *Speaking with Vampires: Rumor and History in Colonial Africa* (Berkeley: University of California Press, 2000); Susan Stanford Friedman, *Mappings: Feminism and the Cultural Geographies of Encounter* (Ithaca: Princeton University Press, 1998).
5 Peter Burke, "History as Social Memory," in *Memory: History, Culture and the Mind*, ed. Thomas Butler (New York: Basil Blackwell, 1989), 100.
6 White, *Speaking with Vampires*, 2–3.
7 Marianne Hirsch and Valerie Smith, "Feminism and Cultural Memory: An Introduction," *SIGNS: Journal of Women in Culture and Society* 28, no. 11 (August 2002): 1–19.

8 Burke, "History as Social Memory," 100; Kristina Minister, "A Feminist Frame for the Oral History Interview," in *Women's Words: The Feminist Practice of Oral History*, ed. Sherna Berger Gluck and Daphne Patai (New York: Routledge, 1991), 30.

9 Jared G. Toney, "Locating Diaspora: Afro-Caribbean Narratives of Migration and Settlement in Toronto, 1914–1929," *Urban History Review/ Revue d'histoire urbaine* 38, no. 2 (2010): 75–87. For a broader discussion of how local and global are positioned with regard to the nation state and bordered concepts of belonging, see Robin Cohen, *Global Diasporas: An Introduction* (Seattle: University of Washington Press, 1997).

10 This community is unique amongst Middle Eastern Christian groups since most of its members can trace their family history back to the village of Telkaif (*Telkeppa*) in the northern province of Mosul, located near the ancient Assyrian ruins of Nineveh. From a community of only 23 people in 1923, Michigan's Chaldean population has grown to well over 100,000 by 2005, concentrated mainly in the Detroit metropolitan area. The most accurate population statistics for Chaldeans in Michigan can be found in the works of sociologist Mary Cey Sengstock, who has worked with community organizations over the past thirty years and produced a solid foundation of work on this community. See Sengstock, "Iraqi-Christians in Detroit: An Analysis of an Ethnic Occupation," in *Arabic-Speaking Communities in American Cities*, ed. Barbara Aswad (New York: Center for Migration Studies and Association of Arab-American University Graduates, 1974), 21–38; *Chaldean Americans: Changing Conceptions of Ethnic Identity*, 2nd ed. (New York: Center for Migration Studies, 1999); *Chaldeans in Michigan* (East Lansing: Michigan State University Press, 2005).

11 Himket Jamil, Sylvia Nassar-McMillan, and Richard G. Lambert, "Immigration and Attendant Psychological Sequelae: A Comparison of Three Waves of Iraqi Immigrants," *American Journal of Orthopsychiatry* 77, no. 2 (2007): 199–205.

12 Louise Cainkar, "Immigration to the United States," in *Arab American Encyclopedia*, ed. A. Ameri and D. Ramey (Detroit: Gale Group, 2000), 35–54.

13 The "Arab Population: Census 2000 Brief" provided the first report on population statistics for Arab Americans conducted by the US Census Bureau. In 1997, the Office of Management and Budget revised the federal standards for the classification of race and ethnicity, noting a lack of consensus regarding the definition of the "Arab" ethnic category, and expressing the need for further study to improve data on this population group. Question 10 of the census asks respondents "What is the person's ancestry or ethnicity?" Ancestry, defined as national origin according to

the census, could also be supplemented by a second category, and another option that complicates this calculation is the category of "Other." As I discuss elsewhere in this book, the Chaldean Federation of America asked community members to list their ethnicity as "Chaldean" under the "Other" category rather than "Iraqi." Since the U.S decennial census does not provide information on numbers according to religious affiliation, these Chaldeans who make up a substantial portion of Iraqis in the US are not included in the total population statistics for Iraqis as an ethnic group. According to the best estimates of the 2000 US Census, the number of Americans of Iraqi descent (including permanent residents) rose from 23,212 in 1990 to 37,714 in 2000 (an increase of 63 per cent overall). These numbers do not include Chaldean-Iraqis, whose numbers in Michigan alone were estimated to be well over 100,000 by 2005. In addition, Kurds are not considered a separate ethnic category; their numbers are instead amalgamated into categories of "Arab" or "Other." By 2000, Iraqis in the US were concentrated in three states, Illinois, Michigan, and California, and were estimated to make up 3.2 per cent of the total Arab American population (excluding those listed as "Arab/Arabic" or "Other Arab" in the census). A more detailed study of Michigan state using US census data in addition to community studies suggests that 10 per cent of Michigan's Arab American population is currently made up of Iraqis and 17 per cent of Assyrian/Chaldean (of which most are likely of Iraqi heritage). According to the Arab American Institute, one-third of Michigan's Arab American population is foreign born, and many of these are new Iraqi refugees who have arrived since the Gulf War of 1991 and the US invasion of Iraq in 2003.

In Canada, similar problems exist in the ways in which ethnic groups are organized by national origin. Estimates suggest that from 1945 to 1975, approximately 200 Iraqis arrived in Canada. The most substantial emigration began after 1979 when Saddam Hussein became president of Iraq. From 1975 to 1992, Census Canada recorded 6,472 Iraqis living in Canada, reflecting approximately 3.5 per cent of the Arab immigrant population of Canada. The greatest concentration of Iraqis, and of Arabs in general, has been in Ontario. Toronto and vicinity (Mississauga, Hamilton, and Markham) received almost 55 per cent of all Arab immigrants to Ontario, including 76 per cent of all Ontario-bound immigrants from the Levant during this period. By 1991, Census Canada recorded 4,790 Iraqis living in Canada, of which 3,525 were of Iraqi ancestry and 1,265 were listed as partial Iraqi ancestry. Community sources, however, suggest that by the mid-1990s, owing to the large numbers of Shi'is and Kurds migrating to Canada to escape persecution, population numbers may have been upward of 25,000 people.

According to UNHCR statistics published online, 183,000 Iraqi refugees were settled in developed/Western countries between 1990 and 2001, of which 31,550 settled in the US and 12,220 settled in Canada. These numbers help to explain the discrepancies in the calculation of estimated Iraqis in Canada in particular, but do not completely account for the differences. Some sources suggest that Iraqis fleeing persecution during the 1990s may have concealed their national identity or identified with other groups such as the Chaldeans, Assyrians, or Kurds, thus altering the numbers of Iraqis listed by Census Canada. In addition, between 1997 and 2001, 3,040 asylum applications were granted for the US and an additional 1,030 were granted for Canada. By 2007, the numbers of Iraqi asylum seekers had risen to 6,000 in the US and 4,000 in Canada. Despite the increase in asylums granted, there has been significant controversy in the US especially, as well as in Europe and Canada, concerning the small numbers of Iraqis that have been admitted in the aftermath of the current war. By 2008, it was estimated that there were over 4 million Iraqis displaced worldwide, and 2.3 million of these were internally displaced people, forced from their homes during the most recent war, some of whom were repatriated following the US invasion. There are also large numbers of Iraqis who were forced to return to Iraq due to their financial situation but were unable to return to their original homes, who are also part of this internally displaced group. The US is estimated to have employed over 100,000 Iraqis during their invasion of Iraq from 2003 to 2009, and only a fraction of these have been granted asylum in the US following the persecution and torture they experienced as a direct result of their work with the US military and armed contract groups. This attempt to compile accurate statistics was made using a range of sources, including Employment and Immigration Canada Reports, 1981–1992; Census Canada, 1991; Statistics Canada, 1991; G. Patricia de la Cruz and Angela Brittingham, "The Arab Population: 2000, Census 2000 Brief," US Department of Commerce, Economics and Statistics Administration, US Census Bureau, File 4, 2000; UNHCR, "Statistics on Displaced Iraqis Around the World: Global Overview," April 2007; UNHCR, "Iraqi Refugee and Asylum-Seeker Statistics," March 2003; Farid E. Ohan and Ibrahim Hayani, *The Arabs in Ontario: A Misunderstood Community* (Toronto: Near East Cultural and Educational Foundation of Canada, 1993); Joseph Sassoon, *The Iraqi Refugees: The New Crisis in the Middle East* (London: I. B. Taurus, 2009); US Census Bureau, "2005–2009 American Community Survey Rolling 5-Year Average"; and the websites http://www.migrationinformation.org/usfocus/display.cfm?ID=113; https://www.canada.ca/en/immigration-refugees-citizenship/corporate/reports-statistics/research/people-iraqi-ethnic-origin-canada.html.

14 Louise A. Cainkar, *Homeland Insecurity: The Arab American and Muslim American Experience after 9/11* (New York: Russell Sage Foundation, 2009), 4–7.

15 Arab Community Center for Economic and Social Services fonds, 98121 Bd 2, Bentley Historical Library, University of Michigan, Ann Arbor; Aliya Hassen papers, 1910–1991, 9820 Aa 2, Bentley Historical Library, University of Michigan, Ann Arbor; RG 76 and RG 25, Library and Archives Canada, Ottawa.

16 John Bodnar, *The Transplanted: A History of Immigrants in Urban America*, Interdisciplinary Studies in History (Bloomington: Indiana University Press, 1987); William I. Thomas and Florian Znanieck, *The Polish Peasant in Europe and America, 1918–1920* (New York: Dovercourt, 1958).

17 Donna R. Gabaccia, "Is Everywhere Nowhere? Nomads, Nations, and the Immigrant Paradigm of United States History," *The Journal of American History* 86, no. 3 (December 1999): 11–17.

18 Nina Glick-Schiller, Linda Basch, and Cristina Blanc-Szanton, eds., *Towards a Transnational Perspective on Migration: Race, Class, Ethnicity, and Nationalism Reconsidered* (New York: New York Academy of Sciences, 1992); Michael Kearney, "The Local and the Global: The Anthropology of Globalization and Transnationalism," *Annual Review of Anthropology* 24 (1995): 547–65; Frank Thistlewaite, "Migration from Europe and Overseas in the Nineteenth and Twentieth Centuries," in *A Century of European Migrations, 1830–1930*, ed. Rudolph J. Vecoli and Suzanna M. Sinke (Champaign: University of Illinois Press, 1991), 17–49.

19 Rudolph J. Vecoli, "*Contadini* in Chicago: A Critique of *The Uprooted*," *Journal of American History* 53 (1964): 404–17. See also Donald Avery, *Dangerous Foreigners: European Immigrant Workers and Labour Radicalism in Canada, 1896–1932* (Toronto: McClelland & Stewart, 1979); William H. Cartwright and Richard L. Watson, eds., *The Re-interpretation of American History and Culture* (Washington, DC: National Council for the Social Studies, 1973); Nathan Glazer and Daniel Patrick Moynihan, *Beyond the Melting Pot: The Negroes, Puerto Ricans, Jews, Italians, and Irish of New York City* (Cambridge, MA: MIT/Harvard University Press, 1970); Milton Gordon, *Assimilation in American Life: The Role of Race, Religion, and National Origins* (New York: Oxford University Press, 1964); J.M.S. Careless, "'Limited Identities' in Canada," *Canadian Historical Review* 50 (1969): 1–10.

20 For a very small sample of these, see Franca Iacovetta, *Such Hardworking People: Italian Immigrants in Postwar Toronto* (Montreal: McGill-Queen's University Press, 1992); Bruno Ramirez, *On the Move: French-Canadian and Italian Migrants in the North Atlantic Economy, 1860–1914* (Toronto: University of Toronto Press, 1991); Kay J. Anderson, *Vancouver's Chinatown: Racial Discourse in Canada, 1875–1980* (Montreal: McGill-Queen's

University Press, 1992); Dirk Hoerder, ed., *"Struggle a Hard Battle": Essays on Working-Class Immigrants* (DeKalb: Northern Illinois University Press, 1986); James Barrett and David Roediger, "Inbetween Peoples: Race, Nationality, and the 'New Immigrant' Working Class," *Journal of American Ethnic History* 16, no. 3 (1997): 3–44; Noel Ignatiev, *How the Irish Became White* (London: Routledge, 1995); Mathew Frye Jacobsen, *Whiteness of a Different Color: European Immigrants and the Alchemy of Race* (Cambridge: Cambridge University Press, 1998); Paul Craven, ed., *Labouring Lives: Work and Workers in Nineteenth-Century Ontario* (Toronto: University of Toronto Press, 1995).

21 Among many others, see Joy Parr, "Gender History and Historical Practice," *Canadian Historical Review* 76, no. 3 (1995): 354–76; Ava Baron, ed. *Work Engendered: Toward a New History of American Labor* (Ithaca: Cornell University Press, 1991); Ruth Frager, "Class, Ethnicity and Gender in the Eaton's Strikes of 1912 and 1934," in *Gender Conflicts*, ed. Franca Iacovetta and Marianne Valverde (Toronto: University of Toronto Press, 1992), 189–228; Nancy Hewitt, "'The Voice of Virile Labor': Labor Militancy, Community Solidarity, and Gender Identity Among Tampa's Latin Workers, 1880–1921," in *Work Engendered: Toward a New History of American Labor*, ed. Ava Baron (Ithaca: Cornell University Press, 1991), 142–67; Ardis Cameron, "Bread and Roses Revisited: Women's Culture and Working-Class Activism in the Lawrence Strike of 1912," in *Women, Work and Protest: A Century of U.S. Women's Labour History*, ed. Ruth Milkman, 2nd ed. (London: Routledge & Kegan Paul, 1985), 42–62; Susan A. Glenn, *Daughters of the Shtetl: Life and Labour in the Immigrant Generation* (Ithaca: Cornell University Press, 1990); Elizabeth Ewen, *Immigrant Women in the Land of Dollars: Life and Culture on the Lower East-Side, 1890–1925* (New York: Monthly Review Press, 1985); Hasia R. Diner, *Erin's Daughters in America: Irish Immigrant Women in the Nineteenth Century* (Baltimore: Johns Hopkins University Press, 1983).

22 In many cases feminist social historians were forced to respond to "vitriolic" attacks made by senior male counterparts who took offence to what they considered to be the decimation of national Canadian history. In the Canadian case, I refer to the well-known case of Howard Palmer's attack on the work of Lynne Marks, a feminist social historian of Jewish immigrant women and religious life in Canada. See Lynne Marks, "Heroes and Hallelujahs – Labour History and the Social History of Religion in English Canada: A Response to Bryan Palmer," *Histoire sociale/ Social History* 34, no. 67 (2001): 169–86; Bryan Palmer, "Historiographic Hassles: Class and Gender, Evidence and Interpretation," *Histoire sociale/Social History* 33, no. 65 (2000): 105–44; Mariana Valverde, "Some Remarks on the Rise and Fall of Discourse Analysis," *Histoire sociale/Social History* 33, no. 65 (2000): 59–72.

23 Donna Gabaccia, *From the Other Side: Women, Gender, and Immigrant Life in the U.S., 1820–1990* (Bloomington: Indiana University Press, 1994); Franca Iacovetta with Paula Draper and Robert Ventresca, *A Nation of Immigrants: Women, Workers and Communities in Canadian History* (Toronto: University of Toronto Press, 1998); Donna Gabaccia and Franca Iacovetta, eds., *Women, Gender and Transnational Lives: Italian Workers of the World* (Toronto: University of Toronto Press, 2002). Other important works that informed the initial conception of this project as a doctoral thesis include Marlene Epp, *Women without Men: Mennonite Refugees of the Second World War* (Toronto: University of Toronto Press, 2000); Tania Das Gupta and Franca Iacovetta, "Whose Canada Is It? Immigrant Women, Women of Colour and Feminist Critiques of Multiculturalism," *Atlantis* 24, no. 2 (Spring 2000): 1-4; Marlene Epp, Franca Iacovetta, and Frances Swyripa, eds., *Sisters or Strangers? Immigrant, Ethnic, and Racialized Women in Canadian History* (Toronto: University of Toronto Press, 2004).

24 Caroline Nagel, "Introduction," in *Geographies of Muslim Women: Gender, Religion and Space*, ed. Ghazi-Waleed Falah and Caroline Nagel (New York: Guildford Press, 2005), 10–12.

25 Khachig Tölölyan, "Rethinking Diaspora(s): Stateless Power in the Transnational Moment," *Diaspora* 5, no. 1 (1996): 3–36; Khachig Tölölyan, "The Nation-State and Its Others: In Lieu of a Preface," *Diaspora* 1, no. 1 (1991): 3–5; James Clifford, ed., "Further Inflections: Toward Ethnographies of the Future," special issue of *Cultural Anthropology* 9, no. 3 (August 1994); Stephen Vertovec, "Conceiving and Researching Transnationalism," *Ethnic and Racial Studies* 22, no. 2 (March 1999): 446–9; Cohen, *Global Diasporas*, x; Michael Reis, "Theorizing Diaspora: Perspectives on 'Classical' and 'Contemporary' Diaspora," *International Migration* 42, no. 2 (2004): 43–7; William Safran, "Diasporas in Modern Society: Myths of Homeland and Return," *Diaspora* 1, no. 1 (Spring 1991): 84; Denise Helly, "Diaspora: History of an Idea," in *The "Muslim" Diaspora and Research on Gender: Promises and Perils*, ed. Haideh Moghissi (London: Routledge, 2006), 5; Michel S. LaGuerre, *Diasporic Citizenship: Haitian Americans in Transnational America* (New York: St. Martin's Press, 1998).

26 See also Nadje Sadig Al-Ali, *Iraqi Women: Untold Stories from 1948 to the Present* (New York: Zed Books, 2007), 17.

27 Arjun Appadurai, "Global Ethnoscapes: Notes and Queries for a Transnational Anthropology," in *Recapturing Anthropology: Working in the Present*, ed. Richard G. Fox (Santa Fe: School of American Research Press, 1991), 192.

28 Benedict Anderson, *Imagined Communities: Reflections on the Origin and Spread of Nationalism* (New York: Verso, 1983); Mathew Frye Jacobsen, *Special Sorrows: The Diasporic Imagination of Irish, Polish and Jewish Immigrants in the United States* (Cambridge, MA: Harvard University Press, 1995), 2, 205–7.

29 Anthony Gorman and Sossie Kasbarian, *Diasporas of the Modern Middle East: Contextualizing Communities* (Edinburgh: University of Edinburgh Press, 2015), 3.
30 Andreas Wimmer and Nina Glick Schiller, "Methodological Nationalism and Beyond: Nation-State Building, Migration and the Social Sciences," *Global Networks* 2, no. 4 (2002): 306.
31 Edward Said, "Zionism from the Standpoint of Its Victims," *Social Text* 1 (Winter 1979): 18.
32 Interview, Mississauga, 2 February 2009.
33 Liisa Malkki, "National Geographic: The Rooting of Peoples and the Territorialization of National Identity among Scholars and Refugees," *Cultural Anthropology Space, Identity, and the Politics of Difference* 7, no. 1 (February 1992): 27.
34 Pierre Bourdieu and Loic Wacquant, *An Invitation to Reflexive Sociology* (Cambridge: Polity Press, 1992).
35 Lamees Al-Ethari, "Defragmenting Identity in the Life Narratives of Iraqi North American Women," PhD diss., University of Waterloo, 2014, 10012/8413, p. 2.
36 Ibid., 114.
37 Wendy Bottero, "Intersubjectivity and the Bourdeausian Approaches to Identity," *Cultural Sociology* 4, no. 1 (March 2010): 3–22.
38 Jasbir K. Puar, *Terrorist Assemblages: Homonationalism in Queer Times* (Durham: Duke University Press, 2007), 1–36.
39 Nagel, "Introduction."
40 Floya Anthias, "Evaluating Diaspora: Beyond Ethnicity?" *Sociology* 32, no. 3 (August 1998): 557–80. See also John Rex, *Ethnic Minorities in the Modern Nation State: Working Papers in the Theory of Multiculturalism and Political Integration* (Basingstoke, UK: Macmillan, 1996), 82–3.
41 Sami Zubaida, "Nations: Old and New: Comments on Anthony D. Smith's 'The Myth of the "Modern Nation" and the Myths of Nations,'" paper presented to the Anthropology Seminar Series, University College, London, 1997.
42 Denise Helly, "Diaspora: History of an Idea," in *Muslim Diaspora: Gender, Culture and Identity*, ed. Haideh Moghissi (New York: Routledge, 2006), 6.
43 Michael Ignatief, *Blood and Belonging: Journeys into the New Nationalisms* (Toronto: Vintage Books, 1993), 4; see also Julia Kristeva, *Nations without Nationalism* (New York: Columbia University, 1993).
44 Nina Glick-Schiller, Linda Basch, and Christina Szanton-Blanc, *Towards a Transnational Perspective on Migration* (New York: New York Academy of Sciences, 1992); Steven Vertovec, "Transnationalism and Identity," *Journal of Ethnic and Migration Studies* 27, no. 4 (2001): 573–92; Nadje Al-Ali, "Trans- or A-national? Bosnian Refugees in the UK and the

Netherlands," in *New Approaches to Migration: Transnational Communities and the Transformation of Home*, ed. Nadje Al-Ali and Khalid Koser (London: Routledge, 2002), 96–117; Nadje Al-Ali and Nicole Pratt, "Women's Organizing and the Conflict in Iraq since 2003," *Feminist Review* 88, no. 1 (2008): 74–85.

45 Vijay Agnew, "Introduction," in *Diaspora, Memory, and Identity: A Search for Home*, ed. Vijay Agnew (Toronto: University of Toronto Press, 2005), 13.

46 Ibid., 4.

47 Ibid., 13.

48 For a small sample, see Bettina Bradbury, *Working Families: Age, Gender and Daily Survival in Industrializing Montreal* (Toronto: McClelland & Stewart, 1993); Ruth Frager, *Sweatshop Strife: Class, Ethnicity, and Gender in the Jewish Labour Movement in Toronto, 1900–1939* (Toronto: University of Toronto Press, 1992); Joy Parr, *The Gender of Breadwinners: Women, Men and Change in Two Industrial Towns, 1880–1950* (Toronto: University of Toronto Press, 1990).

49 For a small sample within the Canadian literature, see Micheline d'Allaire, "Origine sociale des religieuses de l'Hôpital Général de Québec," *Revue d'histoire de l'Amérique français* 33, no. 4 (March 1970): 559–82; Micheline Dumont-Johnson, "Les communautés religieuses et la condition féminine," *Recherches sociographiques* 19, no. 1 (January–April 1978): 79–102; Marta Danylewycz, *Taking the Veil: An Alternative to Marriage, Motherhood, and Spinsterhood in Quebec, 1840–1920* (Toronto: McClelland & Stewart, 1987); Frances Swyripa, *Wedded to the Cause: Ukranian-Canadian Women and Ethnic Identity, 1891–1991* (Toronto: University of Toronto Press, 1993); Epp, *Women without Men*.

For a small sample within the US literature, see Mary Ewen, *The Role of the Nun in Nineteenth Century America* (New York: Arno, 1978); Elizabeth Kolmer, "Catholic Women Religious and Women's History: A Survey of the Literature," *American Quarterly* 30, no. 5 (Winter 1978): 639–51; Glenn, *Daughters of the Shtetl*; Robert A. Orsi, *Thank You, St. Jude: Women's Devotion to the Patron Saint of Hopeless Causes* (New Haven: Yale University Press, 1996); John T. McGreevy, *Parish Boundaries: The Catholic Encounter with Race in the Twentieth-Century Urban North* (Chicago: University of Chicago Press, 1996).

50 See, among many others, Ahmed Yousif, *Muslims in Canada: A Question of Identity*, 2nd ed. (Ottawa: Legas, 2008); Baha Abu-Laban and Michael W. Suleiman, eds., *Arab Americans: Continuity and Change* (Belmont: Association of Arab American University Graduates, 1989); Ernest McCarus, ed., *The Development of Arab-American Identity* (Ann Arbor: University of Michigan Press, 1995); Philip M. Kayal and Joseph M. Kayal, *The Syrian-Lebanese in America: A Study in Religion and Assimilation*

(New York: Twayne, 1975); Barbara C. Aswad, *Arabic Speaking Communities in American Cities* (New York: Center for Migration Studies of New York, 1974); Debbie Miller, "The Syrian Lebanese and Other People of the Middle East," in *They Chose Minnesota: A Survey of the State's Ethnic Groups*, ed. June Drenning Holmquist (St. Paul: Minnesota Historical Society Press, 1981), 511–30; Afif Tannous, "Acculturation of an Arab-Syrian Community in the Deep South," *American Sociological Review* 8, no. 3 (June 1943): 264–71; Baha Abu-Laban, *An Olive Branch on the Family Tree: The Arabs in Canada, a History of Canada's Peoples* (Toronto/Ottawa: McClelland & Stewart/Multiculturalism Directorate, 1980); Mohammed Sawaie, ed., *Arabic-Speaking Immigrants in the United States and Canada: A Bibliographical Guide with Annotation* (Lexington: Mazda, 1985).

51 Haideh Moghissi, "Introduction," in *Muslim Diaspora: Gender, Culture and Identity*, ed. Haideh Moghissi (London: Routledge, 2006), xiv. See also Kirsten E. Schulze, Martin Stokes, and Colm Cambell, eds., *Nationalism, Minorities and Diasporas: Identities and Rights in the Middle East* (London: Tauris, 1996); Gabriel Sheffer, ed., *Modern Diasporas in International Politics* (London: Croom Helm, 1986); Moshe Ma'oz and Gabriel Sheffer, eds., *Middle Eastern Minorities and Diasporas* (Brighton: Sussex Academic Press, 2002); Haideh Moghissi, "The 'Muslim' Diaspora and Research on Gender," in *Diaspora, Memory, and Identity: A Search for Home*, ed. Vijay Agnew (Toronto: University of Toronto Press, 2005), 255–6; Rivka Yadlin, "The Muslim Diaspora in the West," in *Middle Eastern Minorities and Diasporas*, ed. Moshe Ma'oz and Gabriel Sheffer (Brighton: Sussex Academic Press, 2002), 219–30.

52 Moghissi, "Introduction," xvi.

53 Ibid., xvii. There are, of course, vast differences within groups that form what might be considered a "Muslim" diaspora. Muslims are a highly diverse group, differentiated by religious sect, gender, generation, class, ethnicity, and cultural practices. Their multiple identities are complex, woven into the fabric of the collective identities of nations into which they are born. One of the most important and misleading assumptions made about this group is that they are united by religious beliefs. Not only are there many schools of thought within each broad sect of Sunni and Shi'a, there is also a vast and global population of non-religious or secular Muslims who identify with this community on the basis of culture or ethnicity rather than religion. The importance of these differences in addition to the ways in which they coalesce to form around a central Muslim community in Canada is addressed further in Yousif, *Muslims in Canada*.

54 Andrew Shryock, "The Moral Analogies of Race: Arab American Identity, Color Politics, and the Limits of Racialized Citizenship," in *Race and Arab Americans before and after 9/11: From Invisible Citizens to Visible Subjects*, ed.

Amaney Jamal and Nadine Naber (Syracuse: Syracuse University Press, 2008), 2–10.

55 Phil Cohen, *New Ethnicities, Old Racisms* (London: Zed Books, 1999), 2.

56 Stuart Hall, "Cultural Identity and Diaspora," in *Theorizing Diaspora*, ed. Jana Evans Braziel and Anita Mannur (Oxford: Blackwell, 2003), 238–44.

57 Haideh Moghissi, Saeed Rahnema, and Mark J. Goodman, eds., *Diaspora by Design: Muslims in Canada and Beyond* (Toronto: University of Toronto Press, 2009), 6.

58 Fanon describes this kind of racism that links a black person to his or her ancestors' experiences of slavery. A similar mechanism is at play when Muslims are homogenized by Western societies as being an ethnic absolute, negating the diversity within this group. Fanon, "The Fact of Blackness," in *Black Skin, White Masks*, trans. Charles Lam Markmann (New York: Grove, 1967); see also Paul Gilroy, *The Black Atlantic: Modernity and Double Consciousness* (Cambridge: Harvard University Press, 1993), 1–40.

59 Yasmin Jiwani, *Discourses of Denial: Mediations of Race, Gender and Violence* (Vancouver: UBC Press, 2006); Jo-Anne Lee and John Lutz, "Introduction: Towards a Critical Literacy of Racisms, Anti-Racisms, and Racialization," in *Situating Race and Racisms in Space, Time and Theory: Critical Essays for Activists and Scholars*, ed. Jo-Anne Lee and John Lutz (Montreal/Kingston: McGill-Queen's University Press, 2005), 3–29; Sunera Thobani, *Exalted Subjects: Studies in the Making of Race and Nation in Canada* (Toronto: University of Toronto Press, 2007); May Yee, "Finding the Way Home through Issues of Gender, Race and Class," in *Returning the Gaze: Essays on Racism, Feminism and Politics*, ed. Himani Bannerji (Toronto: Sister Vision Press, 1993), 3–37; Sherene Razack, *Casting Out: The Eviction of Muslims from Western Law and Politics* (Toronto: University of Toronto Press, 2008); Patricia Monture, "Race, Gender and the University: Strategies for Survival," in *States of Race: Critical Race Feminism for the 21st Century*, ed. Sherene Razack, Malinda Smith, and Sunera Thobani (Toronto: Between the Lines, 2010), 23–36; Himani Bannerji, *Thinking Through: Essays on Feminism, Marxism and Anti-Racism* (Toronto: Women's Press, 1995); Vijay Agnew, ed., *Resisting Discrimination: Women from Asia, Africa, and the Caribbean and the Women's Movement in Canada* (Toronto: University of Toronto Press, 1996); Aminah B. McCloud, *Transnational Muslims in American Society* (Gainesville: University of Florida Press, 2006); Rima Berns-McGown, *Muslims in the Diaspora: The Somali Communities of London and Toronto* (Toronto: University of Toronto Press, 1999), viii.

60 Shahnaz Khan, *Aversion and Desire: Negotiating Muslim Female Identity in the Diaspora* (Toronto: Women's Press, 2002), 12. See also Parin Dossa, *Politics and Poetics of Migration: Narratives of Iranian Women from the Diaspora* (Toronto: Canadian Scholars Press, 2004), 26; Trinh T. Min-ha, *Woman Native Other* (Bloomingdale: Indiana University Press, 1989), 119.

61 See Yvonne Yazbeck Haddad, "The Dynamics of Islamic Identity in North America," in *Muslims on the Americanization Path?*, ed. Yvonne Yazbeck Haddad and John L. Esposito (Atlanta: Scholar Press, 1998), 19–46; Muqtedar M. Khan, "Constructing the American Muslim Community," in *Religion and Immigration: Christian, Jewish and Muslims Experiences in the United States*, ed. Yvonne Haddad, Jane I. Smith, and John L. Esposito (Walnut Creek: AltaMira, 2003), 174–98; Mark J. Goodman, "Diaspora, Ethnicity and Problems of Identity," in *Muslim Diaspora: Gender, Culture and Identity*, ed. Haideh Moghissi (London: Routledge, 2006), 54–68.

62 Ali Rattansi, "Introduction: Writing 'Race' and the Difference It Makes," in *Race, Culture and Difference*, ed. James Donald and Ali Rattansi (London: Sage, 1992), 25. See also Philip Corrigan, "Race/Ethnicity/Gender/Culture: Embodying Differences Educationally: An Argument," in *Breaking the Mosaic*, ed. Jon Young (Toronto: Garamond, 1987), 20–30; Rodney Clifton and Lance Roberts, "Multiculturalism in Canada: A Sociological Perspective," in *Multiculturalism in Canada*, ed. Augie Fleras and Jean Elliott (Toronto: Nelson, 1992), 120–47.

63 Khan, *Aversion and Desire*, 13.

64 Ibid., 20.

65 Chandra Talpade Mohanty, "Introduction: Cartographies of Struggle: Third World Women and the Politics of Feminism," in *Third World Women and the Politics of Feminism*, ed. Chandra Talpade Mohanty, Ann Russo, and Lourdes Torres (Bloomington: Indiana University Press, 1991), 2.

66 Ibid., 4.

67 Chandra Talpade Mohanty, "Feminist Encounters: Location the Politics of Experience," *Copyright* 1 (Fall 1987): 30–44.

68 Nira Yuval-Davis, *Gender and Nation* (London: Sage, 1997), 7.

69 Ibid., 8.

70 Dorothy Smith, *The Everyday World as Problematic: A Feminist Sociology* (Boston: Northeastern University Press, 1987), 2.

71 Himani Bannerji, *Returning the Gaze: Essays on Racism, Feminism, and Politics* (Toronto: Sister Vision Press, 1993). See also Mohanty, "Introduction," 1–50; Anderson, *Imagined Communities;* Gayatri Spivak, "Gayatri Spivak on the Politics of the Subaltern: Interview with Howard Winant," *Socialist Review* 20 (1990): 81–97; Nadje Al-Ali and Nicola Pratt, "Introduction," in *Women and War in the Middle East: Transnational Perspectives*, ed. Nadje Al-Ali and Nicola Pratt (London: Zed Books, 2009), 5. See also Wenona Giles and Jennifer Hyndman, "New Directions for Feminist Research and Politics," in *Sites of Violence: Gender and Conflict Zones*, ed. Wenona Giles and Jennifer Hyndman (Berkeley: University of California Press, 2004), 313–14; Sherene Razack, Malinda Smith, and Sunera Thobani, "Introduction," in *States of Race: Critical Race Feminism for the 21st Century*, ed. Razack,

Smith, and Thobani (Toronto: Between the Lines, 2010), 2; Razack, *Casting Out*; Thobani, *Exalted Subjects*; Patricia J. Williams, *Seeing a Color-Blind Future: The Paradox of Race* (New York: Farar, Straus and Giroux, 1998); Minh-ha, *Woman, Native, Other*, quoted in Razack, Smith, and Thobani, "Introduction," 3.

72 Lila Abu-Lughod, "Do Muslim Women Really Need Saving? Anthropological Reflections on Cultural Relativism and Its Others, *American Anthropologist* 104, no. 3 (2002): 783–90; Miriam Cooke, "Saving Brown Women," *Signs: Journal of Women in Culture and Society* 28, no. 1 (2002): 468–70; Usha Zacharias, "Legitimizing Empire: Racial and Gender Politics of the War on Terrorism," *Social Justice* 30, no. 2 (2003): 123–32; Leila Ahmed, *Women and Gender in Islam: Historical Roots of a Modern Debate* (New Haven: Yale University Press, 1992), 236–7.

73 Al-Ali and Pratt, "Introduction"; Dahr Jamail and Ali Al-Fadhily, "No Safety for Women in Iraq," *Alternet*, 15 December 2006, https://www.alternet.org/2006/12/no_safety_for_women_in_iraq/.

74 Doreen Ingrams, *The Awakened: Women in Iraq* (London: Third World Center, 1983); Deborah Cobbett and the Committee Against Repression and for Democratic Rights in Iraq, "Women in Iraq," in *Saddam's Iraq: Revolution or Reaction?* (London: Zed Books, 1989), 120–37; Jacqueline S. Ismael and Shereen T. Ismael, "Gender and State in Iraq," in *Gender, Citizenship in the Middle East*, ed. Suad Joseph (Syracuse: Syracuse University Press, 2000), 185–211; Noga Efrati, "The Other Awakening in Iraq: The Women's Movement in the First Half of the Twentieth Century," *British Journal of Middle Eastern Studies* 31, no. 2 (2004): 153–73; Nadje Al-Ali, "Reconstructing Gender: Iraqi Women between Dictatorship, War, Sanctions and Occupation," *Third World Quarterly* 26, no. 4–5 (2005): 739–58; Al-Ali, *Iraqi Women*; Jacqueline S. Ismael and Shereen T. Ismael, "Iraqi Women Under Occupation: From Tribalism to New-Feudalism," *International Journal of Contemporary Iraqi Studies* 1 (2007): 247–68; Al-Ali and Pratt, "Women's Organizing and the Conflict in Iraq"; Orit Bashkin, "Representations of Women in the Writing of the Intelligentsia in Hashemite Iraq, 1921–1958," *Journal of Middle East Women's Studies* 4, no. 1 (Winter 2008): 53–82; Noga Efrati, *Women in Iraq: Past Meets Present* (New York: Columbia University Press, 2012); Yasmin Husein Al-Jawaheri, *Women in Iraq: The Gender Impact of International Sanctions* (London: Boulder, 2008).

75 Zahra Ali, *Women and Gender in Iraq: Between Nation-Building and Fragmentation* (Cambridge, MA: Cambridge University Press, 2018).

76 Friedman, *Mappings*, 19.

77 Iderpal Grewal and Karen Caplan, "Transnational Feminist Practices and Questions of Postmodernity," in *Scattered Hegemonies: Postmodernity and*

Transnational Feminist Practices, ed. Inderpal Grewal and Karen Caplan (Minneapolis: University of Minnesota Press, 1994), 13; Doreen Massey, "A Global Sense of Place, and a Place Called Home?" in *Space, Place and Gender* (Minneapolis: University of Minnesota Press, 1994), 146–74.

78 Eric Davis, *Memories of State: Politics, History, and Collective Identity in Modern Iraq* (Berkeley: University of California Press, 2005).

79 See also Claudia Koontz, *Mothers in the Fatherland: Women, the Family and Nazi Politics* (London: Cape, 1986).

80 Judith Butler, *Gender Trouble: Feminism and the Subversion of Identity* (London: Routledge, 1990).

81 Hirsch and Smith, "Feminism and Cultural Memory," 11–13; see also Franca Iacovetta, "Post-Modern Ethnography, Historical Materialism, and Decentring the (Male) Authorial Voice: A Feminist Conversation," *Canadian Historical Review* 32, no. 64 (1999): 275–93; Joan Sangster, "Telling Our Stories: Feminist Debates and the Use of Oral History," *Women's History Review* 3, no. 1 (1994): 5–28.

82 Sana Al-Khayyat, *Honor and Shame: Women in Modern Iraq* (London: Al-Saqi, 1990), 22.

1. Gendered Narratives of State: The Project for the Rewriting of History

1 Interview, Toronto, 24 January 2010.

2 Marita Eastmond, "Stories as Lived Experience: Narratives in Forced Migration Research," *Journal of Refugee Studies* 20, no. 2 (2007): 251.

3 Dunya Mikhail, *A Diary of a Wave Outside the Sea*, trans. Elizabeth Winslow and Dunya Mikhail (New York: New Directions, 2009).

4 Anna Green, "Individual Remembering and 'Collective Memory': Theoretical Presuppositions and Contemporary Debates," *Oral History* 32, no. 2 (Autumn 2004): 38–43.

5 Samir al-Khalil, *Republic of Fear: The Politics of Modern Iraq* (Berkeley: University of California Press, 1989), 77–8.

6 Susannah Radstone and Bill Schwartz, "Introduction: Mapping Memory," in *Memory: Histories, Theories, Debates*, ed. Susannah Radstone and Bill Schwartz (New York: Fordham University Press, 2010), 4.

7 Saddam Hussein was particularly concerned with the Shi'is and the Kurds, extensively targeting their efforts to gain political independence. The regime's also suppressed smaller ethno-religious minority groups, including the Armenians, Chaldeans, Syriacs, Assyrians, and Iraqi Jews.

8 Parin Dossa, *Racialized Bodies, Disabling Worlds: Storied Lives of Immigrant Muslim Women* (Toronto: University of Toronto Press, 2009), 21.

9 Eric Davis, *Memories of State: Politics, History, and Collective Identity in Modern Iraq* (Berkeley: University of California Press, 2005).

10 Interview, Amman, 23 September 2008, emphasis mine.

11 Zoe Preston, *The Crystallization of the Iraqi State: Geopolitical Function and Form* (Oxford: Peter Lang, 2003), 77. By 1914, Iraq had a population of approximately three million people. Historians estimate the population was 90 per cent Muslim (55 per cent of which were Shi'i), with significant ethnic and religious divides, including a 15–20 per cent Kurdish population to the north, an important Jewish population in the capital city of Baghdad (approximately 3 per cent of the total population at this time), and minorities of Turkomans, Persians, Assyrians, Christians, Mandaeans, and Yazidis. Phebe Marr, *The Modern History of Iraq* (Boulder: Colorado University Press, 1985), 20–7.
12 Al-Khalil, *Republic of Fear*, 77–8.
13 The United Nations even awarded Iraq special recognition for its literacy campaign. Thabit A. J. Abdullah, *A Short History of Iraq*, 2nd ed. (London: Longman, 2011), 131.
14 Ibid., 131–2.
15 Al-Khalil, *Republic of Fear*, 78–82.
16 General Federation of Iraqi Women, Secretariat of Studies and Researchers, *Working Progress of the Iraqi Republic to Improve the Woman's Status: The National Papers Presented to the International Congress for the UN Women's Contract Held in Copenhagen* (Baghdad: General Federation of Iraqi Women, August 1980), 30–4.
17 These significant gains contributed to making Iraqi women some of the most literate and educated women in the Middle East by 1980, although these shifts fail to address improvements made to gendered equality in the home and in the workplace as women began to emerge from the home to occupy a new role in Iraq's public life. General Federation of Iraqi Women, *Working Progress of the Iraqi Republic*, 44.
18 Reva Simon, "The Teaching of History in Iraq before the Rashid Ali Coup of 1941," *Middle Eastern Studies* 22 (1986): 37–51.
19 Hanna Batatu, *The Old Social Classes and the Revolutionary Movements of Iraq: A Study of Iraq's Old Landed and Commercial Classes and of Its Communists, Ba'athists, and Free Officers* (Princeton: Princeton University Press, 1978), 645.
20 Simon, "The Teaching of History in Iraq," 43.
21 Batatu, *The Old Social Classes*, 646–7; Simon, "The Teaching of History in Iraq," 49.
22 Joe Stork, "State Power and Economic Structure: Class Determination and State Formation in Contemporary Iraq," in *Iraq: The Contemporary State*, ed. Tim Niblick (London: Croon Helm/Exeter Center for Arab Gulf Studies, 1982), 27–35.
23 Marion Farouk-Sluglett and Peter Sluglett, "The Historiography of Modern Iraq," *American Historical Review* 96, no. 5 (December 1991): 1413.
24 Marr, *The Modern History of Iraq*, 5–17.
25 Farouk-Sluglett and Sluglett, "The Historiography of Modern Iraq," 1414.

26 Marr, *The Modern History of Iraq*, 10–11.

27 Batatu, *The Old Social Classes*, 22.

28 Craig Calhoun, *Critical Social Theory: Culture, History, and the Challenge of Difference* (Oxford: Blackwell, 1995), 220.

29 Davis, *Memories of State*, 4.

30 Ibid., 5.

31 Elie Kedourie, *Democracy and Arab Political Culture* (Washington, DC: Washington Institute for Near East Policy, 1992), 5–15.

32 Davis, *Memories of State*, 110.

33 Ibid., 148–70.

34 The use of rhetoric and symbols as a mechanism of control has also been noted in similar authoritarian regimes in this region of the Middle East, including in Syria's Assad regime, where the symbolic production of state-sanctioned narratives of the past was closely regulated. As Lisa Wedeen notes, although this means of controlling the production of historical narratives does not necessarily imply coercion is not employed, this was certainly not the case in Iraq or in Syria: rather, coercion was not the exclusive form of control upon which these regimes relied. Lisa Wedeen argues that "symbolic displays of power not only operate in tandem with overt coercive controls, they are themselves a subsystem of coercive control." Wedeen, *Ambiguities of Domination: Politics, Rhetoric, and Symbols in Contemporary Syria* (Chicago: University of Chicago Press, 1999), 27.

35 Ibid., 150.

36 To mask the fact that sectarianism was used as the basis for filling jobs in the state's administration, the Revolutionary Command Council issued a decree in 1978 that forbade Iraqis from using surnames that referred to their tribal or regional backgrounds. The comprehensive study of Iraqi tribes *'Asha'ir al-'Iraq* (The Tribes of Iraq) was also banned during the 1970s and 1980s. Davis, *Memories of State*, 204.

37 Eric Davis and Nicolas Gavrielides, "Statecraft, Historical Memory, and Popular Culture in Iraq and Kuwait," in *Statecraft in the Middle East: Oil, Historical Memory and Popular Culture*, ed. Eric Davis and Nicolas Gavrielides (Miami: Florida International University Press, 1991), 139.

38 See especially Zainab Salbi and Laurie Becklund, *Between Two Worlds – Escape from Tyranny: Growing Up in the Shadow of Saddam* (New York: Gotham, 2005).

39 Hanna Batatu, "Class Analysis and Iraqi Society," in *Arab Studies Quarterly* 1, no. 1 (1979): 230.

40 Yitzhak Nakash, *The Shi'is of Iraq* (Princeton: Princeton University Press, 1994), 30–4; Marion Farouk-Slugett and Peter Slugett, "The Transformation of Land Tenure and Rural Social Structure in Central and Southern Iraq, c. 1870–1958," *International Journal of Middle East Studies* 15 (1983): 494; Marr, *The Modern History of Iraq*, 6–8.

41 Karen Kern, *Imperial Citizen: Marriage and Citizenship in the Ottoman Frontier Provinces of Iraq* (Syracuse: Syracuse University Press, 2011), 149.
42 Ibid., 152.
43 Stuart Hall, "Minimal Selves," in *Identity, the Real Me*, ICA Document 6 (London: ICA, 1987), 44.
44 Cynthia Cockburn, *The Space between Us: Negotiating Gender and National Identities in Conflict* (London: Zed Books, 1998), 5–15.
45 Nadje Al-Ali, "Reconstructing Gender: Iraqi Women between Dictatorship, War, Sanctions and Occupation," *Third World Quarterly* 26, no. 4–5 (2005): 741.
46 Saddam Hussein, "Women – One Half of Our Society," *The Revolution and Women in Iraq*, trans. Khalid Kishtainy (Baghdad: Translation and Foreign Languages Publishing House, 1981), 12.
47 In a speech to the General Federation of Iraqi Women (GFIW) in 1977, an organization that was later absorbed into the state structure, Saddam Hussein argued that women were better suited to family life and raising children than to fighting in the army. By carrying out their traditional role, women in Iraq were fighting on behalf of their nation. Saddam Hussein, "The Revolution and the Historical Role of Women," in *The Revolution and Women in Iraq*, trans. Khalid Kishtainy (Baghdad: Translation and Foreign Languages Publishing House, 1981), 51–4.
48 This "awakening" is largely associated with a focus on improving the literacy, health, education, and legal rights of women in Iraq during the revolutionary period. This was in many ways premised upon an earlier "women's awakening" (*nahda al-nisa'*) during the 1920s that also focused on education as well as on "emancipating" women from the veil. Nadje Al-Ali, *Iraqi Women: Untold Stories from 1948 to the Present* (New York: Zed Books, 2007), 12. See also Salbi and Becklund, *Between Two Worlds*.
49 Noga Efrati, "Competing Narratives: Histories of the Women's Movement in Iraq, 1910–1958," *International Journal of Middle East Studies* 40 (2008): 446.
50 This was also the case in women's movements in the surrounding regions. Ruth Frances Woodsmall and Charlotte Johnson, *Study of the Role of Women, Their Activities and Organizations in Lebanon, Egypt, Iraq, Jordan and Syria* (New York: International Federation of Business and Professional Women, 1956), 45–50.
51 Efrati, "Competing Narratives," 447. The union also received the patronage of Queen Mother Aliya, which they used to their political advantage, remaining neutral on the subject of British involvement in Iraq.
52 The first and most often cited account of the history of the Iraqi women's movement in the English literature is Doreen Ingram's *The Awakened: Women in Iraq* (London: Third World Center, 1983), which was published in 1983. This version became the official account of the women's movement during the Ba'ath regime. Ingrams dedicated the book to the General Federation of Iraqi Women. See Efrati, "Competing Narratives," 445, 461.

53 This alternate narrative received academic attention following the English-language publication of Deborah Cobbett's article "Women in Iraq," published in 1989. Efrati, "Competing Narratives," 445.

54 Ibid., 460.

55 Charles Tripp, *A History of Iraq*, 2nd ed. (Cambridge: Cambridge University Press, 2002), 194–5.

56 Marr, *The Modern History of Iraq*, 279.

57 Interview, Toronto, 13 August 2009.

58 As I mention above, Zeynab is a very close acquaintance of mine, and I know from speaking with her on many occasions both formally and informally that these periods of repression had a devastating effect on her family. Her father, once a notable historian, was pressured by the government to promote the Ba'ath version of the Iraqi past, which he refused to do, leading to his demotion from a prestigious position within the Iraqi Academy and eventual alienation from academic life. Two of her siblings left the country to establish lives in Sweden and America, and she was unable to visit them until she arrived in Canada as a refugee. After marriage, she was forced out of her position as an electrical engineer at the Iraqi National Energy Board due in part to her father's tense relationship with the state and in part to association with her husband's family (many of whom were targeted by the Ba'ath because of their former connection with the communist party).

59 Interview, Toronto, 13 August 2009.

60 Ibid., 10 December, 2009.

61 Al-Ali, *Iraqi Women*, 136–8.

62 Suad Joseph, "Elite Strategies for State Building: Women, Family, Religion and the State in Iraq and Lebanon," in *Women, Islam and the State*, ed. Deniz Kandiyoti (Philadelphia: Temple University Press, 1991), 182.

63 Ibid., 186.

64 This is in direct contrast to states such as Lebanon, where ethno-religious identities were legally incorporated as a basis for formal representation in the state, and the heterogeneous elite organized around competitive and often conflicting political ideologies. Sectarian factions in Lebanon shared control over the population, whereas in Iraq the manipulation of the political processes was dominated by a single head of party and state. Furthermore, Lebanon's programs were designed to keep women in kin/ethnic/tribal groups, whereas the Iraqi state strove to draw in women to its political apparatus by distancing them from their kin/ethnic/tribal groups. Joseph, "Elite Strategies for State Building," 195.

65 Jacqueline Ismael, "Social Planning and Social Change: The Case for Iraq," *Arab Studies Quarterly* 2, no. 3 (1980): 235–48.

66 Joseph, "Elite Strategies for State-Building," 186–7.

67 Aihwa Ong, *Flexible Citizenship: The Cultural Logic of Transnationality* (Durham: Duke University Press, 1999).
68 Hala Fatah, "The Question of the 'Artificiality' of Iraq as a Nation-State," in *Iraq: Its History, People and Politics*, ed. Shams C. Inati (New York: Humanity Books, 2003), 53.
69 Vieda Skultans, "Weaving New Lives from an Old Fleece: Gender and Ethnicity in Latvian Narrative," in *Ethnicity, Gender, and Social Change*, ed. Rohit Barot, Harriet Bradley, and Steve Fenton (New York: Palgrave Macmillan, 1999), 182–3.
70 Muhammad Siddiq, "On Ropes of Memory: Narrating the Palestinian Refugees," in *Mistrusting Refugees*, ed. V. Daniel and J. Knudsen (Berkeley: University of California Press, 1995), 87–9.
71 Luissa Passerini, *Fascism in Popular Memory: The Cultural Experience of the Turin Working Class*, trans. Robert Lumley and Jude Bloomfield (Cambridge: Cambridge University Press, 1987).
72 Jeffrey Olick, Vered Vinitzky-Seroussi, and Daniel Levy, "Introduction," in *The Collective Memory Reader*, ed. Jeffrey Olick, Vered Vinitzky-Seroussi, and Daniel Levy (Oxford: Oxford University Press, 2011), 1–62.
73 Eric Hobsbawm, "Introduction: Inventing Traditions," in *The Invention of Tradition*, ed. Eric Hobsbawm and Terence Ranger (Cambridge: Cambridge University Press, 1983), 1–14.

2. Resisting the State: Shi'a, Chaldean, and Kurdish Women's Counter-narratives

1 Michael Bamberg, "Considering Counter Narratives," in *Considering Counter Narratives: Narrating, Resisting, Making Sense*, ed. Michael Bamberg and Molly Andrews, Studies in Narrative 4 (Amsterdam: John Benjamins, 2004), 360–1.
2 Sidonie Smith and Julia Watson, *Reading Autobiography: A Guide for Interpreting Life Narratives* (Minneapolis: University of Minnesota Press, 2001), 230–6; Nancy K. Miller, "Personal Histories, Autobiographical Locations," in *Getting Personal: Feminist Occasions and Other Autobiographical Acts*, ed. Nancy K. Miller (New York: Routledge, 1991), 90–9.
3 Bamberg, "Considering Counter Narratives," 352.
4 Judith Butler, "Collected and Fractured: Responses to Identities," in *Identities*, ed. K. Appiah and H. Gates (Chicago: University of Chicago Press, 1995), 445–7.
5 Ibid., 367.
6 Parin Dossa, *Racialized Bodies, Disabling Worlds: Storied Lives of Immigrant Muslim Women* (Toronto: University of Toronto Press, 2009), 25.

7 Julie Cruikshank, *The Social Life of Stories: Narrative and Knowledge in the Yukon Territory* (Vancouver: UBC Press, 1998), 71–97.
8 Michael Benson, *Crime and Life Course: An Introduction* (Los Angeles: Roxbury, 2002), 6. See also Mikhail Bakhtin, *The Dialogic Imagination*, trans. C. Emerson and M. Holquist (Austin: University of Texas Press, 1981); Mary Louise Pratt, *Imperial Eyes: Travel Writing and Transculturation* (London: Routledge, 1992).
9 Anh Hua, "Diaspora and Cultural Memory," in *Diaspora, Memory, and Identity: A Search for Home*, ed. Vijay Agnew (Toronto: University of Toronto Press, 2005), 199.
10 Marianne Hirsch and Valerie Smith, "Feminism and Cultural Memory: An Introduction," *Signs: Journal of Women in Culture and Society* 28, no. 1 (2002): 5.
11 Max Scherberger, "The Confrontation between Sunni and Shi'i Empires: Ottoman-Safavid Relations between the Fourteen and Seventeenth Century," in *The Sunna and Shi'a in History: Divisions and Ecumenism in the Muslim Middle East*, ed. Ofra Bengio and Meir Litvak (New York: Palgrave Macmillan, 2011), 64–5.
12 Meir Litvak, "Encounters between Shi'i and Sunni 'Ulama' in Ottoman Iraq," in *The Sunna and Shi'a in History: Divisions and Ecumenism in the Muslim Middle East*, ed. Ofra Bengio and Meir Litvak (New York: Palgrave Macmillan, 2011), 69–70.
13 Ibid., 11.
14 For example, in Basra the landlords of the province in the 1920s were with the exception of one (Shaikh of Muhammarah) all Sunni, whereas the cultivators of their palm gardens were predominantly Shi'i. The same was true of the administration of Basra and several other southern towns, which were run almost entirely by Sunni Arabs while the town was made up of a majority of Shi'a (the only exception here is the Shi'i holy cities). In Baghdad, the socially dominant families were predominantly Sunni even though the two sects were almost evenly matched in terms of total population numbers. Hanna Batatu, *The Old Social Classes and the Revolutionary Movements of Iraq: A Study of Iraq's Old Landed and Commercial Classes and of Its Communists, Ba'athists, and Free Officers* (Princeton: Princeton University Press, 1978), 44–5.
15 Ibid., 12.
16 In the rural regions, Sunni tribal warring "People of the Camel" became the dominant force over the Shi'i tribal peasant marsh-dwellers or "People of the Sheep." In the urban regions, Sunni Ottoman political dominance dictated the ascension of Sunnis into a firmly economic, political, and increasingly military ruling elite. Batatu, *The Old Social Classes*, 45.
17 David Pool, "From Elite to Class: The Transformation of Iraqi Political Leadership," in *The Integration of Modern Iraq*, ed. Abbas Kelidar (London: Croom Helm, 1979), 64.

18 Majid Khadduri, *Republican 'Iraq: A Study in 'Iraqi Politics since the Revolution of 1958* (London : Oxford University Press, 1969), 4–5; Batatu, *The Old Social Classes*, 28–9.
19 Batatu, *The Old Social Classes*, 36; Phebe Marr, *The Modern History of Iraq* (Boulder: Colorado University Press, 1985), 50–4; Pool, "From Elite to Class," 76–8.
20 Eric Davis, "'10 Conceptual Sins' in Analyzing Middle East Politics," http://new-middle-east.blogspot.ca/2009_01_01_archive.html.
21 Jacqueline Ismael, "Social Planning and Social Change: The Case for Iraq," *Arab Studies Quarterly* 2, no. 3 (1980): 183.
22 In addition to Efrati's "Competing Narratives," see also Marion Farouk-Sluglett and Peter Sluglett, "The Historiography of Modern Iraq," *American Historical Review* 96, no. 5 (December 1991): 1408–21; Reva Simon, "The Teaching of History in Iraq before the Rashid Ali Coup of 1941," *Middle Eastern Studies* 22 (1986): 37–51; Amatzia Baram, *Culture, History and Ideology in the Formation of Ba'thist Iraq* (New York: St. Martin's Press, 1991); Eric Davis, *Memories of State: Politics, History, and Collective Identity in Modern Iraq* (Berkeley: University of California Press, 2005).
23 Interview, Toronto, January 17, 2009.
24 Ibid.
25 Ibid.
26 Ibid.
27 Yitzhak Nakash, *The Shi'is of Iraq* (Princeton: Princeton University Press, 1994), 4.
28 Yitzhak Nakash, *Reaching for Power: The Shi'a in the Modern Arab World* (Princeton: Princeton University Press, 2006), 75–8.
29 "Corpse traffic" refers to the transfer of bodies for burial in holy sites located in southern Iraq, dating from at least the tenth century. Ottoman sanitary regulations stipulated that in order to be buried in the holy cities of Najaf and Karbala, bodies transported from Iran to Iraq must be dry-buried for three years prior to their final burial in Iraq. However, this lucrative industry soon resulted in a massive illegal transfer of corpses intended to bypass the three-year wait and fees imposed by Ottoman officials at the border. Towards the end of the nineteenth century, the scale of this industry had transformed the economies of these cities, to the point where the livelihoods of the majority of people depended on this traffic. Active debates amongst Shi'i *mujtahids* in 1911 over the *naql al-jana'iz* customs associated with the practices raised questions about disgraced corpses and the authenticity of practices according to Islamic law. In order to deal with the growing traffic and the illegal smuggling of bodies, the Corpse Traffic Law of 1924 was passed, later replaced by the Corpse Traffic Law of 1967, by which the state further absorbed control over burial dues and the officiating of procedures. In an effort to divert funds away

from the British, Reza Shah sought to abolish this tradition by shifting the Iranian corpse traffic towards the holy cities of Mashhad and Qum in Iran, subsequently enhancing their religious status. Nakash, *The Shi'is of Iraq*, 196–201, 236–7.

30 Elie Kedourie, "The Iraqi Shi'is and Their Fate," in *Shi'ism, Resistance and Revolution*, ed. Mark Kramer (Boulder: Westview, 1987), 153–5; Michael Eppel, "The Elite, the Effendiyya, and the Growth of Nationalism and Pan-Arabism in Hashemite Iraq, 1921–1958," *International Journal of Middle Eastern Studies* 30 (1998): 232–5; Nakash, *The Shi'is of Iraq*, 6–7.

31 Adeed Dawisha, "Arabism and Islam in Iraq's War with Iran," *Middle East Insight* 2 (1984): 31–2; Eric Davis and Nicolas Gavrielides, "Statecraft, Historical Memory, and Popular Culture in Iraq and Kuwait," in *Statecraft in the Middle East: Oil, Historical Memory and Popular Culture*, ed. Eric Davis and Nicolas Gavrielides (Miami: Florida International University Press, 1991), 132–7.

32 Nakash, *The Shi'is of Iraq*, 101–2; Nakash, *Reaching for Power*, 86–7.

33 Malik Mafti, *Sovereign Creations: Pan-Arabism and Political Order in Syria and Iraq* (Ithaca: Cornell University Press, 1996), 30–42.

34 Interview, Toronto, 17 January 2009.

35 Phone interview, 20 February 2009.

36 Ibid.

37 Interview, Toronto, 13 June 2009.

38 Ibid. The definition of *shroogi* is somewhat contentious, though the term is certainly derogatory. Its literal meaning is "east of the Euphrates," and in its modern usage it refers to poor southern Iraqi farmers, the majority of which were Shi'a Arabs, who migrated to Baghdad in the 1930s and 1940s. As they formed slums on the outskirts of Baghdad, they were referred to as *shargawi* or *shroogie*. The term is employed by middle- and upper-middle-class Iraqis to refer to the poor and peasant class of Iraq. It retains its original ethnic connotations even when it is used to refer to other ethnic or racial groups.

39 Interview, Detroit, 6 November 2009.

40 Interview, Detroit, 7 November 2009.

41 Ibid.

42 Shak Hanish, "The Chaldean Assyrian Syriac People of Iraq: An Ethnic Identity Problem," *Digest of Middle East Studies* (Spring 2008): 35; Leslie Goffe, "Chaldeans USA," *The Middle East*, November 1999, 50.

43 Ray Kamoo and Sarhad Jammo, *Ancient and Modern Chaldean History: A Comprehensive Bibliography of Sources* (Lanham: Scarecrow Press, 1991), 60.

44 Wilhem Baum and Dietmar W. Winkler, *The Church of the East: A Concise History* (London: Routledge, 2003), 112.

45 Anthony O'Mahony, "The Chaldean Catholic Church: The Politics of Church-State Relations in Modern Iraq," *Heythrop Journal* 45, no. 4 (2004): 435–6; Anthony O'Mahony, "Eastern Christianity in Modern Iraq," in *Eastern Christianity: Studies in Modern History, Religion and Politics*, ed. Anthony O'Mahony (London: Melisende, 2004), 11–15.
46 O'Mahony, "The Chaldean Catholic Church," 442.
47 Interview, Detroit, 7 November 2009.
48 Mary Cey Sengstock, *Chaldean Americans: Changing Conceptions of Ethnic Identity* (New York: Center for Migration Studies, 1982), 145–54.
49 Hanish, "The Chaldean Assyrian Syriac People of Iraqi," 35; Kamoo and Jammo, *Ancient and Modern Chaldean History*, introduction.
50 Interview, Detroit, 9 November 2009.
51 Interview, Toronto, 8 November 2008.
52 Ibid.
53 Phone interview, 11 January 2009.
54 Ibid.
55 Ibid. Not all Kurdish women responded in this way; in fact, some were adamant that they not be considered as "Iraqis" in the research resulting from their interviews. In a group interview in Detroit, one Kurdish woman claimed that "I'm not Iraqi, I am Kurdish. When you say Iraqi this means Arab or Christian, but I am none of these, I am Kurdish. Yes, I am born Muslim, but that is a relationship between me and God. But who I am, I am Kurdish and very proud of it" (group interview, Detroit, 7 November 2009).
56 Interview, Toronto, 8 November 2008.
57 Ibid.
58 Ibid. The irony of this metaphor is extremely layered and complex, especially in the context of the Ba'ath party's use of "family" and the transitional meaning of "family" in modern Iraq. Belonging to a family means something very different since the regime took power, in comparison to the more primordial use of "family" and "tribe" in pre-modern Iraq.
59 Martin van Bruinessen, *Transnational Aspects of the Kurdish Question*, Robert Schuman Centre for Advancement Studies EUI Working Paper RSC No. 2000/22 (Florence: European University Institute, 2000), 35.
60 David McDowell, *A Modern History of the Kurds* (London: I.B. Taruris, 1996), 343–67; Ismet Cheriff Vanly, "Kurdistan in Iraq," in *People without a Country: The Kurds and Kurdistan*, ed. Gerard Chalian (London: Zed Books, 1993), 143–7.
61 Including remnants of earlier religious Kurdish sects in settlements of Yezidis, Zoroastrians, and Ahl-i Haqq in Iraq. See Nelinda Fuccaro, *The Other Kurds: Yazidis in Colonial Iraq* (London: I.B. Tauris, 1999); Taufiq

Wahby, *The Remnants of Mithraism in Hatra and Iraqi Kurdistan, and Its Traces in Yazidism: The Yazidis Are Not Devil-Worshippers* (London: T. Wahby, 1962); Mary Boyce, *A History of Zoroastrianism*, 2 vols. (Leiden: E.J. Brill, 1982); Cecil John Edmonds, "The Beliefs and Practices of the Ahl-i Haqq of Iraq," *Iran* 7 (1969): 89–106.

62 David McDowall, "The Kurdish Question: A Historical Review," in *The Kurds: A Contemporary Overview*, ed. Philip G. Kreyenbroek and Stefan Sperl (London: Routledge, 1992), 11.

63 Ibid., 18.

64 Mahir A. Aziz, *The Kurds of Iraq: Nationalism and Identity in Iraqi Kurdistan* (London: I.B. Taurus: 2015), 1–14.

65 George Harris, "Whither the Kurds?" in *Global Convulsions: Race, Ethnicity, and Nationalism at the End of the Twentieth Century*, ed. A. Winston (Albany: SUNY Press, 1997), 205–23.

66 John Joseph, *The Nestorians and Their Muslim Neighbors: A Study of Western Influence on Their Relations* (Princeton: Princeton University Press, 1961), xv.

67 Martin van Bruissen, "Kurdish Society, Ethnicity, Nationalism and Refugee Problems," in *The Kurds: A Contemporary Overview*, ed. Philip G. Kreyenbroek and Stefan Sperl (London: Routledge, 1992), 43–5.

68 Interview, Detroit, 10 November 2009.

69 Ibid.

70 Phone interview, 11 January 2009.

71 Lorri Lukitz, *Iraq: The Search for National Identity* (London: Frank Cass, 1995), 153.

72 Hala Fatah, "The Question of the 'Artificiality' of Iraq as a Nation-State," in *Iraq: Its History, People and Politics*, ed. Shams C. Inati (New York: Humanity Books, 2003), 52.

73 Batatu, *The Old Social Classes*, 21.

74 Ibid., 22.

75 Davis, *Memories of State*, 282.

76 Benedict Anderson, *Imagined Communities: Reflections on the Origin and Spread of Nationalism* (New York: Verso, 1983), 12.

77 Aziz, *The Kurds of Iraq*, 46–8.

78 Anthony Smith, *Nations and Nationalism in a Global Era* (Cambridge: Polity, 1995), 5.

79 Portelli, *The Death of Luigi Trastulli and Other Stories: Form and Meaning in Oral History* (Albany: SUNY Press, 1991), 26.

80 Jan Assmann, *Moses the Egyptian: The Memory of Egypt in Western Monotheism* (New Haven: Harvard University Press, 1999), 9.

81 Bamberg, "Considering Counter-Narratives," 365.

82 Marek Tamm, "History as Cultural Memory: Mnemohistory and the Construction of the Estonian Nation," *Journal of Baltic Studies* 39, no. 4 (2008): 499–516.
83 J. Straub, "Telling Stories, Making History: Towards a Narrative Construction of the Psychological Construction of Meaning," in *Narration, Identity and Historical Consciousness*, ed. J. Straub (New York: Berghen, 2005), 44–98.

3. Towards an Affective Methodology: Interviewer, Translator, Participant

1 Annie E. Coombes, "The Gender of Memory in Post-Apartheid South Africa," in *Memory: Histories, Theories, Debates*, ed. Susannah Radstone and Bill Schwartz (New York: Fordham University Press, 2010), 444.
2 Nancy Rose Hunt, "The Affective, the Intellectual, and Gender History," *Journal of African History* 55 (2014): 331–45.
3 Alessandro Portelli, *The Death of Luigi Trastulli and Other Stories: Form and Meaning in Oral History* (Albany: SUNY Press, 1991); Michael Frisch, *A Shared Authority: Essays on the Craft and Meaning of Oral and Public History* (Albany: SUNY Press, 1990); Michael Riordan, *An Unauthorized Biography of the World: Oral History on the Front Lines* (Toronto: Between the Lines, 2004); Donald Ritchie, *Doing Oral History: A Practical Guide*, 2nd ed. (New York: Oxford University Press, 2003); Robert Perks and Alistair Thomson, eds., *The Oral History Reader* (London: Routledge, 1998); Sherna Berger Gluck and Daphne Patai, eds., *Women's Words: The Feminist Practice of Oral History* (New York: Routledge, 1991).
4 Alessandro Portelli, "What Makes Oral History Different," in *The Oral History Reader*, ed. Robert Perks and Alistair Thomson, 2nd ed. (London: Routledge, 1998), 33.
5 Frisch, *A Shared Authority*, 84–6.
6 Clifford Geertz, "Thick Description: Toward an Interpretive Theory of Culture," in *The Interpretation of Cultures: Selected Essays* (New-York: Basic Books, 1973), 3–30.
7 I am indebted to Nadje Al-Ali's work on Iraqi women, and in particular her book *Iraqi Women: Untold Stories from 1948 to Present* (London: Zed Books, 2007). I read the book during a particularly bleak period of reflection, and after I had started the process of interviewing women in Amman and Toronto. Her personal reflections on accessing women through family and professional networks provided guidance at a time when I was starting to doubt my methods and the project itself. *Iraqi Women*, as well as her many other important works on Iraqi women, has helped me immeasurably in my efforts to frame this project and interpret

the interview material, as well as to locate my own voice within the research. See also Leila Ahmed, *Women and Gender in Islam: Historical Roots of a Modern Debate* (New Haven: Yale University Press, 1992), 6.

8 Lynn Abrams, *Oral History Theory* (London: Routledge, 2010), 74; Gluck and Patai, *Women's Words.*

9 Hunt, "The Affective," 332.

10 Chandra Talpade Mohanty, "Under Western Eyes: Feminist Scholarship and Colonial Discourses," in *Third World Women and the Politics of Feminism*, ed. Chandra Mohanty, Ann Russo, and Lourdes Torres (Bloomington: Indiana University Press, 1991), 51–80.

11 Lila Abu-Lughod, "Do Muslim Women Really Need Saving? Anthropological Reflections on Cultural Relativism and Its Others," *American Anthropologist* 104, no. 3 (2002): 785. See also Kathryn Anderson and Dana Jack, "Learning to Listen: Interview Techniques and Analysis," in *Women's Words: The Feminist Practice of Oral History*, ed. Sherna Berger Gluck and Daphne Patai (New York: Routledge, 1991), 11.

12 Nicholas de Genova, "Spectacles of Migrant 'Illegality': The Scene of Exclusion, the Obscene of Inclusion," *Journal of Ethnic and Racial Studies* 36, no. 7 (2013): 1180–98.

13 Interview, Amman, 20 June 2008.

14 Ibid.

15 Alexander Freund, "'Confessing Animals': Towards a *Longue Durée* History of the Oral History Interview," *Oral History Review* 41, no. 1 (January 2014): 1–26.

16 Binaya Subeidi, "Theorizing a 'Halfie' Researcher's Identity in Transnational Fieldwork," *International Journal of Qualitative Studies in Education* 19, no. 5 (September–October 2006): 573–93.

17 Freund, "Confessing Animals," 21.

18 Michal Foucault, *The History of Sexuality, Vol. 1: An Introduction*, trans. Robert Hurley, 2nd ed. (New York: Vintage, 1990), 58.

19 Freund, "Confessing Animals," 22.

20 Interview with the author, Amman, 17 July 2008.

21 Oral history research on women in diaspora, in particular, tend to draw from personal and familial contacts within the community. Accessing the female voice is frequently a difficult task, and this is often (though certainly not exclusively) true of groups migrating from the Third World, where women are more isolated upon settlement in North America. Other important elements that can hinder access to migrant women are linguistic/cultural boundaries, traditional etiquette, and generational shift. See Vijay Agnew "A Diasporic Bounty: Cultural History and Heritage," in *Diaspora, Memory, and Identity: A Search for Home*, ed. Vijay Agnew (Toronto: University of Toronto Press, 2005), 171–87; Pamela

Sugiman, "Memories of Internment: Narrating Japanese-Canadian Women's Life Stories," in *Diaspora, Memory, and Identity: A Search for Home*, ed. Agnew, 48–81; Isabel Kaprielian-Churchill, "*Odars* and 'Others': Intermarriage and the Retention of Armenian Ethnic Identity," in *Sisters or Strangers?: Immigrant, Ethnic, and Racialized Women in Canadian History*, ed. Marlene Epp, Franca Iacovetta, and Frances Swyripa (Toronto: University of Toronto Press, 2004), 341–65; Shahnaz Khan, *Zina, Transnational Feminism, and the Moral Regulation of Pakistani Women* (Vancouver: UBC Press, 2006).

22 On the role of the translator see Nadia Jones-Gailani, "Third Parties in 'Third Spaces': The Multifaceted Role of Translator in Oral History Interviews with Iraqi Diasporic Women," in *Oral History Off the Record: Towards an Ethnography of Practice*, ed. Stacey Zembrzycki, and Anna Sheftel (Toronto: Palgrave Macmillan, 2013), 169–83.

23 Reputation and social standing in Iraqi culture are defined by the class status of the father's family. Access to upper- and middle-class Sunni and Kurdish women through family contacts initially restricted me to this social spectrum of Iraqi society. Hanna Batatu discusses the formation of the class system in Iraq in his foundational work *The Old Social Classes and the Revolutionary Movements of Iraq: A Study of Iraq's Old Landed and Commercial Classes and of Its Communists, Ba'thists, and Free Officers* (Princeton: Princeton University Press, 1978).

24 Homi K. Bhabha, *The Location of Culture* (Abingdon: Routledge, 1994), 1–18.

25 Subeidi, "Theorizing a 'Halfie' Researcher's Identity."

26 Batatu, *The Old Social Classes*, 1–52.

27 Interview, Amman, 12 September 2008.The emphasis on "good" implied that I was a woman of virtue from a respectable family, or a woman of virtue *because* I am from a respectable family.

28 Stacey Zembrzycki discusses the way in which sharing authority with a third participant can create a more intimate setting but at the same time shapes the flow of the discussion and can often change the ways in which the narrator reconstructs shared memories. Zembrzycki, "Sharing Authority with Baba," *Journal of Canadian Studies* 43, no. 1 (Winter 2009): 225.

29 Interview, Amman, summer 2008.

30 This regulation of femininity and sexuality within diasporic communities has become the focus of many excellent women's histories in North America. My discussion of female modesty as it relates to the example of Iraqi women is drawn from the following: Shanaz Khan, *Aversion and Desire: Negotiating Muslim Female Identity in the Diaspora* (Toronto: Women's Press, 2002); Yvonne Haddad, "Islamic Values among American Muslims," in *Family and Gender among American Muslims: Issues Facing Middle Eastern*

Immigrants and Their Descendants, ed. B. Bilge and B. Aswad (Philadelphia: Temple University Press, 1996), 1–13; Fatima Mernissi, *Beyond the Veil: Male-Female Dynamics in Modern Muslim Society* (Bloomington: Indiana University Press, 1987); Al-Ali, *Iraqi Women*; Chandra Talpade Mohandy, *Feminism without Borders: Decolonizing Theory, Practicing Solidarity* (Durham: Duke University Press, 2003); Henry Greenspan, *On Listening to Holocaust Survivors: Recounting the Life History* (Westport: Praeger, 1998).

31 Lila Abu-Lughod, "Fieldwork of a Dutiful Daughter," in *Arab Women in the Field: Studying Your Own Society*, ed. Soraya Altorki and Camilla Fawzi El-Solhi (Syracuse: Syracuse University Press, 1988), 139–61.

32 Interview, Amman, 20 August 2009.

33 A few examples are: P. Thompson, *The Voice of the Past: Oral History*, 3rd ed. (Oxford: Oxford University Press, 2000); Ritchie, *Doing Oral History*; Valerie Yow, *Recording Oral History: A Guide for the Humanities and Social Sciences*, 2nd ed. (Walnut Creek: AltaMira, 2005).

34 Al-Ali, *Iraqi Women*, 744–5.

35 Interview, Amman, 26 September 2008.

36 Interview, Hamilton, 30 April 2009.

37 Interview, Amman, 30 September 2008.

38 I am referring here to a culturally understood notion within the Arab world of how women are perceived in relation to their family, and how their modesty influences their families and their broader kin group. These insights are drawn from personal reflection, and filtered through my own understanding of what it means to stand in between identities more precisely situated as colonizer and colonized. See Homi K. Bhabha, "The Other Question: Difference, Discrimination and the Discourse of Colonialism," in *Out There: Marginalization and Contemporary Cultures*, ed. Russell Ferguson, Martha Gever, Trinh T. Min-ha, and Cornel West (New York/Cambridge, MA: New Museum of Contemporary Art/MIT Press, 1990), 71–88. Shanaz Khan discusses the specific ways in which Muslim and Arab women are shaped by the "simultaneous alienation that occurs at the nexus of desire and aversion" in *Aversion and Desire*.

39 A particularly heart-rending example of the divide between generations in terms of education and understandings of both the past and the present is contained in Zainab Salbi and Laurie Becklund, *Between Two Worlds – Escape from Tyranny: Growing Up in the Shadow of Saddam* (New York: Gotham, 2005).

40 Group interview with two Sabean women, three Kurdish, two Chaldean, and one Sunni Iraqi women in Rochester, Detroit, 5 November 2009.

41 Judith Butler, *Gender Trouble: Feminism and the Subversion of Identity* (London: Routledge, 1990); Abrams, *Oral History Theory*, 58.

42 Mohanty, "Under Western Eyes," 62.

43 I owe a particular debt to Anna Sheftel and Stacey Zembrzycki, who organized a workshop in Montreal (2009) and invited me as a junior doctoral candidate to share my work in conversation with many of the authors cited here who have been instrumental in shaping the field of oral history and memory studies. Each time we gathered at the Canadian Historical Association meeting or at other workshops, we continued our discussions on how to listen and evaluate material that is recorded and that which is "off the record." I am immensely grateful for their encouragement and example as feminists who continue to fight for space in their respective fields. For more on oral history interviews and how we conceptualize the "record," see their thoughtful collection, in which I add my reflections regarding the use of translators in interviews with Iraqi women: Sheftel and Zembrzycki, eds., *Oral History Off the Record: Towards an Ethnography of Practice* (Toronto: Palgrave Macmillan, 2013).
44 Group interview in Rochester, Detroit, 2 November 2009.
45 Group interview conducted with eight Kurdish women and one Arab Sunni woman in Toronto, 8 November 2008.
46 Interview, Toronto, 9 December 2008.
47 Eric Davies, *Memories of State: Politics, History, and Collective Identity in Modern Iraq* (Berkeley: University of California Press, 2005), 282–3.
48 Shahnaz Khan, *Muslim Women: Crafting a North American Identity* (Tampa: University Press of Florida, 2001), 84–100.
49 Georges E. Fouron and Nina Glick-Schiller, "The Generation of Identity: Redefining the Second Generation within a Transnational Social Field," in *The Changing Face of Home: The Transnational Lives of the Second Generation*, ed. Peggy Levitt and Mary C. Waters (New York: Russell Sage Foundation, 2002), 176.
50 Interview with Sabean family, Amman, 30 September 2008.
51 The ongoing struggle of the Sabeans in Iraq is detailed in Ma'oz Moshe, *Middle Eastern Minorities: Between Integration and Conflict* (Washington, DC: Washington Institute for Near East Policy, 1999), 71–91.
52 Interview with Sabean family in Amman, 30 September 2008.
53 Interview, Jordan, 30 September 2008.
54 There were large numbers of middle-class Iraqis living in Amman in 2008 and 2009 when I conducted the interviews, and educated Sunni professionals in particular created social networks of friends and family who lived in close proximity and gathered on a regular basis to celebrate holidays and events. Their situation in Amman was temporary; although many Sunni families lived in relative comfort, their narratives reflected the precarious uncertainly that plagued their lives. See also Jeff Crisp, Jane Janz, and José Riera, "Surviving in the City: A Review of UNHCR's Operation for Iraqi

Refugees in Urban Areas of Jordan, Lebanon and Syria," UNCHR Policy Development and Evaluation Service, Geneva, July 2009, 8–9.

55 Interview, Amman, 15 September 2008.

56 Ibid.

57 Ibid.

58 Ibid.

59 Ibid.

60 Ibid.

61 Ibid.

62 Interview, Toronto, 15 September 2008.

63 Interview, Toronto, 6 September 2010.

64 Ibid.

65 Interview, Toronto, 10 December 2008.

66 Terrence Des Pres's discussion of the ways in which survivors cope with trauma suggests that survivors often recount great suffering without emotion, as a means to cope with painful memories. Des Pres, "Holocaust Laughter?" in *Writing and the Holocaust*, ed. Berel Lang (New York: Holmes and Meier, 1988), 229–30.

67 Davies, *Memories of State*, 273–8.

68 Group interview with five Chaldean-American women in Southfield, Detroit, 6 November 2009.

69 Saskia Witteborn, "Identity Mobilization Practices of Refugees: The Case of Iraqis in the United States and the War in Iraq," *Journal of International and Intercultural Communication* 1, no. 3 (August 2008), 216.

70 R. Radhakrishnan, *Diasporic Mediations: Between Home and Location* (London: University of Minnesota Press, 1996), 203–14.

71 R. Parameswaran, "Feminist Media Ethnography in India: Exploring Power, Gender and Culture in the Field," *Qualitative Inquiry* 7, no. 1 (2001): 69–103.

72 Geertz, "Thick Description," 3–30.

4. *Qahwa* and *Kleiche*: Cookbooks, Coffee, and Conversation

1 Claude Lévi-Strauss, quoted in Mary Douglas, "Deciphering a Meal," in *Food and Culture: A Reader*, ed. C. Counihan and P. Van Esterik, 2nd ed. (New York: Routledge, 2008), 44.

2 C. Spurlock, quoted in Janet M. Cramer, Carlnita P. Greene, and Lynn M. Walters, eds., *Food as Communication, Communication as Food* (New York: Peter Lang, 2011), xi.

3 Claudia Roden, *The New Book of Middle Eastern Food* (New York: Alfred A. Knopf, 2000).

4 Sidney Mintz, *Tasting Food, Tasting Freedom: Excursions into Eating, Culture, and the Past* (Boston: Beacon, 1996).

5 Peter Heine, *Food Culture in the Near East, Middle East, and North Africa* (London: Greenwood, 2004), 1–18.
6 Lames Ibrahim, *The Iraqi Cookbook* (Northampton, MA: Interlink, 2011); Kay Karim, *Iraqi Family Cookbook: From Mosul to America* (Falls Church, VA: Iraqi Family Cookbook LLC, 2006); Chaldean American Ladies of Charity, Ma Baseema*: Middle Eastern Cooking with Chaldean Flair* (Detroit: Huron River Press, 2011); Samira Cholagh, *A Baking Journey: From Samira's Kitchen to Yours* (Detroit: Tata, 2011).
7 David Sutton, *Remembrance of Repasts: An Anthropology of Food and Memory* (Oxford: Berg, 2001).
8 Nawal Nasrallah, *Delights from the Garden of Eden: A Cookbook and a History of the Iraqi Cuisine*, 2nd ed. (New York: Equinox, 2003), 3–12.
9 Ibid., 27–8.
10 Ibid., 30–1.
11 Anne L. Bower, ed., *Recipes for Reading: Community Cookbooks, Stories, Histories* (Amherst: University of Massachusetts Press, 1997).
12 Carole M. Counihan, "Introduction – Food and Gender: Identity and Power," in *Food and Gender: Identity and Power*, ed. Carole M. Counihan and Steven L. Kaplan (Amsterdam: Harwood, 1998), 2–3. See also Linda Keller Brown and Kay Mussell, eds., *Ethnic and Regional Foodways in the United States: The Performance of Group Identity* (Knoxville: University of Tennessee Press, 1984).
13 Arlene Voski Avakian, *Through the Kitchen Window: Women Explore the Intimate Meanings of Food and Cooking* (Boston: Beacon, 2005); Donna Gabaccia, *We Are What We Eat: Ethnic Food and the Making of America* (Cambridge, MA: Harvard University Press, 2000); Hasia Diner, *Hungering of America: Italian, Irish, and Jewish Foodways in the Age of Migration* (Cambridge, MA: Harvard University Press, 2003); Ray Kirshnendu, *The Migrant's Table: Meals and Memories in Bengali-American Households* (Philadelphia: Temple University Press, 2004); Brown and Mussell, eds., *Ethnic and Regional Foodways* .
14 Similar trends are explored in Marlene Epp's recent piece on reading immigrant cookbooks, "Eating across Borders: Reading Immigrant Cookbooks," *Histoire Sociale/Social History* 48, no. 96 (May 2015): 45–65.
15 Annia Ciezadlo, *Day of Honey: A Memoir of Food, Love, and War* (New York: Free Press, 2011), 8.
16 L. Long, "Learning to Listen to the Food Voice Recipes as Expressions of Identity and Carriers of Memory," *Food, Culture and Society: An International Journal of Multidisciplinary Research* 7, no. 1 (2004): 118–22.
17 Janet Carsten, "The Substance of Kinship and the Heat of the Hearth: Feeding Personhood, and the Relatedness among Malays in Pulau Langkawi," *American Ethnologist* 22 (1995): 224.

18 Mary Douglas, "Deciphering a Meal," in *Myth, Symbol and Culture*, ed. Clifford Geertz (New York: Norton, 1971), 62; Franca Iacovetta, "Food Acts and Cultural Politics: Women and the Gendered Dialectics of Culinary Pluralism at the International Institute of Toronto, 1950s–1960s," in *Edible Histories, Cultural Practices: Towards a Canadian Food History*, ed. Franca Iacovetta, Valerie J. Korinek, and Marlene Epp (Toronto: University of Toronto Press, 2012), 359–84.

19 Lisa Heldke, "Let's Cook Thai: Recipes for Colonialism," in *Pilaf, Pozole, and Pad Thai: American Women and Ethnic Food*, ed. Sherrie A. Innes (Amherst: University of Massachusetts Press, 2001), 174–98.

20 Interview, Southfield, Detroit, 5 November 2009.

21 Angela Little, "An Academic Ferment," *Journal of Gastronomy* 2 (1986): 24.

22 Peter Farb and George Armelagos, *Consuming Passions: The Anthropology of Eating* (Boston: Houghton Mifflin, 1980), 111.

23 Paul Connerton, *How Societies Remember* (Cambridge: Cambridge University Press, 1989); Ann Stoler and Karen Strassler, "Castings for the Colonial: Memory Work in 'New Order' Java," *Comparative Studies in Society and History* 48 (2000): 4–48.

24 Connerton, *How Societies Remember*, 39.

25 Michael Lambek, "The Past Imperfect: Remembering as Moral Practice," in *Tense Past: Cultural Essays in Trauma and Memory*, ed. Michael Lambek and Paul Antze (London: Routledge, 1998), 238. The Western bias is best explained by David Howes: "The anthropology of the senses is primarily concerned with how the patterning of sense experiences varies from one culture to the next in accordance with the meaning and emphasis attached to each of the senses … only by developing a rigorous awareness of the visual and textual biases of the Western episteme [can we] hope to make sense of how life is lived in other cultural settings." Howes, "Introduction," in *The Varieties of Sensory Experience* (Toronto: University of Toronto Press, 1991), 4.

26 Leilah Nadir, The Orange Trees of Baghdad: In Search of my Lost Family (London: Key Porter Books, 2007).

27 Nadir, *Orange Trees of Baghdad*, 3.

28 Ibid., 2.

29 Interview, Toronto, 6 January 2008.

30 Group interview, Rochester, 7 November 2009.

31 Nasrallah, *Delights from the Garden of Eden*, 526–7.

32 Examples include Joe Lutrario, "Mezze Momentum: Za'atar, Labneh and Dried Limes: The Rise of Authentic Food from Greece, the Levant and the Rest of the Middle East," *Restaurant* (June 2014): 6–9; Theresa Preston-Werner, "Gallo Pinto: Tradition, Memory, and Identity in Costa Rican Foodways," *Journal of American Folklore* 122, no. 483 (2009): 11–27; Richard R. Wilk, "'Real Belizean Food': Building Local Identity in the Transatlantic

Caribbean," *American Anthropologist* 101, no. 2 (June 1999): 244–55; Merin Oleschuk, "Engendering Transnational Foodways: A Case Study of Southern Sudanese Women in Brooks, Alberta," *Anthropologica* 54 (2012): 119–31.

33 Psyche Williams-Forson, "'I Haven't Eaten If I Don't Have My Soup and Fufu': Cultural Preservation through Food and Foodways among Ghanaian Migrants in the United States," *Africa Today* 61, no. 1 (2013): 69–87.

34 S.E. Colby, S. Morison, and L. Heldeman, "What Changes When We Move? A Transnational Exploration of Dietary Acculturation," *Ecology of Food and Nutrition* 48, no. 4 (2009): 327–43; J. Satia-Abouta, "Dietary Acculturation: Definition, Process, Assessment, and Implications," *International Journal of Human Ecology* 4, no. 1 (2003): 73.

35 Carole Counihan, *The Anthropology of Food and Body: Gender, Meaning and Power* (New York: Routledge, 1999), 47–8.

36 For a study of similar migrant populations in Norway found very different acculturation patterns in first-generation migrants, based on food availability and geographical proximity to sourcing regions, see Laura Terragni, Lisa M. Garnweidner, Kjell Sverre Pettersen, and Annhild Mosdøl, "Migration as a Turning Point in Food Habits: The Early Phase of Dietary Acculturation among Women from South Asian, African, and Middle Eastern Countries Living in Norway," *Ecology of Food and Nutrition* 53, no. 3 (2014): 273–91.

37 Informal conversation with author, 7 May 2011.

38 Stuart Hall, "Cultural Identity in Diaspora," in *Identity: Community, Culture, Difference*, ed. Jonathan Rutherford (London: Lawrence & Wishart, 1990), 223.

39 Carole Counihan and Van Esterik, *Food and Culture: A Reader* (New York: Routledge, 1997).

40 Arjun Appadurai, "Introduction: Commodities and the Politics of Value," in *The Social Life of Things: Commodities in Cultural Perspective*, ed. Arjun Appadurai (Cambridge: Cambridge University Press, 1996), 3.

41 Thomas M. Wilson, "Drinking Cultures: Sites and Practices in the Production and Expression of Identity," in *Drinking Cultures: Alcohol and Identity*, ed. T. Wilson (Oxford: Berg, 2005), 12.

42 For more on histories of drinking, a good number of which are focused on alcoholic drink in historical perspective, see Craig Heron, *Booze: A Distilled History* (Toronto: Between the Lines, 2003); Cheryl Krasnick Warsh, ed., *Drink in Canada: Historical Essays* (Montreal and Kingston: McGill-Queen's University Press, 1993); Janet Noel, *Canada Dry: Temperance Crusades before Confederation* (Toronto: University of Toronto Press, 1995); Julia Roberts, *In Mixed Company: Taverns and Public Life* (Vancouver: UBC Press, 2009); T.E. Brennan, *Public Drinking and Popular Culture in Eighteenth-Century Paris* (Princeton: Princeton University Press, 1988).

43 Wilson, "Drinking Cultures," 12.
44 A.J. Arberry, *The Seven Odes: The First Chapter in Arabic Literature* (London: Macmillan, 1957), 146–7.
45 Heine, *Food Culture*, 4.
46 Nasrallah, *Delights from the Garden of Eden*, 17. See also Ralph Hattox, *Coffee and Coffeehouses: The Origins of a Social Beverage in the Medieval Near East* (Seattle: University of Washington Press, 1985), 15–23.
47 Heine, *Food Culture*, 4–5.
48 Ibid., 122.
49 Wilson, "Drinking Cultures," 10.
50 Ibid.
51 Richard Tapper, "Blood, Wine and Water: Social and Symbolic Aspects of Drinks and Drinking in the Islamic Middle East," in *Culinary Cultures of the Middle East*, ed. Sami Zubaida and Richard Tapper (London/New York: I.B. Taurus/Centre of Near and Middle Eastern Studies, University of London, 1994), 215.
52 Claudia Rodin, *Coffee: A Connoisseur's Companion* (New York: Random House, 1994), 37–9.
53 Jewish Iraqis do not feature prominently in this research since many had a very different migration narrative from women who left Iraq and settled in North America. Many Jewish Iraqis currently living in Canada and the US arrived as immigrants from Israel following their exile there after the 1948 Arab-Israeli war. See Orit Bashkin, *New Babylonians: A History of Jews in Modern Iraq* (Stanford: Stanford University Press, 2012).
54 Interview, Toronto, 8 November 2010.
55 Carol Bardenstein, "Transmissions Interrupted: Reconfiguring Food, Memory, and Gender in the Cookbook-Memoirs of Middle Eastern Exiles," *Signs: Journal of Women in Culture and Society* 28, no. 1 (Autumn 2002): 353–87.
56 Carlnita Greene, "Competing Identities at the Table: Slow Food, Consumption, and the Performance of Social Style," in *Food as Communication, Communication as Food*, ed. Janet M. Cramer, Carlnita P. Greene, and Lynn M. Walters (New York: Peter Lang, 2011), 76–7.
57 Wilson, "Drinking Cultures," 4.
58 Lynn Abrams, *Oral History Theory* (London: Routledge, 2010), 74.
59 Ruth Behar, *The Vulnerable Observer: Anthropology That Breaks Your Heart* (Boston: Beacon, 1996), 19.
60 Interview with Sabean family, Amman, 30 September 2008. For more on the struggle of the Sabeans in Iraq, see Ma'oz Moshe, *Middle Eastern Minorities: Between Integration and Conflict* (Washington, DC: Washington Institute for Near East Policy, 1999), 71–91.
61 Interview, Amman, 30 September 2008.

62 Iraqis continue to live in fear of retribution generations after leaving the homeland, owing mainly to their ongoing ties to communities, family, and friends in Iraq. In the most recent displacement of refugees, these threats have become a reality, as many have suffered the loss of loved ones and acquaintances in the sectarian violence that continues to destabilize the country. In interviews with Iraqi women, approximately 80 per cent report having lost family or friends as a result of the Ba'th regime's repressive policies and the violence following its overthrow. Also see Joseph Sassoon, *The Iraqi Refugees: The New Crisis in the Middle East* (London: I.B. Taurus, 2009), 23–31.
63 Interviews and conversations conducted with the author predominantly in Amman, summer 2008.
64 Clifford Geertz, "Thick Description: Toward an Interpretive Theory of Culture," in *The Interpretation of Cultures: Selected Essays* (New York: Basic Books, 1973), 3–30.
65 Brown and Mussell, "Introduction," *Ethnic and Regional Foodways*, 9.
66 Sutton, *Remembrance of Repasts*, 162–3.
67 Shameem Black, "Recipes for Cosmopolitanism: Cooking across Borders in South Asian Diaspora," *Frontiers: A Journal of Women Studies* 31, no. 1 (2010): 1–30.

5. Policing Women's Bodies in Diaspora: Toronto and Detroit in Comparative Context

1 Sana Al-Khayyat, *Honor and Shame: Women in Modern Iraq* (London: Al-Saqi, 1990), 22.
2 Toronto Iraqi Muslims have a complex relationship with the hyphen, but Chaldeans in Detroit have embraced a hyphenated identity, adopting "Chaldean-American" as their official status in most community and government-affiliated organizations. See also http://www.chaldean.org/; http://chaldeanchamber.com/.
3 In Detroit, the city is divided into suburbs of the metropolitan downtown and then larger districts within which distinct communities are formed. Southfield is one of these districts, as is Dearborn, though the latter is closer to the downtown. Toronto is the core of the Greater Toronto Area or GTA that includes distinct towns and cities falling within the spatial limits of this designated space. All of the cities or large towns mentioned in these pages (Hamilton, Mississauga, Burlington), with the exception of Windsor, are within the GTA.
4 A. Naff, "Arabs in America: A Historical Overview," in *Arabs in the New World*, ed. S.Y. Abraham and N. Abraham (Detroit: Wayne State University Center for Urban Studies, 1983), 89; J. Zogby, *Arab-America Today: A Demographic Profile of Arab Americans* (Washington, DC: Arab-American

Institute, 1990); "The Arab Population: 2000: Census 2000 Brief," *United States Census 2000* (US Department of Commerce, Economics and Statistics Administration, December 2003).

5 The Detroit community is now estimated to be the largest population of Chaldeans anywhere in the world, since the exodus of this ethnic group from Iraq following persecution under Saddam Hussein's regime and the 2003 US invasion. See also "The Arab Population," *United States Census 2000.*

6 Mary Cey Sengstock, *Chaldeans in Michigan* (East Lansing: Michigan State University Press, 2005), 31–3.

7 Ibid., 28–9.

8 Ibid., 41.

9 Examples of these trends can also be found in Louise Cainkar, "Palestinian Women in American Society: The Interaction of Social Class, Culture, and Politics," in *The Development of Arab-American Identity*, ed. Ernest McCarus (Ann Arbor: The University of Michigan Press, 1994), 89–90.

10 Ken Marten, "The Greatest Generation: CIAAM Honors Its Elders," *Chaldean News*, December 2006, 40.

11 Interviews with women in the Chaldean community in Southfield and Dearborn, 5–8 November 2009.

12 Group interview with Chaldean American Ladies of Charity executive members in Southfield, Detroit, 6 November 2009.

13 For more information, see http://calconline.org.

14 Group interview conducted with members of the Chaldean Angels in Southfield, Detroit, 7 November 2009.

15 Discussions of the changing post-1945 roles of women in ethnic organizations can be found in the following (among many others): Ethel Vineburg, *The History of the National Council of Jewish Women* (Montreal: National Council of Jewish Women, 1979); Joanne Meyerowitz, *Not June Cleaver: Women and Gender in Postwar America* (Philadelphia: Temple University Press, 1994); F. Iacovetta, *Gatekeepers: Reshaping Immigrant Lives in Cold War Canada* (Toronto: Between the Lines, 2006).

16 "Middle Eastern Christians" is a term frequently used in Chaldean community literature as well as in my discussions with Chaldean men and women living in Dearborn, Southfield, and Sterling Heights, 5–8 November 2009.

17 Detroit Arab American Study Team, *Citizenship and Crisis: Arab Detroit after 9/11* (Detroit: Russell Sage Foundation, 2009).

18 Tom Hundley, "Arab or American? Either Choice Brings Built-In Conflicts," *Detroit Free Press*, 28 April 1986, 2B.

19 "An Appeal: A Letter of Concern to the Youth of the Chaldean Community," Barbara Aswad Papers, Bentley Historical Library, University of Michigan, Ann Arbor.

20 Hundley, "Arab or American?," subheading "Keeping Their Respect," 3B.
21 Ibid.
22 Ann Antone, chair of the Chaldean Ladies of Charity, interview, Detroit, 6 November 2009.
23 Vanessa Denha-Garmo and Joyce Wiswell, "Changing Faces: Chaldeans Yesterday, Today and Tomorrow," *Chaldean News*, February 2006, 34.
24 These issues are discussed in greater detail in Yvonne Haddad, "Maintaining the Faith of the Fathers: Dilemmas of Religious Identity in the Christian and Muslim Arab-American Communities," in *The Development of Arab American Identity*, ed. E. McMarus (Ann Arbor: University of Michigan, 1994), 61–85.
25 Ken Marten, "Ruffling Feathers: Teacher Challenges the Mainstream View," *Chaldean News*, June 2006, 38–9.
26 Ibid., 39.
27 "Filled with Fallacy," letter to the editor, *Chaldean News*, July 2006, 10.
28 Denha-Garmo and Wiswell, "Changing Faces," 35.
29 Ibid., 38.
30 "Filled with Fallacy," 39.
31 Jennifer Korail, "All in the Family: Working Women Turn to Nannies for Help," *Chaldean News*, January 2007, 30.
32 "Women Are Caught between Cultures," *Detroit Free Press*, 30 November 1983, 3B.
33 Ibid.
34 Ibid.
35 Vanessa Denha-Garmo, "CALC Working Women: Female Entrepreneurs Share Their Expertise," *Chaldean News*, June 2006, 50.
36 Interview with Chaldean Angels members in Southfield, Detroit, 7 November 2009.
37 Jennifer Korail, "Leaving the Nest: More Students Are Going Away to College," *Chaldean News*, September 2006, 31.
38 Ibid.
39 Joyce Wiswell, "On Their Own: Single Women Enjoy Their Independence," *Chaldean News*, May 2006, 36.
40 Ibid.
41 Ibid.
42 A discussion of measures of gender traditionalism and how we can evaluate women's support for traditional family roles, feminist issues, and non-traditional public roles can be found in Jen'nan Ghazal Read, *Culture, Class and Work among Arab-American Women* (New York: LFB Scholarly Publishing, 2004), 37; Ibrahim Hayani, "Arabs in Canada: Assimilation or Integration?" in *Arabs in America: Building a New Future*, ed. Michael W. Suleiman (Philadelphia: Temple University Press, 1999), 284–303; and Sharon McIrvin Abu-Laban and Baha Abu-Laban, "Teens Between: The

Public and Private Spheres of Arab-Canadian Adolescents," in *Arabs in America,* ed. Abu-Laban and Abu-Laban, 113–28.

43 Min Zhou and Alessandro Portes, "The New Second Generation: Segmented Assimilation and Its Variants," *Annals of the American Academy of Political and Social Sciences* 530, no. 1 (November 1993): 80–3.

44 Ibid.

45 Abu-Laban and Abu-Laban, "Teens Between," 122.

46 Jovan Kassab, "Spiritual Quest: E.C.R.C.'s Programs Appeal to All Ages," *Chaldean News,* January 2006, 36.

47 Christina Guppy, "CASA Catches On: College Clubs Connect to the Community," *Chaldean News,* January 2007, 32 (emphasis mine).

48 Interviews with author, Detroit, 2009–2011.

49 Yvonne Haddad, "Islamic Values among American Muslims," in *Family and Gender among American Muslims: Issues Facing Middle Eastern Immigrants and Their Descendants,* ed. B. Bilge and B. Aswad (Philadelphia: Temple University Press, 1996), 1–13.

50 Read, *Culture, Class and Work,* 37, 117.

51 Ibid., 117–20.

52 Sengstock, *Chaldeans in Michigan,* 66–8.

53 Milton Gordon, *Assimilation in American Life: The Role of Race, Religion and National Origins* (New York: Oxford University Press, 1964). On the importance of social class as the main marker of identification in Iraqi society, see Nadje Al-Ali, *Iraqi Women: Untold Stories from 1948 to the Present* (London: Zed Books, 2007), 65; and Batatu, *The Old Social Classes and the Revolutionary Movements of Iraq: A Study of Iraq's Old Landed and Commercial Classes and of Its Communists, Ba'athists, and Free Officers* (Princeton: Princeton University Press, 1978). Similar patterns of ethclass associations were also found in communities of Palestinian women in the US; see Cainkar, "Palestinian Women in American Society," 89–90.

54 Interview, Mississauga, 8 November 2008.

55 The ways in which these freedoms affected the lives of Iraqi women in the 1960s and 1970s is explored in much greater detail by Nadje Al-Ali in her discussion of interviews with Iraqi women, *Iraqi Women,* 47–9.

56 Interview, Mississauga, 8 December 2008.

57 Interview, Mississauga., 10 December 2009.

58 Nadje Al-Ali, "Reconstructing Gender: Iraqi Women between Dictatorship, War, Sanctions and Occupation," *Third World Quarterly* 26, no. 4–5 (2005): 745; T. Wright, "Managing Gender Expectations upon Resettlement: The Experiences of Iraqi Kurdish Muslim Women in the UK," *Gender, Place and Culture* 21, no. 6 (2014): 733–4.

59 Al-Ali, "Reconstructing Gender," 747–50.

60 Ibid.

61 Group interview, Mississauga, 8 November 2008.
62 Ali Al-Wardi, *A Study of the Nature of Iraqi Society* (Baghdad: Matba'at al-'Ani, 1965), 105–7.
63 Al-Ali, in her interviews with Iraqi women in the US and UK, also found evidence of women following Western fashions in the sixties; *Iraqi Women*, 98.
64 Interview, Hamilton, 9 November 2010.
65 Interview, Hamilton, 2 May 2009.
66 Interview, Hamilton, 9 November 2010.
67 These second-generation participants are best described as the "1.5 generation." The notion of a 1.5-generation is explored in the work of Ruben G. Rumbaut, among others, in an attempt to expand the statistical boundaries of the second-generation in order to explore the complexities between foreign-born immigrants who are partly socialized abroad and native-born immigrants born to foreign parents. Ruben G. Rumbaut, "Severed or Sustained Attachments? Language, Identity, and Imagined Communities in the Post-Immigrant Generation," in *The Changing Face of Home: The Transnational Lives of the Second-Generation*, ed. Peggy Levitt and Mary C. Waters (New York: Russell Sage Foundation, 2002), 48.
68 Interviews, Hamilton and Toronto, 12 December 2010 and 27 November 2011.
69 Georges E. Fouron and Nina Glick-Schiller, "The Generation of Identity: Redefining the Second Generation within a Transnational Social Field," in *The Changing Face of Home: The Transnational Lives of the Second Generation*, ed. Peggy Levitt and Mary C. Waters (New York: Russell Sage Foundation, 2002), 180.
70 Zhou and Portes, "The New Second Generation," 85.
71 Barbara Aswad, "Strengths of the Arab Family for Mental Health Considerations and Therapy," in *The Arab American Family: A Resource Manual for Human Service Providers* (Ypsilanti: Eastern Michigan University/ACCESS, 1988), 93–101.
72 S.H. Mathews and T.T. Rosner, "Shared Filial Responsibility: The Family as the Primary Caregiver," *Journal of Marriage and the Family* 50, no. 1 (1988): 185–95.
73 Timothy Williams and Abeer Mohammad, "What Not to Wear, Baghdad Style: Fashion Rules Begin to Change," *New York Times*, 5 June 2009.
74 Due to the scope and focus of my research on different ethno-religious groups of Iraqis, there are relatively few veiled women as participants, and I include only the taped and official interviews conducted with women in hijab in the text. However, there were other women with whom I had more casual conversations with regarding their decision to wear the hijab. Some of these would not sign consent forms and did not want to be part of the research. While I entirely respect their decision to remain off the record, I

have included their narratives in my overall assessment of the interview material. These young veiled women were quick to identify other Iraqi women who had also made the decision to wear hijab, indicating a small though important trend amongst this generation, and one that I intend to explore further in future research.

75 Interview, Hamilton, 17 December 2010.

76 Al-Ali, "Reconstructing Gender," 739–58.

77 These differences between first- and second-generation responses to Islamic dress in North America indicate that most parents would prefer that children fit in and not "other" themselves from society regardless of religious codes. In a study that spanned a number of urban centres in Canada and the US, Nimat Hafez Barazangi found that very few of the parents in their study were aware of the proper Quranic codes of dress for women (although all felt that modest dress was appropriate), whereas the youth response was more in line with the actual teachings of the Quran. The author suggests that there is a greater understanding of religious text in the youth response and far more diverse reactions to proper modes of Islamic dress. Barazangi, "Arab Muslim Identity Transmission: Parents and Youth," in *Arab-Americans: Continuity and Change*, ed. Baha Abu-Laban and Michael W. Suleiman (Belmont: Association of Arab-American University Graduates, 1989), 65–75.

78 Interview, Hamilton, 17 December 2010.

79 Interview, Mississauga, 5 March 2010.

80 Group interview, Hamilton, 17 December 2010.

81 Interview, Mississauga, 10 December 2009.

82 Group interview, Hamilton, 17 December 2010.

83 Interview, Hamilton, 17 December 2010.

84 Indeed, I was so fascinated by this idea that I spent three months in 2009 (under the guidance of several Iraqi female participants) wearing the hijab and observing the same customs that these young women have adopted. In the place of attending mosque and daily prayers (although this was not something that all five women observed on a weekly basis), I spent time reading a translated copy of the Qu'ran and silently meditating.

85 Haideh Moghissi, Saeed Rahnema, and Mark J. Goodman, eds., *Diaspora by Design: Muslims in Canada and Beyond* (Toronto: University of Toronto Press, 2009), 14.

86 Some researchers have even documented the increasing number of teenagers from non-practicing and secular Muslim families who are influenced by more religious friends to following conservative and often fundamentalist practices. Saeed Soltanpour, "Iranian-Islamic Centers in Toronto," part 2, *Shahrvand Weekly*, 11 February 2005, 926.

Conclusion

1 John Hutchison and Anthony D. Smith, eds., *Ethnicity* (Oxford: Oxford University Press, 1996), 367.
2 Gabriel Sheffer, "Middle Eastern Diasporas – An Overview," in *Middle Eastern Minorities and Diasporas*, ed. Mosh Ma'oz and Gabriel Sheffer (Brighton: Sussex Academic Press, 2002), 200.
3 Ibid., 202.
4 Ibid., 203.
5 Ibid.
6 Ruben G. Rumbaut, "Severed or Sustained Attachments? Language, Identity, and Imagined Communities in the Post-Immigrant Generation," in *The Changing Face of Home: The Transnational Lives of the Second Generation*, ed. Peggy Levitt and Mary C. Waters (New York: Russell Sage Foundation, 2002), 48.
7 Rivka Yadlin, "The Muslim Diaspora in the West," in *Middle Eastern Minorities and Diasporas*, ed. Moshe Ma'oz and Gabriel Sheffer (Brighton: Sussex Academic Press, 2002), 219–22.
8 Shanaz Khan, *Muslim Women: Crafting a North American Identity* (Tampa: University of Florida Press, 2001); Vijay Agnew, ed., *Diaspora, Memory, and Identity: A Search for Home* (Toronto: University of Toronto Press, 2005); Haideh Moghissi, *The "Muslim" Diaspora and Research on Gender: Promises and Perils* (London: Routledge, 2006); Parin Dossa, *Racialized Bodies, Disabling Worlds: Storied Lives of Immigrant Muslim Women* (Toronto: University of Toronto Press, 2009); *Politics and Poetics of Migration: Narratives of Iranian Women from the Diaspora* (Toronto: Canadian Scholars Press, 2004).
9 Chandra Talpade Mohanty, "'Under Western Eyes' Revisited: Feminist Solidarity through Anticapitalist Struggles," in *Feminism without Borders: Decolonizing Theory, Practicing Solidarity* (Durham: Duke University Press, 2003), 221–52.
10 Gayatri Chakravorty Spivak, "Can the Subaltern Speak?" in *Marxism and the Interpretation of Culture*, ed. Cary Nelson and Lawrence Grossberg (London: Macmillan, 1988), 24–8.
11 These were common responses to this question over the course of my interviews in Amman, Toronto, and Detroit from 2007 to 2011.
12 Samira Yako Cholagh, *Treasured Middle Eastern Cookbook*, 2nd ed. (Saline, MI: McNaughton & Gunn, 2008). The book was first published in 1998, and by popular demand a second edition was released on the ten-year anniversary of the original publication date. Interview, 6 November 2009, Southfield, Michigan.

13 Jan Nederveen Pieterse and Bikhu Parekh, "Shifting Imaginaries: Decolonization, Internal Decolonization, Postcoloniality," in *The Decolonization of Imagination: Culture, Knowledge and Power*, ed. Jan Nederveen Pieterse and Bhikhu Parekh (London: Zed Books, 1995), 1–19.

14 A small sample includes Loretta Baldassar and Donna R. Gabaccia, eds., *Intimacy and Italian Migration: Gender and Domestic Lives in a Mobile World* (New York: Fordham University Press, 2011); Loretta Baldassar, Cora Vellekoop Baldock, and Raelene Wilding, *Families Caring across Borders: Migration, Ageing and Transnational Caregiving* (New York: Palgrave Macmillan, 2007); Deborah Bruceson and Ulla Vuorela, eds., *The Transnational Family: New European Frontiers and Global Networks* (Oxford: Berg, 2002); Ann Laura Stoler, "Tense and Tender Ties: The Politics of Comparison in North American History and (Post) Colonial Studies," *Journal of American History* 88, no. 3 (2001): 829–65.

15 Raeling Wilding, "Virtual Intimacies: Family Communications across Transnational Borders," *Global Networks* 6, no. 2 (2006): 125–42.

16 Pnina Werbner, *Imagined Diasporas among Manchester Muslims: The Public Performance of Pakistani Transnational Identity Politics*, World Anthropology Series (Santa Fe: SAR Press, 2002).

17 Nadine Naber, *Arab America: Gender, Cultural Politics, and Activism* (New York: New York University Press, 2012); Minoo Moallem, "Ethnic Entrepreneurship and Gender Relations among Iranians in Montreal, Quebec, Canada," in *Iranian Refugees and Exiles Since Khomeini*, ed. Asghar Fathi (Costa Mesa: Mazda, 2005), 43–69; Werbner, *Imagined Diasporas among Manchester Muslims.*

Index

Abu-Lughod, Lila, 67, 69
activism: labour, 9; political, 17, 57; religious, 114; women's, 33; young Iraqi women's, 134
agency, 59, 63, 104, 125, 130; women's, 124
Agnew, Vijay, 13
Al-Ali, Nadje, 17, 71
al-Baghdadi, Ibn al-Khateeb, 86
Al-Ethari, Lamees, 12, 22
Ali, Rashid, 28
Ali, Zahra, 17
Al-Khayyat, Sana, 105
Al-Warraq, Ibn Sayyar, 86
American Community Center for Economic and Social Services of Detroit, 62
Amman: interviews, 68, 72; United Nations Refugee Agency in, 25; women in, 47, 76, 81
Anderson Benedict, 37, 58
Anthias, Floya, 13
Arab Americans, 14, 110–12
Arab Muslims, 7, 14, 74, 109, 112, 116
Arab religions. *See under* religion
Arab Socialist Ba'ath, 4, 24, 26; administration, 5, 6, 117; Iraqi Socialist Ba'ath, 4, 21–2, 74; pan-Arab nationalism, 36; party, 36–7, 49, 50, 54, 56; regime, 29, 32; social state, 18, 33; state nationalism, 25
Arab women. *See* women, Arab
Arab world, 30, 95, 111
Armelagos, George, 89
ascendancy, 39, 40, 58; Sunni, 4, 26
Assmann, Jan, 59
Assyrian Canadian National Federation, 62
Assyrian Iraqis, 4, 127
Assyrians, 5, 7, 30, 50, 137n13, 138n13, 148n7
asliyyun, 47
authenticity, 29, 31–2, 97, 155–6n29

Bagdad Twist (film), 12, 22
Bamberg, Michael, 59
bamieh, as metaphor for Iraq, 3–4, 5
Bannerji, Himani, 16
Bardenstein, Carol, 97
Barzani, Mustafa, 55
Bashkin, Orit, 17
Basra, 50, 154n14
Batatu, Hanna, 29
Behar, Ruth, 82, 98
belonging, 73–5, 86–7, 91–4, 102, 111; national, 22, 45, 58, 59; sense of, 38, 52–5, 86
Benson, Michael, 41

Bourdieu, Pierre, 12
British Mandate, 17, 25, 28; government, 43; system, 46
Burke, Peter, 5

Canada: Iraqis in, 79, 137–8n13; life in, 66, 79, 117, 140n22; women in, 66, 120–2
CARE (organization), 62, 72, 76–7
Caritas, 62
Center of the Assyrian-Canadian Federation, 3, 62
Chaldea, 50
Chaldean-American Chamber of Commerce, 109
Chaldean American Ladies of Charity, 62, 81, 109–15
Chaldean-American Student Association, 115
Chaldean Angels, 108–9, 115
Chaldean Federation of America, 62, 107–9, 137n13
Chaldean-Iraqi American Federation of Michigan, 107
Chaldeans, 7, 14, 18, 30, 36, 38, 50, 52, 109–10; American-born, 128; American identity, 80, 109, 112; church, 51, 111–15, 127; community, 81, 105–6, 109–12, 116, 118, 121, 132; in Detroit, 50–1, 79, 81–4, 106, 115, 121, 127, 129 (*see also* Detroit); women, in US, 80–1, 105–8, 110–11, 114, 128–9. *See also* second generation; third generation
Cholagh, Samira, 125, 132
Christians, 7, 27–9, 44–9, 50–1, 107–9, 111–12, 149n11, 170n16
Ciezadlo, Annia, 86
citizenship, 49, 54; diasporic, 129; Iraqi, 47, 54; women's, 31
class: middle, 33–6, 71, 108, 116, 120, 123, 128, 161n23; professional, 6, 43, 62, 91, 117; social, 37, 43, 98–9
coffee: in Bedouin culture, 95; in Iraqi culture, 83, 96–9; serving of, 19, 96, 98, 101–2
colonialism, 54, 131; and dominance, 87; and food, 87; internal, 133; and policy, 43; and powers, 42, 43; and structures of power and knowledge, 65
common origin, myth of, 26, 31, 38
community (Arab), 105–6, 110, 127; Community Center of Toronto, 62; Detroit, 106
confession, 64–6, 70
cookbook, 19, 83–8, 125, 132
Coombes, Annie, 61
counter-narrative, 3, 4, 22–5, 40–2, 52–9, 60, 75–7, 80, 101–2, 132; collective, 44; vs. collectivized state memory, 41; women's, 18, 41, 60
cuisine. *See* food
culture (Arab), 104, 113

Davis, Eric, 18, 25, 30, 75
Dearborn (Michigan), 49, 106, 109–10, 113–15
decolonization, internal, 133
Detroit, 50–2; Chaldean community in, 106, 121; migration to, 50, 107; women in, 80–1, 126. *See also* Chaldeans
diaspora: Assyrian women in, 50; communities in, 81–7, 131, 133; diasporic citizens/citizenship, 46, 129; diasporic imagination, 9, 81, 127–31; ethnic, 9, 13, 127; global, 88; Iraqi, 3, 5, 6, 42, 52, 73–6, 77, 87, 89, 91–4, 129, 131–2, 134; and Iraqi women, 9, 15, 18, 20–6, 77, 84, 101, 105, 123; Muslim, 14, 130, 144n53; and solidarity, 127–8; women in, 32–5, 62, 125

displacement, 22, 38, 41, 48, 81, 90, 98, 169n62
Dossa, Parin, 41
Douglas, Mary, 84

Efrati, Noga, 17, 32–3
emotion, 4, 12, 61–2, 80, 98
embodied ethnographic method, 62
ethnicity, 14, 15, 87–9, 94–7, 112, 131–2, 136–8n13; and absolutism, 14, 15; Assyrian, 50; and diasporas, 9, 13, 127, and exclusivity, 28, 114–15, 130; and identity, 54, 89, 94, 111–13, 115, 130–1; and methodology, 23; and race, 13, 16, 121, 130, 136n13
ethnography, 9, 19, 82, 130; of emotion and the senses, 61
ethno-nationalism, 7, 13, 59; group, 8, 13, 38, 43, 54, 88, 94, 105, 132; and identities, 40, 104, 130–2; Iraqi, 89, 127–9; and minorities, 127
ethno-religiosity: and communities, 4, 40, 52, 105, 129; and group, 7–8, 12–13, 38, 41, 77, 81, 120, 173n74; and identity, 13, 19, 40, 128–9; Iraqi, 13
exclusion, 14, 27, 35, 45–7, 49, 52–5, 63, 125
exile, 9, 10, 12, 14, 39, 52–5, 84, 117, 127–8, 168n53

family: and community, 62; and friends, 17, 76, 116; history of, 73, 81, 90–2, 136n10; and home, 92–8, 113–21; and immigrant economies, 9; interviewing, 74, 124; and kin, 104; members, 23–4, 34, 41, 64, 66–7, 76–7, 79, 91, 105–7, 118, 122–3; and migration, 66; multigenerational, 35; planning, 115; ties, 20, 105; transnational, 8, 121. *See also* honour; reputation
Farb, Peter, 89
Faysal, King, 43
femininity, 63
feminism, 16, 20, 104, 124, 130; feminist history, 9, 63, 131; and holistic reflexivity, 6; and Marxist theory, 16; methodology, 5, 62, 63, 82, 133; migration scholars, 131; Muslim, 124–5; religious, 18; transnational, 8, 18; and the veil, 124–5
first generation, 106, 109–10, 120, 123; Iraqi-born Sunni women, 116; Kurdish migrants, 92; migrants, 17–18, 167n36; parents, 113, 174n77; Sunni Iraqi women, 117–20; women, 74, 108
food, 19, 20, 83–4; Iraqi, 3, 84, 85, 87, 132; as metaphor, 3–4, 5, 19, 88–9, 102; and nostalgia/memory, 19, 84–9, 93, 102
Freund, Alexander, 64, 65
Frisch, Michael, 62

Geertz, Clifford, 82, 102
gender: and class, 16; and equality, 149n17; histories, 61; and identities, 18, 20, 102; and memory, 39, 62; and obedience to state, 18; and race, 13; relations, 86; and religious conservatism, 17; and subjectivities, 13, 90, 102; and traditions/traditionalism, 108–16
General Federation of Iraqi Women (GFIW), 36–7, 151n47
globalization, 9, 10, 134
Goodman, Mark, 125
gossip, 4, 75, 100, 116, 122, 126
grassroots movements, 22, 33
Guha, Ranajit, 40
Gulf War, 27, 116, 137n13

halfie researcher, 64, 65, 67–8
Hashemite monarchy, 33, 43

Hashemites, 33, 43
headscarf, 119, 120, 122
Heine, Peter, 95
hijab, 15, 116, 122, 126, 130, 173–4n74; first-generation Sunni perception of, 123; religious symbolism of, 119; tradition of wearing, 124
history/histories: of Armenian persecution in Iraq, 98; Chaldean, 51; of food, 83–4; Iraqi, 27, 28, 30, 56, 89; Iraqi women's, 5, 33; Middle Eastern, 87; national, 9, 28, 89, 133 (*see also* identity); of nation vs. state, 10; official, 33, 89, 90, 101, 129; personal, 48; women's oral, 63, 160n21. *See also* family; migration
holistic life narrative approach, 34
home: claims to, 38; fluid imaginings of, 18; life, 115; politics of, 6; recollections of, 4. *See also* family; memory
homeland, 4, 8, 9, 13, 45, 57, 76–7, 99, 103, 109, 114, 116, 119, 131, 134; Arab, 28, 31; connection to, 78, 81, 121, 126, 127, 129; and ideals of female behavior, 125; outside the, 87, 94, 122–28; and politics, 104; and rituals, 20; and roles of Iraqi women, 79; and traditions, 110
"honor and shame," phenomenon of, 20, 105
honour, 17, 20, 95, 101, 105, 119; Chaldean/Arab ideas of, 110; family, 121; women's, 32
hospitality, 95–6
humour, 10, 11, 19, 51, 71
hybridity, 82

identity: Chaldean-American, 80, 109, 112; collective, 8, 25–6, 60, 93–4, 144n53; communal, 89, 105–7, 130; and ethnicity, 54, 89, 94, 111–13, 115, 130–1; Iraqi, 4, 11, 12, 25, 29, 38, 58, 92; national, 4, 9, 13, 18, 27–9, 31–5, 58–9, 60, 95–6, 138n13; overlapping identities, 29, 48, and politics, 15, 94, 130; postcolonial, 133; and religion, 25, 38, 40, 55, 97, 106. *See also* gender
intimacy, 61, 94, 98, 99, 117, 132; and food/drink, 19, 83, 88; virtual, 134
inconsistency, in historical account, 7, 24, 35–8, 71
indigeneity, Iraqi. *See under* Iraqis
interview. *See* oral history/histories
Iran-Iraq War, 23, 30, 91
Iraqiness, 12, 45, 53–8, 86
Iraqis: indigenous, 38, 47, 49, 54, 78; refugees, 21, 44, 59, 70, 72, 74, 85, 100, 137n13, 138n13; second-generation women, 130; third-generation women, 130; women in diaspora, 9, 15, 20
Iraqi Women's Union, 32–3, 36
inclusion/exclusion, 35, 63, 89
Intifada, 7, 43–7, 51
Islam, 14, 30, 117, 124–5, 134; political, 125, 130
Islamism, 17
Islamophobia, 112, 117

Jews, 7, 22, 36, 44, 107

Karbala, 46, 155–6n29
Khan, Shahnaz, 15, 75
kleiche, 91–3, 97, 102, 132
Kurdishness, 57
Kurdistan, 54–9, 80; Iraqi, 74; Regional Government, 55
Kurds/Kurdish, 4, 7, 11, 27–9, 30–1, 38, 43–9, 54–6, 59, 74, 106, 128–9, 137n13, 138n13; Christian, 55; historical imaginaries of, 18; Iraqi, 11, 44, 55, 80, 127–8; Iraqi women, 41, 76; migrants, 52, 92, 129; movement, 53–7; Muslim women, 73; and nation

state, 129; refugees, 18, 129; Sunni women, 58; women, 52–4, 80–1, 118, 157n55, 161n23. *See also* migration
Kuwait, 7, 22–3, 27, 34, 91

language, 15, 17, 28, 47, 50–1, 71–3, 84–9, 97, 115; Arabic, 27; and cultural distinctiveness, 55; and cultural heritage, 52; and ethnic culture, 59
life narrative, 3, 5, 18, 38, 41, 102
Little, Angela, 89
League for the Defense of Women's Rights, 32

madrasas, 46
Makiya, Kanan, 24
Malkki, Liisa, 12
mallaks, 43
marginalization, 15, 130
marriage, 81, 104–6, 114, 123; early, 86; endogamous, 121–2; laws, 31; partner, 31, 79, 119, 122–6; prospects, 116, 120–2
marriageability, 101
memory: collective, 4, 26, 36, 44, 58, 73–7, 84–8, 102; collectivized state memory, 41; communal, 18, 129; counter memory, 75; cultural, 42, 90; dialectic of, 75; and food, 19, 84–9, 102; and gender, 39, 62; historical, 27–9, 31, 35, 37, 39, 53–4, 58, 75, 87; of home, 3, 53, 90; inherited, 6, 39, 89, 90–1, 94; Iraqi women's, 60; making, 19, 22–4, 46–9, 50–1, 63; multigenerational, 6, 19; national, 18, 40, 60; nostalgic, 84; sensory, 19, 83–9, 91–4, 102; and state, 18, 24–6, 45–8; women's, 6, 13, 18, 33
Mesopotamia, 29–30, 78, 80–4
Mesopotamianism, 30
metaphor, 41, 59, 61, 84–8, 157n58; *bamieh* as metaphor for Iraq, 3–4, 5; consumptive, 20; of family, 55; food as, 3–4, 5, 19, 88–9, 102; and meaning, 18; poisoned dish as metaphor for Iraq, 88–9; sensory, 3; and silence, 62; use of, 10, 11
Middle East, 6, 14, 84, 96, 118, 131
migrants, 7, 8, 9, 10, 51–3, 57, 84, 93, 108, 114, 128–31; Chaldean, 107; diasporic, 90; Iraqi, 3, 5, 6, 94; Iraqi women, 3, 5, 6, 17, 20–2, 41–4, 49, 54, 79, 81, 87–8, 94, 105, 132–4; Kurdish, 129; Kurdish women, 52; Muslim, 14, 132; Muslim women, 63, 124; Sunni Arab Muslims, 106; women, 13, 15, 19, 63, 105. *See also* third generation
migration, 5, 12, 51, 52, 74, 76, 129; American and Canadian literature of, 8; chain, 50, 107, 118; forced, 50, 54, 64, 66, 84, 99, 127; global, 9, 17, 127; history of, 9; from Iraq, 7, 50, 64–6, 107; migration studies, 9; North American migration studies, 13. *See also* transnationalism
Mikhail, Dunya, 23
Mintz, Sidney, 84
Mitnaz Law Group, 62, 76–7
mnemohistory, 59
modesty, 68, 109, 113, 115–16, 162n38; as defensive, 122; women's, 17, 20, 70, 104–5, 106, 110, 114, 126, 161n30
Moghissi, Haideh, 14, 125
moral regulation, 68, 108
Mosul, 3, 25, 49, 50–3
Mother of God Chaldean Church, 107
mujtahids, 46–7, 155–6n29
multiculturalism, 15, 131
Muslim al-Sham region, 42

Nadir, Leilah, 83, 90–1
Najaf, 42–3, 46, 155–6n29
Nasrallah, Nawal, 85

National Center for Human Rights, 62, 100
nation, Arab, 30–1
nationalism, 4, 6, 9, 17, 29, 30–8, 58, 81–9, 94, 133; Arab, 47; civic, 13; Iraqi, 25–9, 59; methodological, 10; new, 13, 44; state, 18, 21, 25–6, 33–7, 45
National Kurdish Congress of North America, 53
9/11, backlash against Arabs and Muslims, 8, 14, 109–11, 116, 127
1968 coup, 22
1924 Nationality Law, 47
Nineveh, 44, 136n10
North America, 7, 8, 12, 63, 83–4, 86
nostalgia, 19, 42–4, 48, 56, 86; and food, 84–9, 93, 102; and cookbooks, 85; and longing for home, 44, 48–9, 84

Ontario, 7, 8, 25, 66, 91
oppression, 16, 18, 21, 49, 54–6, 60, 80, 128
oral history/histories, 5, 9, 35, 40, 51, 61, 92, 96, 132, 163n43; Chaldean women's, 58; and confession, 64–6; feminist method of, 62–3, 82, 98; in interviews, 23–4, 70–5; interviews off the record, 23, 80, 163n43, 173–4n74; and safety, 21, 24, 75–7
Ottoman Empire, 28, 42, 50–5

pan-Arabism, 18, 22, 26, 27, 28, 29–31, 38, 58
Passerini, Luisa, 39
Patai, Daphne, 131
patriarchy, 16, 17, 134; collective narrative of, 132; and gender relations, 32; and religious ideologies, 15
persecution, 41, 48, 49, 51, 80, 137n13, 138n13; of Armenians in Iraq, 98; of Chaldeans in Iraq, 81; of Iraqi ethnic/religious minority groups, 6, 25, 76, 77, 98, 99, 127; by state, 13, 22, 50, 106
policing: of female conduct, 123; of women, 104–5
politics: community, 109; of dislocation, 17; and identity, 15, 94, 130; Iraqi, 73, 92, 128; nationalist, 4; transnational, 128. *See also* home; homeland
Portelli, Alessandro, 59, 61
Portes, Alessandro, 114, 74–5
positionality, 25, 41, 47, 54, 57
postcolonial research/discourse, 13, 16, 18, 19, 63, 82, 90, 131. *See also* identity
power: colonial, 42–3; state, 26, 43–5; structures of, 19, 22, 102, 125, 131
Pratt, Nicola, 17
Project for the Rewriting of History, 26–9, 30–1, 33, 35–6, 45, 58

Qasim Revolution (1958), 30

Rahnema, Saeed, 125
reflexive methodology, 23, 67
refugees: Armenian, 98; Chaldean, 49; Iraqi women, 116; Jewish, 97; Kurdish, recent, 35, 59, 66, 93, 111–17; refugee camps, 77, 100; Sunni community, 98, wave of, 6; women, 3, 5, 17, 20, 40–4, 129, 131. *See also under* Iraqis; Kurds/Kurdish; Sunni
religion, 43, 48, 49, 54, 127, 129, 130, 131, 132; Arab Christian, 106; Arab Muslim, 14; Chaldean-Americans, 108, 109, 111; and conservatism, 122 (*see also* gender); and ethnicity, 89; and identity, 25, 38, 40, 55, 97, 106; Shi'a, 30, 156n38; and subjectivity,

13, 14, 73; Sunni, 30, 35–7, 117, 123, 124, 125, 129, 154n14; women and, 15, 16, 73, 74, 105, 106, 123–5
remembering, 20, 35, 39, 59, 66, 83, 90; act of, 39, 42; collective, 45; multigenerational, 6, 19, 90; process of, 64, 75, 102
reputation, 20, 69, 101, 110, 113–14, 123, 125–6; familial, 17, 68, 104, 105; female, 116–22; good, 95, 108, 119, 120–5; moral, 68
resistance: consumptive metaphors and, 20; history of, 6, 57; narrative as tool of, 18, 25, 40–1, 44–5, 49, 50–1, 59, 80–1, 101–2, 125; political, 40, 52
resistant counter-remembrance, 44
Roden, Claudia, 84

Saddam, Hussein, 4, 22, 27, 29, 31, 49, 58, 137n13, 148n7, 151n47, 170n5
Saddamism, 38
Said, Edward, 10
Salbi, Zainab, 22
second generation, 31, 76, 80, 116, 126, 173–4n74; Chaldeans, 106–7, 110–14; Chaldean women, 108–10, 115; Iraqi women, 120, 130; women, 74, 81, 109, 113, 122–3, 124, 129, 130
sectarianism, 18, 42, 74, 99, 150n36; and divides, 4, 26, 74; Iraq vs. Lebanon, 152n64; and violence, 38, 44, 169n62
sensory experience, 84, 90
sexuality, 16, 18, 122–6, 132; female sexuality, 104–5
shame, 20, 71, 101. *See also* "honor and shame," phenomenon of
Sheffer, Gabriel, 129
Shi'a, 5, 7, 18, 22, 25, 28–9, 35, 41, 46–7, 49, 58, 64, 72–3, 129, 144n53, 154n14, 154n16; Arab Iraqi women, 80; Arabs, 30, 156n38; Iraqis, 4, 22–4, 46, 106; population, 22, 42–4, 78; Sunni-Shi'a rift, 42; women, 37, 45, 47, 49
shrine/shrine cities, 42–3, 45–6, 47
silence, in narrative, 4, 17, 61, 62, 131
situated intersubjectivity, 12
Skultans, Vieda, 38
Smith, Anthony, 59
society, Arab, 105, 121
solidarity, 114, 127–9
speech acts, 40
Spivak, Gayatri, 67, 132
storytelling, 19, 61
subaltern, 13, 90, 132
subjectivity, 5, 8, 12, 13, 17, 39, 73, 98; women's political, 13. *See also* gender
Sunni, 5, 18, 22, 25, 28–9, 30, 35, 38, 43; Arab Iraqis, 7, 24; Arab supremacy, 25; Arab women, 36, 124–30; Iraqi women, 24, 38, 116–18, 126; Muslim women, 104–5; refugee women, 3; Sunni-Shi'a rift, 42; Sunni state, 18; women, 4, 31, 38, 106, 119
Sunnification, 21, 34–5
Syria, 7, 10, 55, 74–6, 83, 118, 120, 133
Syriacs, 7, 50

Talabani, Jalal, 55
Tamm, Marek, 60
technology/technologies: of memory, 39; of power, 66; of the self, 66
testimony, 5, 18, 23, 38–9, 41, 61, 65–6
thick description, 62, 82, 84, 102
third generation: Chaldeans, 106, 116; Chaldean women; 51, 108; Iraqis, 94; Iraqi women, 130; migrants, 109; women, 108, 113–15, 126
Third World, 16, 131–3

translator (in interviews), 19, 66–7, 70
transmigrants, 17, 67, 70–2
transnationalism: and diaspora movement, 18, 54; and migration, 6, 9, 11; and nationalism, 10, 17; and politics, 128; as web, 6, 91. *See also* feminism
trauma, 23, 42, 74–5, 77, 80–1, 99, 102–3, 129; personal, 34, 64; state-induced, 48
traumatic past, 80, 129
tribal affiliations, 44–8, 58
tribalism, 55
tribal loyalties, 46, 58
tribal values (Arab), 30

ummah, 14, 15
UNHCR (United Nations High Commissioner for Refugees), 7, 11, 62–3, 66, 100, 120, 138n13
unity (Arab), 22, 47
US invasion of Iraq, 16, 77, 80, 86, 116, 120, 122, 125, 137n13, 138n13, 170n5

veil, 23–5, 105, 116, 119–20, 123, 130, 151n48, 173–4n74; and feminism, 124–5
victimhood, 130
virginity, 20, 69, 105

waqf, 46
women, Arab: bodies, 15, 17, 20, 31, 32, 36, 104, 105–6, 110, 117, 121–3, 124, 125–6; dress codes, 117–19; modesty, 17, 20, 104–5, 110, 114, 126; narratives (*see* women's narratives); and purity, 125; as refugees, 17, 20; stories, 41, 68, 71–7; as reproducer of the nation, 31–2; sexuality, 104–5; socialization, 37; women's organizations, 5, 31; and women's rights, 16
Women's League Society, 32–3
women's movement, Arab, 33, 151n50, 151n52; pre-1958, 32–3
women's narratives, 9, 12, 24, 41; Chaldean, 49; Iraqi, 9, 104; Kurdish, 80; Shi'a, 49; Sunni, 58, 65
womanhood, 63, 73, 105, 112, 116; Iraqi, 20

Zhou, Min, 114

STUDIES IN GENDER AND HISTORY

General Editors: Franca Iacovetta and Karen Dubinsky

1 Suzanne Morton, *Ideal Surroundings: Domestic Life in a Working-Class Suburb in the 1920s*
2 Joan Sangster, *Earning Respect: The Lives of Working Women in Small-Town Ontario, 1920–1960*
3 Carolyn Strange, *Toronto's Girl Problem: The Perils and Pleasures of the City, 1880–1930*
4 Sara Z. Burke, *Seeking the Highest Good: Social Service and Gender at the University of Toronto, 1888–1937*
5 Lynne Marks, *Revivals and Roller Rinks: Religion, Leisure, and Identity in Late-Nineteenth-Century Small-Town Ontario*
6 Cecilia Morgan, *Public Men and Virtuous Women: The Gendered Languages of Religion and Politics in Upper Canada, 1791–1850*
7 Mary Louise Adams, *The Trouble with Normal: Postwar Youth and the Making of Heterosexuality*
8 Linda Kealey, *Enlisting Women for the Cause: Women, Labour, and the Left in Canada, 1890–1920*
9 Christina Burr, *Spreading the Light: Work and Labour Reform in Late-Nineteenth-Century Toronto*
10 Mona Gleason, *Normalizing the Ideal: Psychology, Schooling, and the Family in Postwar Canada*
11 Deborah Gorham, *Vera Brittain: A Feminist Life*
12 Marlene Epp, *Women without Men: Mennonite Refugees of the Second World War*
13 Shirley Tillotson, *The Public at Play: Gender and the Politics of Recreation in Postwar Ontario*
14 Veronica Strong-Boag and Carole Gerson, *Paddling Her Own Canoe: The Times and Texts of E. Pauline Johnson (Tekahionwake)*
15 Stephen Heathorn, *For Home, Country, and Race: Constructing Gender, Class, and Englishness in the Elementary School, 1880–1914*
16 Valerie J. Korinek, *Roughing It in the Suburbs: Reading* Chatelaine *Magazine in the Fifties and Sixties*
17 Adele Perry, *On the Edge of Empire: Gender, Race, and the Making of British Columbia, 1849–1871*
18 Robert A. Campbell, *Sit Down and Drink Your Beer: Regulating Vancouver's Beer Parlours, 1925–1954*
19 Wendy Mitchinson, *Giving Birth in Canada, 1900–1950*

20 Roberta Hamilton, *Setting the Agenda: Jean Royce and the Shaping of Queen's University*
21 Donna Gabaccia and Franca Iacovetta, eds., *Women, Gender, and Transnational Lives: Italian Workers of the World*
22 Linda Reeder, *Widows in White: Migration and the Transformation of Rural Women, Sicily, 1880–1920*
23 Terry Crowley, *Marriage of Minds: Isabel and Oscar Skelton Reinventing Canada*
24 Marlene Epp, Franca Iacovetta, and Frances Swyripa, eds., *Sisters or Strangers? Immigrant, Ethnic, and Racialized Women in Canadian History*
25 John G. Reid, *Viola Florence Barnes, 1885–1979: A Historian's Biography*
26 Catherine Carstairs, *Jailed for Possession: Illegal Drug Use Regulation and Power in Canada, 1920–1961*
27 Magda Fahrni, *Household Politics: Montreal Families and Postwar Reconstruction*
28 Tamara Myers, *Caught: Montreal Girls and the Law, 1869–1945*
29 Jennifer A. Stephen, *Pick One Intelligent Girl: Employability, Domesticity, and the Gendering of Canada's Welfare State, 1939–1947*
30 Lisa Chilton, *Agents of Empire: British Female Migration to Canada and Australia, 1860s–1930*
31 Esyllt W. Jones, *Influenza 1918: Disease, Death, and Struggle in Winnipeg*
32 Elise Chenier, *Strangers in Our Midst: Sexual Deviancy in Postwar Ontario*
33 Lara Campbell, *Respectable Citizens: Gender, Family, and Unemployment in the Great Depression, Ontario, 1929–1939*
34 Katrina Srigley, *Breadwinning Daughters: Young Working Women in a Depression-Era city, 1929–1939*
35 Maureen Moynagh with Nancy Forestell, eds., *Documenting First Wave Feminisms, Volume 1: Transnational Collaborations and Crosscurrents*
36 Mona Oikawa, *Cartographies of Violence: Women, Memory, and the Subjects of the Internment*
37 Karen Flynn, *Moving beyond Borders: A History of Black Canadian and Caribbean Women in the Diaspora*
38 Karen Balcom, *The Traffic in Babies: Cross-Border Adoption and Baby-Selling between the United States and Canada, 1930–1972*
39 Nancy M. Forestell with Maureen Moynagh, eds., *Documenting First Wave Feminisms, Volume II: Canada – National and Transnational Contexts*

40 Patrizia Gentile and Jane Nicholas, eds., *Contesting Bodies and Nation in Canadian History*
41 Suzanne Morton, *Wisdom, Justice and Charity: Canadian Social Welfare through the Life of Jane B. Wisdom, 1884–1975*
42 Jane Nicholas, *The Modern Girl: Feminine Modernities, the Body, and Commodities in the 1920s*
43 Pauline A. Phipps, *Constance Maynard's Passions: Religion, Sexuality, and an English Educational Pioneer, 1849–1935*
44 Marlene Epp and Franca Iacovetta, eds. *Sisters or Strangers? Immigrant, Ethnic, and Racialized Women in Canadian History, Second Edition*
45 Rhonda L. Hinther, *Perogies and Politics: Radical Ukrainians in Canada, 1891–1991*
46 Valerie J. Korinek, *Prairie Fairies: A History of Queer Communities and People in Western Canada, 1930–1985*
47 Julie Guard, *Radical Housewives: Price Wars and Food Politics in Mid-Twentieth-Century Canada*
48 Nancy Janovicek and Carmen Nielson, *Reading Canadian Women's and Gender History*
49 L.K. Bertram, *The Viking Immigrants: Icelandic North Americans*
50 Donica Belisle, *Purchasing Power: Women and the Rise of Canadian Consumer Culture*
51 Allyson D. Stevenson, *Intimate Integration: A History of the Sixties Scoop in Saskatchewan and the Colonization of Indigenous Kinship*
52 Nadia Jones-Gailani, *Transnational Identity and Memory Making in the Lives of Iraqi Women in Diaspora*